THE MORAL DECISION

THE MORAL DECISION

RIGHT AND WRONG IN THE LIGHT OF AMERICAN LAW

by Edmond Cahn

Indiana University Press
Bloomington

TO

JUDGE JEROME FRANK

CHAMPION OF ENLIGHTENMENT
AND OF HUMANE JUSTICE

New Midland Book Edition 1981

Permission has kindy been granted by Oxford University Press to quote from *The Present Age* by Søren Kierkegaard; and by Constable & Co., Ltd. to quote from *Scepticism and Animal Faith* by George Santayana.

Manufactured in the United States of America

Library of Congress Cataloging in Publication Data

Cahn, Edmond Nathaniel, 1906–1964.
The moral decision.

Reprint. Originally published: Bloomington: Indiana University Press, 1955. With new introd.
Bibliography: p.
Includes index.
1. Law—United States—Cases. 2. Law and ethics—Cases. I. Title.
KF379.C33 1981 340'.112'0973 81-47586
ISBN 0-253-33875-1 AACR2
ISBN 0-253-20273-6 (pbk.) 1 2 3 4 5 85 84 83 82 81

Contents

Foreword

Edmond Cahn was not the first philosopher to probe the relationship between law and morals. As he recognized in the introductory portions of this book, the tension between "law as is" and "law as it should be" has provided much grist for the scholar's mill. What was it, then, that made *The Moral Decision* so different when it first appeared twenty-six years ago, and why, today, is it still as timely as this morning's newspaper, still providing us with profound insights into life and law? The answers to these questions tell us why Edmond Cahn occupied a unique place in American jurisprudence and why the republication of *The Moral Decision* is cause for rejoicing by all who look to the law as a source of moral nourishment.

Edmond Cahn differed from traditional legal philosophers in that he looked for the relationship between law and morals through a study of actual legal cases rather than from a more theoretical point of view. According to traditional legal philosophers, law and morality either had no necessary connection (the positivists) or had to be bound together in order for the legal system to have validity (the natural law believers) or were so unrelated that it was not worth the time to consider the connection (the legal realists). There are, of course, many variations on these themes, and to say that the approach of traditional philosophers differed from Cahn's does not denigrate the value of their insights or minimize their importance in the development of Cahn's thinking. It is not a question of right or wrong. It is a question of recognizing and appreciating the difference.

A rare combination of philosopher and practicing lawyer, Edmond Cahn studied real cases and tried to extract from them certain moral judgments—the moral decisions—which judges made as they coped with the problems of life, death, marriage, sexual relationships, business dealings, and racial discrimination. This book eschews broad theories about the relationship between law and morals. It demonstrates instead that there are moral values in the inner workings of the law and that positive law and morality influence each other. Nor is there any articulation of a set of overarching moral values which Cahn may have regarded as providing the underpinnings for a humane and democratic society, although he had strong views on moral issues, as can be readily gleaned from this book and his other writings.

Thus, with Cahn the case is the starting point of analysis. The cases he selected for this book are not landmark decisions, but their unexceptional status is a useful reminder of the pervasive presence of morality in law. Through these cases we learn how courts view the obligations of business associates toward each other, the privacy of sexual relationships, the individual's decision to die, or society's attitudes toward racial differences. The moral insight we acquire from the cases are then used as a springboard from which to consider analogous real-life situations and to speculate on cases that loom on the horizon.

Cahn wrote for the ordinary reader, and that is why the book is fun to read. The cases are real, the facts are readily recognizable, we can identify with the parties, we can understand the problems, and we can appreciate the difficult choices of the judges. I would not hesitate to recommend *The Moral Decision* for vacation reading as well as for required reading in a philosophy course. The life of the law is experience, as Holmes admonished, and Edmond Cahn knew how to draw on that experience brilliantly. It is a skill that needs emulating today.

What is more important, Cahn's approach forces us to consider all the nooks and crannies of moral judgments that arise in particular cases rather than only the very broad issues. There has been a near-obsession among scholars in recent years with two aspects of the relationship of law and morality. Both are in the domain of constitutional law. One concerns the moral justification for courts' overriding the decisions of the democratic majority expressed through the votes of a popularly elected legislature. This is, of course, our country's oldest continuing constitutional road show—the legitimacy of judicial review—which has been playing the intellectual circuit at least since *Marbury* v. *Madison*, in 1803, and which has now been recast in a new production, featuring moral philosophy and political theory, with law in a supporting role.

The second concern of the current group of moral-constitutional philosophers is an intense interest in moral criticism of law. It probably derives from an attempt to create a moral framework for the consideration of those constitutional issues that are difficult to resolve by reference to constitutional text or history, e.g., the outer limits, if any, of a woman's right to terminate a pregnancy; the extent to which the Fourteenth Amendment protects the right of poor persons for equal education, housing, or subsistence; or the extent to which the Constitution protects private decisions regarding sexual conduct.

Approaching both of these subjects from the perspective of general principles, rather than specific cases, almost inevitably channels our attention toward the broadest issues: What types of cases justify judicial intervention? Are anti-adultery laws constitutional? Should society punish prostitution or homosexuality? What are the permissible interferences with the right of individuals to co-habit? Does our Constitution protect "process" or "rights"?

The moral criticism of law, if viewed primarily from the perspective of broad philosophical concepts, encounters serious analytical problems. In the world of law, moral issues do not arise from a study of philosophical theory. Rather, they arise initially in a case when someone sues someone else for specific relief. These cases generally do not confine themselves to neatly defined and broad moral principles. They involve delicate personal relationships which require that judges apply a moral sensitivity to a myriad of fact situations. This is sharply illustrated in the discussion in chapter IV of a New Mexico decision which holds that a husband's suit for divorce on grounds of incompatibility could not be defeated by proof of the husband's adultery, and which holds also that the husband must pay alimony. Although the discussion contains some stereotypical descriptions of the role of men and women (remember this book was written in the early 1950s), the attitude towards laws regulating private sexual conduct is strikingly modern and "liberated."

Moreover, the entire chapter is replete with moral insights into marriage and other relationships between men and women. There is no discussion of constitutional issues (in 1955 these were not of constitutional dimension), but we learn much more about the way the law deals with these moral issues than we do by asking the broad questions about the constitutional right of consenting adults to freedom of private sexual behavior.

Thus, the cases provide the forum and the ingredients for the moral decisions. From them the moral principles evolve. Without cases, such as those discussed in chapter IV, the constitutional litigation of the 1960s and 1970s would not have emerged as they did. It was Edmond Cahn's genius that made us realize that through the process of deciding cases moral decisions emerge which then become the building blocks of the moral constitution.

Cahn's approach to moral issues might also help with the important question of the permissible limits of judicial review. That debate, which has recently been renewed with great intensity in academic circles, rages between those who would limit the Supreme Court's role to interpreting the history and text of the Constitution and those who would recognize the legitimacy of the Court's infusion of moral values into the Constitution even though that involves a more activist role for the Court. To judges deciding constitutional cases, however, these arguments, while raising important issues of American constitutional and political theory, may have an aura of unreality. For the debate views judicial review from what Edmond Cahn would have called "the imperial perspective"—that of the Supreme Court. But hundreds of lower-court judges, state and federal, also decide constitutional questions, and they, too, contribute to the democratic colloquy between the people and their judges.

How does a lower-court judge, for example, decide whether federal and state governments may deprive a woman of reimbursement, from public funds, for the cost of medically indicated abortions, while providing such reimbursement for other medical procedures including normal childbirth? Edmond Cahn would not deny that this case raises serious questions about the extent to which the Supreme Court should overthrow legislative judgments that public funds should not be used to encourage abortions. But judges hearing the cases are faced with precise and immediate issues. How does the case compare with previously decided cases establishing a woman's right to terminate a pregnancy during the first trimester? Is the denial of reimbursement so related to a religious belief as to constitute an establishment of religion? Is the decision to terminate a pregnancy a medical decision in the same sense as a decision to remove an appendix? If there is a state law involved, does it conflict with federal laws or policies? Should the case be deferred until the state has had an opportunity to interpret its own law? What are the medical consequences to the mother and child of the denial of reimbursement? All these questions, which may be considered by many judges including those of the Supreme Court, influence evolving theories of the legitimacy of judicial review, and, in turn, the judges will be influenced by those philosophical concepts. Cahn reminds scholars, who might otherwise forget, of the importance of concrete cases in determining the appropriate scope of judicial review in a democratic society. Political theory, like morality, has room for "the consumer perspective."

It is from the perspective of a judge that Edmond Cahn's approach may be most valuable. Moral philosophers can easily develop a body of literature that conveys to judges a most unfortunate impression: that moral judgments are to be made by judges only after they immerse themselves in moral philosophy. Judges, after all, are not customers at a constitutional county fair at which their only role is to decide which philosophical ticket to purchase in order to acquire the moral vision to decide hard cases. Nor is it realistic to expect busy judges to be able to delve into the depths of moral philosophy in order to decide cases.

Edmond Cahn, of course, would have been the last person to discourage judges from reading all they could about jurisprudence and moral philosophy. But he would have been among the first to recognize that judges are, for the most part, practicing lawyers who have been given a robe and some status, and that for better or worse these mortal judges must decide actual cases on the basis of the facts, applicable law, arguments of counsel, and such wisdom as they can bring to bear on the cases. A critical message in *The Moral Decision*, emphasized in the concluding chapter, is that the responsibility for the moral decision lies with the judge. A judge must decide whether a state law prohibiting the use of laetrile is constitutional or whether lawyers may be permitted, or required, to reveal certain client confidences. While the judge can, and should (if time permits), consider the moral value of personal autonomy in decision-making with regard to death, or the ethical considerations involved in the relationship of lawyers to clients, the moral decision will not come from heavenly voices, or from an abstract moral construct. It comes from the mind and character of the judge.

This is the real world in which judges live and work. Edmond Cahn appreciated the burden of the judge, and he also helped them to revel in the glory of their responsibilities. For he made it clear in this book that the law itself is the embodiment of moral values, that the individual case, decided by one lone judge with a yellow pad and a well-worn pen, is a proper forum for moral adjudication. And in a democratic society should it really be any other way?

If one looks for well-ordered moral structures, for a broad conceptual framework within which difficult moral decisions should be made, *The Moral Decision* will not be very satisfying. For Edmond Cahn has provided us with a process and not with a result, an approach to the making of moral decisions and not a superimposed philosophy, a set of brilliant insights and not an all-purpose revelation. He has described the world of law, and of morals, as it really functions.

Shortly after Edmond Cahn's death in 1964, I observed, "As long as this nation lives under representative government Edmond Cahn's voice will span the years and help with the work of the hour." That sentence looked good then. A generation later, it looks even better.

New York University School of Law
April 1981

Norman Redlich

The Purpose of This Book

What moral guides can be found in American law?

In every mature society, there is a considerable overlap between legal questions and moral questions. A man who violates the law against murder likewise violates a moral precept against killing; fraud and theft are condemned not only by courts but also by consciences; in short, law and morals frequently do their work with the very same item of human behavior. In a democratic society like ours where the law reflects many of the people's basic values, this overlap becomes all the more extensive and important. Under the official appearance of deciding the legal issues presented to them, American judges are often required to assess moral interests and resolve problems of right and wrong. It is realistic to look at the law not merely as a technical institution performing various political and economic functions but also as a rich repository of moral knowledge which is continually reworked, revised, and refined.

The purpose of this book is to draw upon the supply of moral insight and experience that American courts have gradually developed and accumulated. Our venture is a new one, rife with the attractions and pitfalls of novelty. It is not a study of legal philosophy, political doctrines, law reform, sociology of law, or theoretical ethics. It does not assume that the reader is learned in philosophy or law. It assumes only that he is a literate individual who is affected or troubled by the moral confusion of the times.

But how can one take the dry abstractions of technical law and transform them into notions that respond to the needs of flesh and blood? How is one to confer life on the abstract and make it pulse so that the reader may say: "This predicament I have truly known; I have not merely understood it in my mind, I have felt it in my bones, it belongs to me; through it, I have acquired a wiser moral insight"?

A new enterprise seems to suggest the adoption of a new method. In the main body of this book, each topic will begin with the statement of an authentic case, summarized from the law reports. Reading it, we observe the behavior of very specific human protagonists, the drama that rises gradually among them, the climax and ultimate resolution. The case operates as a prism: it reveals an entire spectrum of moral forces—personal ambitions, group standards, lusts, sufferings, and ideals. Thus the abstract concept becomes fit for our own experience.

Are we to consider the judge's legal decision as possessing authority in the sphere of morals? Is the author's comment on the decision necessarily correct? Is a reader expected to accept decisions or interpretations without criticism? Manifestly not; an individual's right to reason for himself is among the proudest of human attributes, which this book constantly reaffirms. "Prismatic" cases have been chosen just because they prompt the reader to cultivate skill and wisdom when he exercises moral judgment. They offer him an invitation to engage in free enterprise of the mind. As for the author's interpretations—whether one agrees or disagrees with them in whole or in part, they will assuredly launch a process of analysis and reflection. Whenever possible, the author takes definite and reasoned positions, for he suspects that the practice of answering merely "on the one hand" and "on the other hand" can become the opiate of responsible thinking.

In ancient days, there was a vision that appeared almost simultaneously to the best minds of the Hellenic and the Hebraic worlds. Great sages voiced the hope that the law could serve as a pedagogue to the people, instructing them in the maxims of enlightenment, righteousness, and self-rule. No less than the Psalmist in the Bible, Plato and Aristotle believed that the law should be employed as "a lamp unto the feet and a light unto the path." In recent times a few prominent jurists have revived the outline of this vision, but none has seen fit to convert it into practical, concrete guides. For this book, we have chosen the way of the concrete. As we draw on the law's experience, we shall deal with the homely concerns of human existence from birth and the beginning, through the entire cycle of growth, love and ambition, desire and anxiety, until we come to death and the end.

It is time to consult the law.

PART ONE

The Legal and the Good

I

Morals As a Legal Order

1. A WAY TO BEGIN: "RIGHT AND WRONG"

According to popular understanding in the United States, the law will not punish a man for committing a crime if he cannot tell the difference between right and wrong. If he does not know what is right and what is wrong, he is believed to be "not guilty by reason of insanity." But if this is the legal test of mental competence, are we bound to infer from it that all the rest of us in the twentieth century are insane? For who, if put under oath, could claim that he knew and was able to explain what is right and how it differs from what is wrong? How many would be willing to have their own sanity judged by their ability to pass that test?

It is unnecessary to rehearse here all the influences that have made for moral confusion in our times. Probably not since the days when the Sophists carried their skepticism from city to city in ancient Greece have men been so afflicted with uncertainty. Dazzling economic and social transformations, the popularization of scientific method and the cynicism bred of world wars, the observation of foreign societies and exotic customs, the growth of relativism and hedonism in philosophy, and the development of a sophisticated semantics—all have challenged the established landmarks and eradicated the familiar lines between moral and immoral. A society changing at an unprecedented pace has simply brushed away the inhibitions of the past. In their place, there seem to be only doubts—not merely the healthy doubts of a critical examination but the sickening and panicky doubts that come when one's bearings fade out of view. Until recently, the answers of the clergy were likely to be accepted as sufficient; now, even where the clergy itself is not infected with the same misgivings as the laity, ecclesiastical pronouncements are considered unauthoritative at the very best. If, therefore, it is a legal axiom that any sane human being must be deemed to know the difference between good and evil, right and wrong, and ought and ought not, then our law is uttering a judgment of mental incompetence on almost all Americans, including those of us who argue at the bar and preside on the bench. This would seem to be no light paradox.

Fortunately, the paradox is easy to resolve. The conclusion we reached was entirely false: the law does not adjudge the American people to be deficient in sanity. And the error of the conclusion followed from the error of our first premise: the test of sanity used in the overwhelming majority of our criminal courts is not whether a man has the capacity to distinguish between right and wrong *in general*. Such an absurdly abstract test would be enough to perplex the brain of an Aristotle: certainly no judge or jury would be able to administer it with any hope of obtaining intelligent results. The test we do employ is quite different. In effect, if evidence has been received of some mental disease (that did not disable the accused person completely from understanding what he was doing), the jury has to decide the question: was he disabled from knowing that *what he was doing* was *wrong*? If he was so disabled, he was insane; if not, he was sane and responsible. Although the rule has its faults, it does not require the impossible.

What has an inquiry like ours to learn from the criminal law's test of sanity? In this book, we are interested in American law not for its own sake but as a repository of knowledge and experience in resolving moral issues. Our purpose is to learn what we can about good and evil and other moral concerns by looking critically at the way American law deals with them. Such being our purpose, the legal test for determining sanity or insanity seems to provide an excellent lead, because it suggests that an analysis of the moral experience should (1) focus on the doing of specific acts, and (2) focus on the notion of wrong.

To the American lawyer, there would be nothing strange about putting our emphasis on specific acts, for these correspond in his professional vocabulary to specific cases and controversies. He has made it a habit to concentrate on the techniques and processes that culminate in a decision, and a decision is the resolution of some highly specific collision of demands. A decision is not only a resolution; it is a victory and a promise of peace after a real conflict. American judges will not decide cases unless they represent genuine controversies. They refuse to give advisory opinions governing possible future circumstances that may or may not ever develop. So far as the moral experience is comparable to the judicial process, the American lawyer would applaud our concentrating on what is unique, immediate, and apprehensible in each specific moral crisis. He would say that for too many centuries men have looked up to the distant and immutable stars as ensigns of the moral law; that though such heaven-gazing may be useful to inculcate sentiments of reverence and humility, it furnishes little or no understanding of the concrete values that collide at any human crossroads.

As for focusing on the notion of wrong, what could seem more profitable to lawyer and layman alike? How often when we cannot decide which of many alternative courses is *right*, we find ourselves utterly certain that one particular course is *wrong*! The criminal law punishes a man for doing an act that it calls wrong; to be punishable for such an act, is it not enough that he was able to recognize its wrongness? On the other hand, what is right neither he nor the judge would probably ever be capable of saying, and while we waited to assess a thousand jarring definitions and ideals, the moral as well as the legal order might fall into a collapse. That is why the really bold attempts to dogmatize about the general nature of goodness will not be found in our court opinions but rather in the literature of ethics, for in ethical writings the feeling of responsibility does not seem so very solemn or immediate.

2. ANOTHER CLEW FROM THE LAW: THE WAY TO "GOODNESS"

In ethical literature the good is generally treated as the goal of moral conduct, and it has been located and marked off with unlimited ingenuity and—sad to say—with at least equal variety. What is the good and how to reach it are questions that have had innumerable earnest and systematic answers during the course of about three millennia, and there are few important respects in which any two of the answers can be said to agree. Nevertheless, if we give consideration only to the main emphases in this luxuriant proliferation of systems, they do tend to fall into a crude but manageable order of classification. There are the ethical systems that emphasize the good as *happiness* and there are those that emphasize the good as *righteousness*.

The exponents of happiness, furthermore, may be divided into those who really believe that happiness is attainable by human beings and those who suspect—though generally without admitting—that it is not. The former say that happiness can be achieved by maintaining a conscious equilibrium or harmony as among the various intellectual, emotional, and instinctive aspects of our personalities. They sometimes recognize that, despite the most perfect equilibrium, a man cannot be happy unless he also has material security, good health, and the grace of favorable luck; and they confess that it is not enough to have all these unless one can retain them as long as he lives. This view may be called aristocratic in its scope, because only a few could possibly attain and preserve such a degree of inner harmony; and only a few among those few would be endowed with the necessary economic, organic, and social advantages. It may also be called aristocratic in its psychological requirements, because for each gifted individual it contemplates a reign by a limited roster of disciplined and mutually deferential impulses in his makeup. If the aristocracy within him degenerates, that is, if some single impulse aggressively declines to respect the territories of the others, civil war may lead to civil anarchy in his personality.

The utilitarians constitute the second group of those who emphasize the good as happiness. They suspect that happiness conceived as an enduring human state is at best impossible and at worst a dangerously seductive delusion. Happiness—the only happiness men really know—is the temporary afflatus that comes from the cure of some disease, the lifting of some yoke, the reconciliation of some conflict, or the satisfaction of some appetite. This view may be called democratic in scope, just because it deals with the suffering, the anxiety, and the continual succession of problems that have always filled so large a part of human lives. It may be deemed psychologically democratic insofar as virtually every internal resource is supposed to be called into play for the resolution of any presented problem or the removal of any felt need. But this democracy too may degenerate whenever the individual happens to lack a scheme of order or self-discipline. Then his dominant appetite is likely to establish a tyranny of capricious expediencies.

The writers who emphasize the good as righteousness generally advocate a more unitary rule. Since the good is equivalent to the right, they say, morality has no concern with other values; the conscience may perhaps consult an advisory cabinet of worldly advantages and utilities, but it must finally arrive at and live by its own determinations. At its conceived best, this view may be called monarchic: it not only establishes a single internal ruler of the individual's moral commonwealth but also anoints him, the individual man, as sovereign of the good in his own life. But nothing can be worse than the corruption of this best; nothing can be crueler than righteousness, obsessed with its own claim to authority, playing the irresponsible despot.

If these are the main ideals of the good in their desired and in their degenerate forms, they must not be thought of as separate or unrelated. On the contrary, their differences are only distinctions of emphasis and, however important those distinctions may appear, no one ideal would benefit by the categorical exclusion of the others. Those who tell us to set our gaze on happiness are never indifferent to righteousness as a means to that end, and the advocates of righteousness consider that its practice, though justified in itself, generally makes men happy. Certainly, the American lawyer would have us carry our use of political analogies to what in his expectation is their logical conclusion: the formula of a "mixed government." In his political philosophy, he has been accustomed to treating the aristocratic, democratic, and monarchic principles not as intercontradictory standards of which only one can be chosen, but as working elements of a successful and balanced republic. The good, according to his political precedents and analogies, should comprise happiness and righteousness alike, excluding neither but distinguishing and balancing their respective functions. He would not choose once and for all; he would distinguish and would choose from time to time according to the needs of the particular function and the facts of the occasion.

For example, he might observe that the operations of the good *qua* happiness tend to resemble those of a successful *administrative* process. They call more for judgment in the sense of a human resource than for judgment in the sense of an acquittal or condemnation. They call for expertness, adaptability, and a talent for accommodation. To be happy, one must make elastic plans, must know the strength of one's materials, and calculate on the possibility of unexpected future demands. On the other hand, the good *qua* righteousness invokes the incidents of a *judicial* process. It operates like a court; it enjoins, it acquits or condemns. Thus, there are certain moral conflicts that call for a process of administration; and there are others that call for a process of adjudication.

Under our law, once an administrative decision has been reached (for example, a government board has determined the manner in which labor relations should be conducted in a certain industry), it may be subjected to the examination and approval or disapproval of the court. This kind of court control we call "judicial review." But in order not to discard the benefits of the administrative process or the special expertness of the administrative judgment, the typical "judicial review" is a strictly limited investigation: the judge will generally consider himself bound to accept the administrative determination even though he doubts its wisdom or correctness, unless he can find no substantial basis in the case to support the way the administrative decision would manage the problem. With this analogy in mind, the American lawyer might suggest there are many moral problems that are best suited to an administrative disposition subject to a judicial review, that is, moral problems that we may handle best by concerning ourselves primarily with values in human happiness and by bowing to the rigorous mandate of conscience only when conscience can find no acceptable basis whatever for the course we have chosen.

If this approach is sound, it would follow that happiness will depend almost as much as righteousness does on the authority and the wisdom of conscience's court. That is why the balance of this chapter is devoted to describing what one experiences when he submits to the court of his conscience.

3. THE MORAL CONSTITUTION

We find a bright example of conscience doing its work if we turn to the Bible story of that celebrated poet and sensualist—King David. We are told that David, while waging war against the Philistines, had only a few of his best soldiers along with him, that a Philistine garrison was encamped in Bethlehem where a well of water could be found, and that David suffered from thirst and yearned audibly for a drink from the captive well. So three of his men broke through the enemy's army, drew water out of the well, and brought it back to their king. David, however, all of a sudden found himself loath to drink; he felt he could not even take a sip. And piously he poured the water upon the ground for an oblation, saying "Shall I drink the blood of men that went in jeopardy of their lives?"

The general human characteristics that lie behind an incident like this may be together regarded as the moral constitution. Without the moral constitution it is difficult to see how there could be any moral legislation or any specific moral decisions. In fact, social life as we know it is close to unthinkable in the absence of the resources and patterns of behavior that furnish the constitutional equipment for morality.

In the first place, we are all of us—like King David—prone to dramatize our selves to ourselves. We consciously or unconsciously *enact* the transactions we meet with. We are not quite so sad as sorry for ourselves, not so glad as rejoicing with ourselves, not so passionate as absorbed in the impulsions to be expected of a lover. The self we know is multiple; it is forever watching itself and sharing the rises and falls of its own course. Partly detached yet never so detached as not to care at all, partly committed yet rarely so committed that it ceases to be an observer, the multiple self is a dramatist that cares along with the *dramatis personae* it creates. David stood off and solemnly approved of himself as he poured out the precious liquid.

In the second place, the self is always incompletely and imperfectly identified with the particular body or physical organism to which chance has happened to assign it. By dint of dramatizing the experiences of that embodiment it becomes skillful at the histrionic art and thus more or less expertly prepared to play a variety of dramas on the stages of other people's predicaments. None of us is wholly content with the casual confinements of a single career, a single sex, a single lifetime and concatenation of scenery. Each desires to live out all kinds of lives, to exert all powers and receive all adulations, to suffer and enjoy every sort of passion, to possess all the women that ever yielded or refused to yield—in short, to play the Faust in an endless metempsychosis of exploits and triumphs. These compulsive lusts drive the self out beyond the boundaries of its own body and send it to enact comedies, tragedies, tableaux, and epics elsewhere. The self very frequently projects itself to other organisms, or by identification with them lives through some part of the poignance of their doings. And in this way, it can learn, to some limited degree at least, to care with them almost as for its own embodiment, and to feel entangled in their condition. So it is that to "know thyself" means eventually to know in this partial measure each and every other member of the human community, and to feel somehow and at some time involuntarily committed to an unlimited *self* preservation. David, for example, could hardly proceed to slake his thirst with what he might have identified in imagination as his own blood.

In the third place, the moral constitution comprises a certain biological equipment, which may be called "the sense of wrong." Our reaction to an act of moral wrong is a blend of reason that recognizes, of emotion that evaluates, and of glands that pump physical preparations for action. In a single combined response, our muscles tighten and our judgment condemns, anger fills us with heat or our spirits slide down with sorrow. A wrong is apprehended in one process on every psychic level as equivalent to an assault, that is, an assault on the self in its own fleshly body or on the self projected by imaginative drama to some other body. Therefore, for a man to do an act of conscious wrong is simultaneously to insult and lacerate one facet of his self within and another facet outside.

These, then, are the working elements of the moral constitution. What we dramatize, what we project, what we care about, what we inflict hurt on—is our selves. There are certain fine occasions when we are joyfully ready to sacrifice every other interest in order to preserve the outside, other self, and this joyous readiness is what we call "love" or *caritas*. Thus love too is involved in the vitality of the moral constitution: anyone can notice at a time of crisis how very cogent it is in intensifying the feeling of commitment. For the humdrum hours of life, however, Kant was entirely right when he asserted that love is a product rather than a cause of our beneficent acts; we learn to love those we benefit because we have given to them, more often than we give because we have learned to love. Perhaps at our best it is the delight of anticipating, not their gratitude but the growth of our own love, that really prompts the giving.

However that may be, the clews furnished by the law at the opening of this chapter can now begin to fulfill their office. It was suggested that the inquiry should focus on the concrete case and on the notion of wrong. The moral constitution, as we have described it, accords very profitably with these clews. For it is only in the concrete case that rational speculation can draw to it the flesh and blood of imaginative projection, and an abstract personal subject can be converted into a vibrant personality. The concrete case alone offers a stage suitable for projected drama, where it prompts the emotions, the glands, and the viscera to join with the faculty of reason in the experiences of a moral evaluation. In a concrete case, the sense of wrong is informed with some genuine personal commitment; in other words, there is real water in the cup and its presence there has put real lives at stake. That is why it is fitting that judges should whenever possible shy away from answers to supposititious cases; human wisdom is on its mettle only where there is a practical risk, which imports responsibility and the felt burden of a personal involvement.

It must be remembered, however, that moral constitutions seem, at least at this early stage of our inquiry, somewhat remote from the making of particular decisions. We should therefore next consider how rules of moral legislation come to be established and enforced.

4. THE NATURE OF MORAL LEGISLATION IN GENERAL

HERE WE are dealing with the central area of the age's confusion in moral matters. Not many of us are disposed to challenge the factual existence of the moral constitution or the beauty of those general standards that stem directly from it.

Almost everyone agrees: that an individual should not injure his other, projected selves but should seek to benefit them; that he should love his neighbors as manifestations of his own self; and that he should do unto other selves as he would have them do unto him. The authority of such propositions continues on without widespread attack precisely because they are general, that is to say, because they appear rather too distant from the unique conditions of any particular time and place to exert an immediate, coercive control over our specific moral decisions. Traditionally, the control that did claim to govern our specific decisions was very much more definite; it consisted of collections of rules and prohibitions (known as the "moral code"), of handsome rewards as incentives to obedience, and—most eloquently elaborated—schedules of punishment as deterrents to infringement. And this, the legislation of morality, is what now stands in the shadow of a spreading skepticism.

Who will be so bold as to deny that there are sensible reasons for doubt? The doubts are uncomfortable; they feel at times like a visitation of vertigo from a torpid liver. A doubt without an eventual answer can become wretched company for any mind. But, on the other hand, there are doubts that cleanse the system of old poisons and make it ready for vital, new efforts. If, in our own generation, we take a retrospective look at the operations of past moral legislation, what now feels like a condition of discomfort and illness may come to be identified as the inescapable twinges of our convalescence.

No one can say how long ago the illness began. It goes back at least as far as the animistic rites and sacrifices of the most primitive cults, when men first deluded themselves with the belief that nature would respond mimetically to a dance or a hymn or a sexual coupling in a sacred grove. The way to bring rain and to make the crops grow was to perform the ceremony; the ceremony was what would please the local divinity and put his magic in motion. The gods seem to have been powerful for long ages before they began to become good. Hence, the moral codes, when they did finally break into the teachings of primitive worship, found themselves combined, tangled, and confused with all the antecedent theologies and ritual observances. Goodness was only a new species of obedience to the irresistible powers, a new way to please them and to avoid provoking their wrath. And—most important in this development—the very same priestly group that regularly dispensed the mysteries and performed the ritual, by like authority and with like finality announced what kind of conduct was or was not to be considered good. The good was generally set down in commands too terse and dogmatic to provide space for exceptions of time, place, and circumstance, and, since the commands came from an assumedly unchanging source, they were themselves unchangeable. If after the lapse of centuries some adjustment or adaptation became overwhelmingly necessary, why then, the same group that had transmitted the commands might through its successors in office reinterpret them. So all vexing questions of decision and application were to be referred to a member of this group. He, however, could rarely be expected, in view of the importance of his own ritual functions, to segregate moral requirements from requirements relating to observance of the cult ceremonial.

As we know, individuals of every description—including some of the wisest and loftiest in human history—have rebelled against these conditions, and some of them have attained at one time or another a measure of local success. The success, such as it was, would soon disappear in the establishment of some new dogmatic cult, announcing its own set of inflexible moral commands and its own exclusive authority to construe them. What, therefore, is genuinely new in our era is not the outbreak of local rebellion but the fact of general revolution, not a momentary breaking away from chains but a persistence in remaining emancipated. Obviously, the spread of literacy has been one of the new disruptive causes, and the rapidity of technological change has been another. Yet, whether we welcome them or not, it will do little good to list the various causes of the revolution, for what signifies most in our lives is the day-to-day consequences it has brought. To us it involves more than an independent search for moral standards: it involves a heavy unaccustomed responsibility for construing the standards and applying them to concrete cases.

Moral standards, it should be noted, have their peculiar "textures" and degrees of pliability, and moral excellence is impossible to anyone who deals with a standard without taking its texture into account. Some standards can be bent without injury and some will not bend at all; some standards allow for the urgency of passing needs; some standards will become peremptory only in a precise and rather specialized social setting and will yield everywhere else to the demands of custom or convenience. Finally, there are the merely ceremonial standards. In almost every contemporary society they have been required to dismount from their authority, and doing so, they have seemed to drag genuine moral legislation along with them. The ritualistic and the ethical had been entwined so long that only the most sophisticated observer could distinguish between them. As the naive saw it, the two fell off together and so the social behavior of men appeared to be riderless. Of course that was not and is not the case; moral legislation still emerges and evolves with all needful vigor, and if anything, it gains a special respect from the unseating of the obsolete reverence for rituals. That much becomes evident as soon as we understand how the legislation operates.

It may be said that moral legislation begins as well as ends with enforcement. Bentham complained that the law teaches us right conduct the same way we instruct a dog what to do: we beat him when he does wrong. But Bentham did not deny that a dog does in fact acquire civilized manners by that kind of pedagogy, and if we understand "beating" to include a wide variety of other possible discomforts, most human puppies have been learning in a similar fashion since time immemorial. They learn group standards from the tone their parents use to say "liar" or "thief" and the excited whispers their playmates reserve for gutter-talk about obscene occupations and supposedly shameful natural functions. They are taught very impressively when wrong conduct is followed by some group gesture of rejection, for rejection is a rod that even the most favored child will feel at one time or another.

All these kinds of external policing are designed to make themselves eventually unnecessary by creating and training an internal monitor alert and strong enough to take over. The objective .o be gained is a disciplined conscious self or *conscience*, who will speak within on behalf of the outer community and will enforce its moral standards. The external police cannot always be on the scene, to arrest every offender and punish every infraction. Fear of being caught, powerful as it is in the operations of morality, is not enough to maintain the process. It is not enough because human beings are so ingenious in their evasions and inventions. It is not enough because the community needs a steady flow of new recruits to its force of moral police, and needs also to feel that the norms and standards it asserts have the power to evoke spontaneous, uncoerced acts of adherence. For these reasons, the enforcement process must do more than announce certain mandates and illustrate the danger of disobeying them. It must build up the varieties of moral habit that it identifies with a "good character." The habit and character so developed are expected to be there on guard whenever an occasion arises for making a moral decision.

This expectation may be disappointed in many different ways, and so the fear of being detected has to continue indefinitely as a significant element in everyone's internal discipline. But that is no basis for underestimating the force and firmness of habit, which has been rightly called "second nature" and is almost irresistible when its direction does not disagree too sharply with the impulses of "first nature." Habit makes the ruts that hold our wheels on the road and keep us from jolting off. Habit is what so largely predetermines the rational and emotional elements that make up our moral decisions.

The *decision* is the summation and epitome of the whole process. Of course, we are entitled to evaluate a man as "good" or "evil" though he is not at the moment engaged in any event of moral import. A good man is good even when he is asleep; his character, which comprises several other factors in addition to mere habituation, consists in his moral readiness, the wisdom of his judgment, the sensitiveness with which he can project himself to where other selves stand, and the firmness he can show in defending a vision of right. But, as was said by Isocrates (the Greek sage of the fourth century B.C. who repeatedly expressed what we now call the "Golden Rule"), we "should test justice when a man is in want, temperance when he is in power, continence when he is in the prime of youth." Only in such circumstances will there be any occasion for making the moral decision, and a character untempted is a character unproved.

Is the principle implicit in a man's decision nothing more than the outcome of his group's external legislation? Certainly not. There are three important stages in the movement by which group moral legislation becomes individual moral decision; the stage we have just considered—impressing the group command on the individual—is only the first. He has still to rework that command in the distinctive machinery of his own character, temperament, and intellect (and in the crucible of the "moral constitution") before it becomes an implement of self-police. He has still to make use of it—as so reworked and reshaped—in the disposition of his own moral controversies. Doing so, he executes the third stage in the command's evolution; he re-legislates it for the public edification of some particular group; he transmits, not the imperative he has received, but the one he has rephrased by his own use. It is impossible, thus, for anyone to escape acting as a moral legislator, for, whether he builds or weakens the total order, he inevitably modifies it.

At this point, we find two massive roadblocks standing in our way. They are (1) the skeptical contention that morals are only community mores or customs and (2) the authoritarian contention that our uncertainties would all disappear like dew in the warmth of the midday sun if we would only subscribe to a list of natural and immutable moral precepts (to be supplied to us, since we shall probably not be able to agree on them among ourselves). This second, authoritarian view need not delay us long, for the history of continual mutations in its so-called "immutables" is too familiar. If what ultimately counts in the moral process is the making of particular moral decisions, then no one can relieve us of that burden or deprive us of that power unless he makes the concrete decisions for us; whoever may formulate the precepts, they mean as much as they are made to mean in specific factual applications.

Shall we say then, as the skeptics say, that morals are only socially established mores? Here too we run into a kind of authoritarianism, one that is subtler and more deceptive because it is less manifest in its despotic implications. To equate morals with mores is to tell the individual conscience that it must abdicate in favor of external legislation and must become the vassal of group behavior. Perhaps that is thought to be a convenient way out of all our doubts and responsibilities: we should look for the decisions the community has made and go along with them.

But this exit also is locked tight. We cannot tell whether "mores" means (1) what the society desires, or (2) what it popularly articulates, or (3) what it practices, or (4) some combination of these. If "mores" means what the community practices, then we cannot tell which of the disparate practices of the numerous indistinct groupings in the society we should follow. And if we could conceivably define the precise practice of the specific group that ought to control, we should still discover it in a process of motion, modification, variation, and evolvement. Every average would necessarily comprise innumerable deviants; every observed conformity would involve an inquest into the conformers' ephemeral and highly individual reasons for conforming. Finally, the very act of selecting one guiding signal out of all the bewildering diversity of signals would entail the exercise of an evaluative preference, that is to say, it would entail a moral decision. What people in general do cannot cancel the responsibility for what they ought to do. But even if it could, a completely dependable pattern of uniform mores simply does not exist.

Morals and mores, we may safely say, are not interchangeable. That, of course, is the reason why we are capable of passing moral judgments on what we believe to be accepted and customary social practices. Whenever we conform merely for the sake of conforming, we are obeying the mores as we then and there interpret them; and it is quite generally desirable that we should do so. Mores are entitled to a certain prestige. They create expectations that no one should wantonly disappoint; they facilitate our daily intercourse and our communication with one another. On the other hand, convenient and familiar as they are, they sometimes assert a claim to ultimate, even to divine, authority; and then our conscience is compelled to protest. Would it not be a very tame divinity that would guarantee whatever, in our little province, our group may happen to be accustomed to?

As I see them, although the moral rules and precepts do not furnish us with specific decisions, they are considerably more than mere restatements of social custom. What practical purposes can they be said to serve? We know that they assist in *pedagogic* efforts to prepare and refine individual character, and that they are indispensable to any *critical* evaluation of behavior. What we are interested in most, however, is their role, if they have any, in the paramount *decisional* process; for if the precepts do not affect our decisions, they are worth comparatively little.

They do. In the first place, precepts can assist the individual self to project into and to care about other selves. This they can do because of their form. Because they are couched in general and generic terms, they can summon the self to recognize all that is generically human in the moral predicaments of other individuals. In the second place, precepts furnish the deliberative grist for the sense of wrong. The sense of wrong, we noted, is a blend of rational activity with emotional and organic affections. When our reasoning power turns to its work, it finds the precepts ready and waiting to be processed. Our moral choices are not made in an unformed, chaotic mist; every factor we observe resembles some kind of precedent, every interest seeks its place somewhere in some pre-established category. We are free to decide, but our deliberations have their stuff prepared for them. The taught moral precepts constitute that stuff; it is with them we work, whether we decide to use them or reject them; the only thing we cannot do is altogether ignore them. We can choose which precept we shall apply and how we shall apply it, but the register of our choice remains finite and our conscience knows the language it must speak and the phrases it must work with.

The intensity of particular phrases in this language—which ones are usually pronounced sternly and which ones indifferently —we learn from day to day by observing the practices of our society. We receive a constant stream of information concerning the texture of one moral standard or another as it is applied, showing the permissible areas of compromise, the places where literal compliance will be insisted on, and the points at which a standard is so remote from the general behavior that it sounds like nothing more than hypocritical unctuousness. Thus, although the mores do not necessarily create the specific moral precept, they can intimate the probable social consequences of infringing it and they can present a chart of alternative practical choices. The chart would, however, remain too abstract for most of us, were it not incarnated and animated in what we call "moral types."

Moral types should be recognized as one of the most potent varieties of moral legislation. A "type" illustrates some set of personal qualities which are usually expressed in a cluster of mythical anecdotes or apothegms. For example, Cato the Censor was long the Roman type for patriotic zeal, inflexible moral severity, and primitively simple frugality. He in turn was inspired by the example of Manius Curius Dentatus, an earlier consul, whose meager cottage was nearby Cato's country seat. It was to this cottage that the ambassadors of the Samnites came to offer Dentatus a bribe on behalf of their nation, and there they found him preparing some turnips for his meal. Cato never forgot Dentatus' answer: "A man who can be satisfied with such a supper has no need of gold."

What an inviting summons to imaginative projection and self-dramatization we have here! Cato could choose at one and the same time both to honor the maxims of antique virtue and to identify himself with the hero of the cottage; in like manner, some exceptional Roman of a later generation, as he strolled abstemiously away from a beautiful woman, could mutter that Rome was not yet devoid of Catos. There are a variety of dressings a man can use to make a supper of turnips more palatable.

Moral types, like moral precepts, should not appear so extreme in their exactions that compliance calls for a cruel and self-afflicting discipline. Of course, there have always been a certain number of voluntary ascetics; they are destined to be respected rather than emulated. Generally, their retirement from the world is considered commendable, if for no other reason than the annoyance that would be occasioned by their remaining among us. If they do remain—because, for example, their religious denomination is not considerate enough to furnish them with a place of withdrawal—they are likely to interfere with everyone else's harmless enjoyments.

The moral types that seem to compete on the American scene are three in number. Two types exemplify the more or less continuous traditions of ethics and the third expresses some rather sporadic and localized social conditions.

The two moral types that are traditional may be called "the muscular" and "the eupeptic."

The muscular species emphasizes strength of will, purity of purpose, and a somewhat narrow channeling of human aspiration. Parson Weems' Washington, the abolitionists, the woman-suffragists, and the popular image of Woodrow Wilson are instances.

The eupeptic type (taking as its motto: *mens sana in corpore sano*) stands for a more varied responsiveness to the moral possibilities of life, and a more flexible, even opportunistic policy. With all his morbid traits, Abraham Lincoln yet appears to be our arch example of this type; Benjamin Franklin was an equally genuine one. They were famous for warmth and humor.

Currently, we have a third moral type, which we call "the well-adjusted individual." The name is somewhat flattering. In actuality, "the well-adjusted individual" tends to resemble what zoologists call a "cryptic mimic," i.e., an animal that conceals and preserves itself by means of protective coloration and other kinds of imitation. The American who commits himself to a gray-green ideal like this has wholly identified morals with mores, and has decided, along with ancient Pindar, that "Custom is king."

From time to time, there appear certain extraordinary men who insist that their society is doing evil and that it must change and adjust its practices. These men, like other creative individuals, are usually quite "maladjusted." They make up a moral type we are accustomed to call the "prophets," and societies being what they are, the prophets meet almost always with hatred and frequently with martyrdom. There are false prophets and true prophets. A prophet is true as far as he adheres to the moral constitution when he challenges some established precept or national practice; in all other respects, he is unauthorized or false. Since the constitution is the only lasting criterion by which to condemn a community, a prophet's authority derives from it. When he protests that the standard of social behavior must comply with the moral constitution, he fulfills the highest function of the moral type: he speaks then to a limited community on behalf of a less limited, possibly a universal, community.

The prophet is not, however, a creator of pure novelties, any more than the rest of us. What he brings to the society was there all the time; he has learned it there, as indeed might everyone else in the audience he addresses. What he contributes of his own is the intense reworking of some familiar moral theme. He may evolve the primitive version; he may confer a new emphasis on it; he may advance it to heights no one in his society contemplated before. On an imposing scale—sometimes the scale of genius—he executes the three stages we have already identified in the universal process of moral legislation. The prophet walks on the very same path, however far he may climb.

Now, at least, it appears that there is a path, a common one —though directions may differ and branches may fork off. That a common path of moral legislation actually exists is something we need to appreciate in order to locate ourselves on it. Too long has the way been hidden from our feet by false theoretical separations. It is as though someone had laid on it two rows of open grocery-boxes, requiring us to step in the box on this side or in the one on that side, and always preventing us from having access to the path underneath. Moral legislation, we have been told persistently, is *either* societal *or* individual, *either* objective *or* subjective, *either* immutable precept *or* arbitrary, local convention: so whatever way we choose, we are forced to limp.

Must we? Our analysis of moral legislation would seem to show that we need not, that we may be able to push those factitious grocery-boxes aside and replace the static either-or's with the both-and's of an ongoing human process. Moral legislation is produced by the group at work in individuals. We see it in objective behavior because a subjective individual has enacted it in his conscience. Of course, moral legislation will always reflect the mutations of times and places—but it does so in the mirror of an expanding moral constitution, and the mirror is not a merely passive or neutral one.

5. THOU SHALT NOT'S, A TYPE OF MORAL LEGISLATION

In the course of this book, we expect to learn a great deal more about moral legislation in general and about certain important moral precepts in particular. But there is one class of precept that needs to be described here by way of introduction, because it represents the most direct and familiar bridge between morals and the law. We receive our first intimation of the interplay between the moral order and the legal order when we examine negative or prohibitive precepts, that is to say, what are popularly called "thou shalt not's."

"Thou shalt not's"—the simple, authentic ones that the unsophisticated conscience is quick to approve, not the host of impostors put forward by clerical ritualists and fanatics—are exceedingly useful precepts. In form they may seem to be only negative and sometimes we resent them as though they were dead-end barriers to human experience. But if we take their pragmatic effects into account, the "thou shalt not's" look more like cross-roads or (at worst) detours. One of the clearest lessons of legal history is that negative legislation is the typical instrument of a laissez-faire policy. Whatever is not prohibited is looked upon as exempt from interference, and thus the negative statutes, unless they are multiplied to an extreme, leave us spacious areas for individual selection and movement. It is rather the positive command that strips us of our choice, because by prescribing one defined course, it inevitably closes the way to all other possibilities.

But if "thou shalt not's" do in fact leave the routes clear to human freedom, why do they so often engender bitterness and rebellion?

One reason is not altogether pleasant to face. It is that the ancients were all too accurate in their observation that "stolen waters are sweet and bread eaten in secret is pleasant." Where conscience operates effectively as a monitor, it stirs up the resentments that are heaped on any monitor, even the most tolerant. Expressing these resentments by defying one's conscience is like adding a spicy sauce to the dish of immoral pleasure: it heightens the immediate enjoyment at least, though it may and often does jade the palate in the long run. In this sense, whatever is banned is thereby made more desirable. The wise moral legislator will therefore dispense his "thou shalt not's" rather parsimoniously.

The second reason, related to the first, is that we have not yet learned the techniques that might enable us to enforce prohibitions on ourselves without excessive psychic cost. Perhaps the monitor would not build up such stores of resentment if forbidding—where forbidding is sensible and necessary—were to take the form of directing impulses and interests toward some definite alternative that would offer substitute satisfactions. Here we are on ground that every mother knows very well: a "no" will not do without a simultaneous, attractive "yes" to draw the will away from the prohibited objective. Generally, the licit will not make us forgetful of the illicit unless it is different enough not to remind us constantly of the forbidden fruit: the man who wants to banish images of his neighbor's wife from his mind has more chance of success if he fastens his attention, not immediately on his own wife, but on some matter of business or sport or civic interest. The decision to do so—or where possible to put geographical distance between oneself and some magnetic temptation—is a moral decision and a prudent one, because it relieves the conscience of an avoidable strain and thus spares it the impact of subsequent resentments.

In the third place, any "thou shalt not" that attempts to stigmatize the mere entertaining of certain forbidden thoughts or feelings is simply impossible to comply with. The most unsuccessful of the Ten Commandments is the tenth ("Thou shalt not covet"); it alone is concerned with regulating the content of men's imaginations. Covetousness is a foul and noisome disease, yet a disease with which every living individual is afflicted. We may be able to reduce its ravages by fixing our attention on what we have as distinguished from what we lack; but to lay down an absolute prohibition of coveting is to demand a society composed exclusively of saints and, because of the sheer cruelty of that demand, to wind up with one composed mainly of scoffers. The suggestion we began with—let us recall once more—is that the analysis should focus on an *act* of wrong.

Before we turn to the law and ask how it agrees with and how it differs from morals, we might glance back at the ground we have traversed. In our discussion there has been no trace of what is traditionally termed "mathematical certainty"; we had not been naive enough to expect any. On the other hand, the moral constitution as we saw it intimates a promise that at times we may reach what is called "moral certainty." Concededly, such a promise will not satisfy the kind of mentality that is afraid to lean on anything less rigid than an "irrefutable" syllogistic demonstration. In some individuals there are, we must admit, fears so deep and obsessive that they are beyond discourse's power to exorcise; as for such, all we can do is pause a moment in compassion, and then go forward.

II

Law As a Moral Order

1. AMERICAN ATTITUDES TOWARD THE LAW

AMERICAN attitudes toward the law from our national beginnings down to the present day make up a history of fierce and unresolved tension. On the one side, there has been an uncritical and excessive trust in what can be accomplished through legislation and policing, while, on the other side, there has been an equally unwarranted mistrust of the law and of social control by means of government.

We are wont to associate the former attitude—which may be called "legalistic"—with the early Puritans, and the latter—the "anti-legalistic"—with Jean-Jacques Rousseau and his eighteenth century American followers. But both traditions may be traced much farther back and may be found in many other cultures. For example, in the millennial history of Confucianism there have been several swings of the pendulum back and forth between a contemptuous rejection of law and an extreme subservience to it. Plato recapitulated these developments in a single lifetime: in his prime he wrote the anti-legalistic *Republic* and when he grew old, he wrote the legalistic *Laws*. Americans—whether or not they have heard of Plato—are likely to shift between the two conflicting attitudes in an even briefer space of time and, in extreme cases, to voice both of them simultaneously.

But there is nothing to apologize for in this, nothing derogatory of American intelligence. Wisdom—that is, the ability to make the best possible bricks in an existence that offers very little straw for the purpose—wisdom never amounts to much more than learning from experience to live with antitheses and, where one can, to make use of them. This special antithesis (of repulsion from and attraction to the law) had been spelled out with the utmost clarity as long ago as the Old and New Testaments. The Five Books of Moses, although themselves by no means consistently legalistic, taught legalism to the Puritans.

In the New Testament, on the other hand, were many opposing, even anarchistic passages, bitterly repudiating the law as such. True, these denunciations of law were more or less linked in the text with an expectation that all mundane life was soon to come to its final end and judgment; nevertheless, after the lapse of so many centuries during which that expectation was deferred, the sentiments antagonistic to law were accepted without regard to context, that is, as though they were intended to apply with equal force to an ongoing human society. Thus the Scriptures offered support for views at both extremes. And, if an American, finding himself sympathetic with neither extreme legalism nor anarchism, desired instead to advocate some moderate measure of confidence in the laws, then he would only have to echo certain fine phrases out of the moral prophesies in the same corpus of ancient literature.

In our own day, legalism takes two forms. The first of them is what we generally call "positivism." According to this view, the law is only the established and existing list of official commands; and speculation on what the rules of law ought to be constitutes a waste of effort. Positivism is something like the Queen of Hearts, who frightened Alice in Wonderland for a while. The Queen was forever shouting, "Off with his head!" and then going on with whatever she had been doing at the time the unfortunate offender happened to cross her path. No one's head was ever really chopped off in the story, because—as Alice noticed—many things can intervene between an official command and its literal execution to deflect or even frustrate the command. In practice, what the law is will always depend to some extent on what it ought to be. Moral influences are among the most powerful and persistent factors in shaping both the general rules and the decisions in particular lawsuits. When a jury renders a verdict or a judge finds the legally decisive "facts of the case," the evidence given in court has first passed through a series of filters, one of the filters being composed of a collection of silent moral presuppositions—prejudices sometimes, at other times sacred convictions. There is no understanding the law without paying attention to its moral side.

On the other hand, in Wonderland there was also the Duchess. She—poor, ugly, tedious creature—insisted on extracting a moral from everything, every turn of conversation and episode of life's experience. "Everything's got a moral," she would say, "if only you can find it." So it is with the second kind of legalism. This kind, far from taking an amoral attitude toward the law, insists that law and morals are one and the same, that every colorless legal issue is charged with the greatest moral significance, and that any effort on the part of law to adjust its methods to social convenience or economic need presents an affront to moral values. This sort of moralistic-legalistic attitude we must be careful to avoid. For our purposes there is plenty of genuine moral ore immediately at hand in the rules and practices of the law; we can readily dispense with all far-fetched or fine-spun notions. Law, like the rest of human institutions, is full of the morally neutral, i.e., what may be called "inert ingredients."

The Queen, we may be certain, is mistaken, for morals are by no means irrelevant to the law. The Duchess too is mistaken, for law and morals are clearly not to be identified one with the other. If, then, the two are related but are not the same, what would Americans say is the nature of the difference between them? How do we distinguish the good from the good-in-law?

2. POPULAR DISTINCTIONS BETWEEN LAW AND MORALS

OFTEN the law deals with a question that is characteristically within the realm of morals. The moral issue regulated by law may be ancient and familiar (e.g., taking of human life in order to save one's own life); sometimes it is a new manifestation of an old moral issue (e.g., the question of euthanasia of persons suffering from incurable disease); and from time to time, the moral issue appears to be precipitated by really novel technological conditions (e.g., the permissibility of artificially inseminating a married woman whose husband is sterile).

In these areas, law and morals undoubtedly concern themselves with the same subject matter, which each endeavors to control according to its own regulations and standards of good behavior. Consequently, these are the areas that we intend to emphasize. Where the legal doctrine so conspicuously overlaps with what we are used to call morals, it should have momentous lessons to teach us. And this will be true even though the law on a specific point seems to lag behind the movement of accepted moral evaluations, for we can always learn as much if not more from a colorful contrast as from a gray similarity.

What, then, are the ways we usually differentiate law from morals? If we examine the various lines of distinction that have gained popular acceptance, we shall find a strange mixture of truth and error and some unexpected sidelights on the nature of moral standards. The first popular distinction is:

> *That the law enforces only those* minimum *standards of moral behavior that are indispensable for community existence, whereas morals deals with the standards suitable to an* ideal *human being.*

This first line of distinction has a rich historical background, particularly in America because of our frontier experience. Under frontier conditions, the duties assigned to the law are very limited, and no one turns to it unless personal safety or some basic property right is threatened or perhaps a marriage ceremony is desired. Even as to these, fending in a virile manner for oneself is deemed more honorable than depending on the assistance of the legal machinery. Self-help and "common-law marriage" keep many items of business away from the courts. In various rural sections of the United States, this pioneer attitude still persists; resort to law is considered mean if not unmanly. Influenced by these historical souvenirs and by the political dogma that a government is best when it governs least, Americans are prone to conclude that law not only does but ought to stop at minimum standards of moral behavior. When it has controlled violence and maintained order, they would say it has discharged its office.

The new industrial age having made this attitude obsolete, it is time that Americans adjusted their notions of law to the twentieth-century facts. Ours has become an urbanized society, and our frontiers—in so far as they remain national in character—are now in the vertical dimension. The community moves upward and downward rather than outward. The legal system is as mature and complete on one coast as on the other, and official regulation touches the existence of every citizen at innumerable points. If the line between law and morals is asserted to be one of relative standards (minimum or ideal), then outgrown historical data are not enough to maintain the distinction.

But at least this contrast between the frontier conditions of the recent past and the urban milieu of today does have one immediate use. It compels us to notice not only that many duties are now assigned to the law which used to be fulfilled by other methods of social ordering, but what is more significant though less familiar—the considerable rise that has occurred in the moral level of legal standards. The more duties the law took on its shoulders during the new industrial era, the more responsive it became to a number of human needs it had previously neglected or ignored. Its moral level rose concomitantly with its obligations, perhaps because it could no longer send so many human interests to other institutions to seek satisfaction. These days, judges do not say as readily as they did a century ago, "Plaintiff may have a moral right but he has no legal right," because so much of the old territory of morals has been put under mandate of the law that yesterday's moral-but-not-legal right frequently becomes today's moral-and-legal right. The becoming, i.e., the impulsion by which advancing moral standards grow into the law, is a central interest of our study.

Is it not possible that some similar process may be identified within the standards of morals? If it could, we might uncover a new meaning in that apparently invidious phrase "minimum standards," which up to now has been reserved for the law side of the comparison. Is there any movement in the realm of morals like the one we have seen in the realm of law?

Patently there is. It is a misleading over-simplification to talk of a moral standard as though it were something single and static. At any given time, we have to acknowledge at least three moral standards by which we pass judgment: they are (1) the standard we require, (2) the standard we desire, and (3) the standard we revere. The *first* we generally enforce by group punishment for infractions, and the *second* we usually seek to bring about by preaching and praising the *third.* Since we so often use the third—what might be called "saintly" or "heroic" morality—for purposes of exhorting others and gratifying our own emotional mysticism, we may take it for granted that this standard does not have much practical reference—that is, unless some genuine "saint" or moral "hero" happens to come into view. If he does, then likely as not, we shall find ourselves preferring people on the minimum moral level to any such literal incarnation of the ideal we profess so ardently in our rhetoric. In fact, people confronted with the actual presence of a moral hero may sink disgracefully below the minimum in the way they treat him. His example instills feelings of guilt and resentment. He ought to know men find it more comfortable to revere him at a distance.

The real purpose of moral ideals is to teach; they are time-tested tools for educating ourselves. Once we recognize this, the old static diagram of commands and precepts changes before our gaze into a fluid, moving process—similar to the process we observed in the workings of the law. The ideal level pulls and strains away to lift the desired, the desired exerts a similar attraction on what is required, and so the entire moral fabric continually shifts and changes. If the social basis should sink because of bad economic conditions or the ravages of war, then the minimum plane can drag the others down with it. And if the desired level in some department of conduct becomes increasingly convenient and accepted, it will sooner or later be identified with the required. Thus what was heroic may become commonplace, and to give one's life for some realizable ideal may be treated no longer as the monopoly of the saints.

This moving process in the life of morals does not, of course, fail to engender similar movement in the life of the law. What was legally optional in one generation may, in this manner, become a strict obligation in the next. For example, giving voluntary assistance to the unemployed may be converted by statute into paying mandatory contributions for unemployment insurance, and what a broker used to consider spontaneous candor in dealing with investors may now amount to nothing more than compliance with Securities and Exchange Commission regulations. The volunteer who thus becomes a conscript has not gone down in possibilities of moral worth; there will always be an advance social patrol for which he can enlist if he chooses to.

There is also a technical aspect to this subject of "minimum standards." We must allow for the fact that American courts deal with the vast majority of civil wrongs by compelling the wrongdoer to pay *compensation*—that is, dollars. Now this circumstance bears on our subject in a variety of ways, two of which are particularly pertinent here.

In the first place, the law very frequently refuses to award any relief whatever where no economic (that is, pecuniary) loss can be shown, despite the conspicuous grievousness of the moral wrong. There are historical reasons for this condition, arising out of the development of the law of civil wrongs or torts in England. A few primitive torts (such as an assault and battery) were called "trespasses," and for these injuries a man could recover nominal and even exemplary damages without offering proof that he had suffered a pecuniary loss. But the list of "trespasses" was a closed one, and the new varieties of tort which the courts gradually came to recognize as the social setting evolved were classified as "actions on the case." These actions could not be maintained unless the plaintiff could prove he had sustained a *money* injury. Such is still the general state of American common law, and its consequence, of course, is that advancement in moral standards in the field of tort law remains limited in some measure to cases of pecuniary damage. That is indeed a disadvantage—but not an insuperable one. The legislature can overcome it with a statute that grants relief regardless of money damage, and sometimes the courts themselves achieve the goal by issuing injunctions before threatened wrongs can materialize.

In the second place, what may look like a refusal by the law to recognize a certain right is sometimes only a refusal of money in a situation where money ought neither to be asked nor accepted. For instance, lawsuits for alienation of affections, having been used all too often for purposes of scandal and blackmail, were finally abolished in several states by enactment of the legislature. It does not require a very sensitive morality these days to determine that losing the affection of one's wife should not be considered compensable by a payment of dollars. This example is important; it may supply part of the answer to a criticism from time to time directed at the law—that the law protects a man's reputation but does not protect his honor. If the law is at fault in this respect, the fault is due to its depending to the extent it does on awards of money. There is no fault in assuming that money-damages will not salve a wound to any honor worthy of the name.

The second popular distinction between law and morals is:

> *That the law is preoccupied with* external *conduct only, which it judges according to the standard of a "reasonable"* or generic *man, whereas morals is preoccupied with the* subjective *intention of the* individual.

Those who rely on this distinction think of law as being like the Chinese peasant in an old folk-anecdote. The peasant decided to buy a pair of shoes to cover his bare feet, so he carefully measured his feet and then trudged several miles to town, where there was a shoe store. When he arrived, the store was soon to close for the night, but he declined to go in and instead turned back toward his farm—because he found he had forgotten to bring the measurements. And when he was asked why the size could not be determined by trying the shoes directly on his feet, he replied, "I trust the measurements more than I do the feet."

There may be somewhat more to this story than appears on the surface, and our indulgent smiles at the peasant's naiveté may have to change into admiration for his good sense. For since he had walked miles in his bare feet, was it not possible that on his arrival in town they were swollen to an abnormal size? The measurements, on the other hand, had been taken at a time when he could feel sure that his feet were of the size he wanted the shoes to fit.

Now it is true that most legal rules and procedures are patterned to the normal generic foot and are difficult to adjust to one that is idiosyncratic or swollen. Lawyers point to this fact with some measure of pride, claiming that it shows that law is no respecter of persons and no one is exempt from its standards. Then, by way of further defense, they will go on to explain that special rules are established for types of individuals (such as minors, persons relying on a confidential relationship, and insane persons) who cannot fairly be expected to protect their own interests like "reasonable" men. Finally, the lawyers may call attention to the individualized procedures in the "children's" and "family" courts and to the new therapeutic practices adopted in several states to treat offenders who are psychopathic. These and similar developments do indicate a certain trend toward progressive individualization in the law. However, it must be granted that many of the reforms came in response to criticism from outside the ranks of the profession, and so they are only modest occasions for pride and none at all for complacency.

Granting as much, American lawyers would be nonetheless

astonished by the suggestion that the system they administer is unlike morals because it is indifferent to the states of men's minds, and they would experience no difficulty in furnishing an impressive list of instances to prove the contrary. Whether we talk of homicide or of contracts, of interference with business relations, of dispositions in a last will, or of tax evasions, the courts are unceasingly busy with ascertaining subjective mental states and with adjudging legal effects in accordance with them. Sometimes a distinction is made between the intent to do an act and the motive for doing it, but surely these are both operations attributable to the mind.

In certain situations—usually situations where the one who acts has much less to lose by literal obedience than others may lose by his disobedience—the law will not pay heed to subjective defenses or excuses. If a motorist exceeds the speed limit, a professedly innocent purpose on his part will not reduce the risk he imposes on the public. To be innocent in the eyes of the public, he must adjust his state of mind to the regulations governing the highway; and the vital fact is that most motorists do. Knowing that even commendable excuses will not be received, they concentrate on the business of safe driving. And this consequence —the conscious obedience to the ordinance—should be attributed to the law along with the instances of infraction, trial, and punishment. The good-in-law is realized not only when a thief is arrested, though that may be the kind of good the public can discern. There is an increment to good whenever a tempted cashier, taking it for granted that thieves are generally detected and arrested, closes the till and leaves it intact. This he does from day to day, and perhaps eventually he builds the habit of honest dealing. Would that be a small benefit?

It is not easy to obtain a forthright answer. For many centuries, the clergy of various denominations so heavily emphasized the moral importance of states of mind that nothing else seemed really meaningful. Why the clergy felt impelled to do so is scarcely mysterious. They were concerned primarily with faith, belief, the subjective dedication to a creed. To them religion involved an inner conversion, that is, a kind of renascent change in the whole spirit of the believer. And certain clergymen may have entertained a special purpose: since every man some time or other is bound to think a forbidden thought, even one who acts righteously will have to seek remission for his sins—provided that a mere thought, linked to no overt action, can constitute a moral offense. In point of fact, a morality which is administered by ecclesiastics can afford to indict the whole of mankind, and perhaps can find advantage in a judgment of universal human guilt. This the law cannot do. It cannot hold the citizenry—or even too large a minority of them—to be felons. On the contrary, law can retain authority only by assuming that, whatever crimes and lapses may take place, the mass of the populace are lending it the support of their daily compliance.

A responsible morals cannot be developed out of private mental states, subjective beliefs, or vaporous reveries. It requires a more social foundation. Whenever we are compelled—at times we are compelled—to pass judgment on another's behavior, we cannot escape drawing inferences from his public actions. As in the courts, the judgment we reach will certainly attach importance to motives, and so it should. But how are we to discover motives? In practice, we are bound to infer them primarily from our neighbor's overt and observable conduct. What a man does is surely one of the guides to what he intends, and sometimes it is the only trustworthy guide.

3. A WORKABLE DISTINCTION BETWEEN LAW AND MORALS

SOME people, sophisticated enough to see the difficulties in the two popular theories we have been discussing, propose a third distinction between morals and the law. They say:

> *There are moral values in the law and there are moral values outside the law; the only practical difference between them is in the respective* methods *by which they are* enforced.

Those who hold this view will insist that there is absolutely no formula of division by which one can determine *a priori* where a specific moral value will be given its enforcement. A moral problem may summon the sheriff, the school, the home, the business association, the social group, the church, or any combination of these, depending exclusively on how the community at that particular stage in its development has chosen to assign the functions of prevention and punishment. To rely on any advance hypothesis as a criterion of allocation they consider futile, because community history and its local incidents decide the question arbitrarily until some further, equally arbitrary pages of history are ready to be written. Can it be expected that all these chance factors and processes will submit to a preconceived system of classification? Surely not.

Now, this pragmatic position is entirely right, within its own limits. It is positivistic without dogmatism; it acknowledges the active existence of moral values along with other, non-moral elements in the law. Rightly, it asserts that while some moral precepts are enforced by the courts, others are not, and that only the conventions and customs of the times determine whether to enforce a precept here or to remit it there. It is, moreover, correct in implying that the development and enforcement of morals do not belong by superior right within the jurisdiction of any church. This is the authentic American view of the subject, guaranteed by our Constitution. If moral rules and behavior were considered mere subdivisions or corollaries of ecclesiastical tenets, no government could legislate concerning them without violating the First Article of the Bill of Rights. ("Congress shall make no law respecting an establishment of religion, or prohibiting the free exercise thereof . . .") Whatever errors we Americans may have committed, we have certainly avoided this one.

Finally, this position has the advantage of directing our attention to the difference between enforcement procedures in the organs of law and those elsewhere in the social community. We are reminded that both morals and law are concerned with techniques of administering and adjudicating. While the two overlap in respect of their subject matter, they likewise overlap in respect of the methods they use to handle and process it.

Thus far and within its limits, the pragmatic view appears unexceptionable; but unfortunately, it does not go nearly far enough. As yet it intimates nothing concerning the really indispensable clews, i.e., clews that might tell us what to look for when we see a familiar moral precept being enforced in the courts as a rule of law. Assuredly, where a rule that previously operated only in some informal social group graduates into becoming a proposition of law, one may expect to notice some change in the rule. And when the man who is confronted with a moral choice has to decide it not as an ordinary citizen but in his official capacity as a judge, does not that circumstance have some effect on the outcome? If it does, then we should need to know in just what respects.

Perhaps there are a few identifying marks that appear on the surface of the good when it manifests itself as the good-in-law;

at least we may suggest certain kinds of phenomena that seem meaningful enough to put a reader on the alert for them. In other words, as we progress in the stages of a study such as this, is there anything in particular we should be watching for?

4. ATTRIBUTES OF THE GOOD-IN-LAW

IN VIEW of the fact that in examining the law we shall be dealing with a highly specialized social institution, we propose to watch in every chapter for the way this institution impresses its own distinctive characteristics on the moral precepts it enforces. There are good reasons to expect that a standard or precept moving along through the machinery of law will show some such marks as the following:

Imprint of the Mode of Trial

Certain moral precepts outside the law are couched in language too abstract, as far as the average citizen is concerned, to convey any powerful impulse to action. Phrases like "human dignity" or "the value of human life," although possessing some incantative usefulness, do not generally move him to project himself into another person's position or predicament. Something more specific, more concrete is necessary. And what proves most effective for the purpose is one form or another of—living *drama.*

There is a story, undoubtedly an apocryphal one, of an incident that is supposed to have happened to Goethe when he was in Rome on his celebrated Italian journey. He observed a number of blind beggars crouching at their several posts and displaying their crudely scrawled appeals near the entrance to St.

Peter's, and he grew more and more intrigued as he noticed the worshipers and visitors pass by most of these unfortunates but almost invariably pause to drop a coin in the cup held out by one—always the same one. Not infrequently, a stroller who had thoughtlessly gone on would turn about, come back to this specially favored blind man, donate something, and then resume his promenade. Filled with curiosity, Goethe thrust himself into the procession of visitors and read as he moved along, again and again in one style or another, "Help the blind." Finally he reached the sign that seemed to work such wonders. It said simply, "It is April, and I am blind."

Dramatization has a magical capacity to arouse our moral constitutions, that is, if the drama is genuine and sincere in nature. One notorious defect of American law is that some of its dramas are fraudulent both as to personnel and as to plot. There are court trials that degenerate into contests of wit between the lawyers, who, while entertaining the onlookers with their surprises and stratagems, completely becloud the factual merits which ought to decide the controversy. Too often we find that we have become spectators at a game of legal swordplay, where objective truth seems nearly irrelevant. As clients see it, a candid disclosure by the attorney to the judge would be tantamount to betrayal, and even an intellectually honest assessment of the applicable rule of law would seem treacherous. The adversary in the case must not be left with a shred of respectability or virtue; each piddling dispute must be puffed up and exaggerated. Accordingly, the trial lawyer goes on to display every pose and device in his histrionic repertoire and if, as he bellows and struts, his client's cause seems by degrees to recede from attention and fade into the background, why that is rather precisely what most laymen expect when they retain the services of a virtuoso. As a by-product of this performance, the moral precept which was too remote and abstract outside the law to summon our power of projection, now summons it well enough—but to the wrong stage and the wrong protagonist. If we identify ourselves, as in the subconscious we often do, with one of the lawyers and his collection of forensic shifts, then we too may come to be more concerned with victory than with a just result.

Fortunately the exhibitions we have been discussing are not necessarily representative of trials in American courts. The judge has authority to maintain effective control over the course of the courtroom drama; and when he does so, the public trial uncovers a host of latent moral values and fairly compels us to cross over into that other self, the one on the witness stand, who has either inflicted or suffered some deprivation of right, some act of outrage. When the lawyers switch on the lights and —either voluntarily or under procedural compulsion—keep their own personalities aside where they belong, the beams center on the accused or the litigant; and as we hear his testimony and cross-examination, we sense the integrity or the malice in him with a sureness of conviction we cannot fully articulate, much less hope to justify in logic. But we know then, nevertheless, that we have found whatever is genuine in the marrow of the man; we have lived through the emergence of his predicament —to the extent he himself is able to apprehend it. When such an instance occurs, it is fitting to say that the formal ideal has taken on flesh and reality by virtue of being involved in a trial at law. "Human dignity," for example, can never again sound like a mere abstraction to anyone who has watched a Negro recount under oath how he was turned out of some public place or conveyance because of his race.

It is for this reason that in the ensuing chapters our study will be based on selected principal cases. Occasionally we shall use a case just as a lawyer would at his daily work—for demonstrative purposes (to prove that some principle or other is the established law) or for illustrative purposes (to show by example how the courts have handled analogous situations). But mainly a case will represent something different to us in this book. It will represent an opportunity to discover an entire spectrum of hidden moral interests and values. The specific personalities and incidents of the case, refracting as they do what would ordinarily appear to be some very simple abstract proposition, serve to break it up into a rainbow sweep of component factors. Hence, when we make use of a court decision, our purpose will generally be neither demonstrative nor illustrative, but prismatic. And although, because it seems kinder to do so, we may sometimes designate the litigating parties by their initials instead of full surnames, that will not imply that there is anything fictional or imaginary about their litigation.

The principal cases, which we intend to use in this prismatic way, arose under American laws and were decided by American courts. Why only American? Because it seems desirable at least, if not strictly necessary, that the decisions grow out of economic conditions and cultural circumstances in a single national society. What happens in the cases is easier to understand when we already know the whole social context.

Imprint of the Professional Discipline

Just as some moral precepts are too abstract to inspire any species of practical action, others are too vague to indicate what kind of action should be taken and what kind should be avoided. When we are told "thou shalt not kill," it is as though someone had tied a thin bandage over our eyes; through it we can make out lights and shadows but the outlines appear fuzzy and imprecise, because we know that there are times and occasions when killing may possibly be justified or even obligatory. Something is needed to confer edges on the areas of light.

In the system of law, statutes and judicial principles mark off the edges with a sharpness which—though by no means invariable or exact—is at least sufficient to unite the community behind the enforcement officials and thus to serve warning on all concerned that this specific precept defined in these concrete terms cannot be transgressed with impunity. It is in this fashion that what we described in chapter 1 as the *sense of wrong* makes its appearance in the law courts and legislatures as the firmer and more precise *sense of injustice.*

The task of making the rules definite and developing the refinements and exceptions is put by the community into the practiced hands of lawyers and judges. Generally speaking, they execute their assignment with considerable skill, and if the results sometimes are unsatisfactory, that is more likely to be due to too much than to too little concentration on technical detail.

For it must be admitted that the kind of men who become attorneys really enjoy what Shakespeare called the "nice sharp quillets of the law." They relish the intellectual chess-game of definitions, fine distinctions, and neat exceptions—particularly when these carry with them a fragrance redolent of age and history. Law is, to some limited extent, a sort of solidification of past social experience, and if for purposes of reform we do away with a body of concepts developed in the course of legal history, we seem in the view of many lawyers to be discarding all the tried and tested wisdom that these concepts were intended to epitomize. So it is that the notorious conservatism of the majority at the bar does not consist nearly so much in adhering immovably to political, economic, or moral convictions, as in using old and verbose phrases, procedures, and technicalities. To the type of mentality that makes a competent lawyer, a page of esoteric verbiage in fine print can look like a sumptuous repast.

Thus, in the matter of precision, the law has the ability to lift a corner of the blindfold that obscures our moral judgment. But whether that ability is exercised advantageously must depend on where the law directs us to fix our eye. There are occasions when we had better grope our way freely in the usual half-light than be allowed to see the issue clearly and yet be forced far away from it at the point of a technicality.

Imprint of the Social Function

It is worth considering that the abstractness and vagueness of a moral precept can prove very convenient, at least on those occasions when the precept goes against the grain of our inclination. When this occurs, we are likely to comfort ourselves with the thought that, though we want to do what is right and cease doing what is wrong, no precise signposts are visible to announce the appropriate way. Indecisiveness is then only a technique we use for escaping conscience's compulsion. True, in our own estimation, we appear merely inert and unable to choose a path; in actuality we are continuing along in the familiar company of something identifiably illicit.

We expect to find the judge or administrator at the opposite pole from this kind of self-indulgent indecision. The community confers his office on him precisely in order to obtain authoritative decisions, which though highly imperfect in many cases will at least set disputes at rest. He may and probably often will err, but since he is a judge he must be able to make up his mind.

Moreover, the community looks for rather similar attributes in the procedures its legal system provides for it. If some personal wrong is committed or some social evil makes an appearance, people demand that the institution of law take remedial steps, not remain neutrally inert but move and intervene.

Legislatures and judges are constantly reminded of this demand.

At times the consequences are harmful. Judges may decide controversies either before they are ripe for wise analysis and decision, or according to a criterion that is more decisive than intelligent. They may use what—in chapter I—we termed a "judicial" process of developing the good-in-law where the nature of the problem calls for an "administrative" process. For instance, where a husband and a wife come into court to submit their conflicts and disagreements, the judge may base his entire disposition of the many ramified and subtle relations among the various members of the family exclusively on some kind of "guilt" imputed by him to one of the spouses. He may be compelled to this imputation by the statutes of his state; for legislatures, particularly in this country, sometimes have a way of making themselves absurd by meddling in concerns beyond their competence and insisting on nostrums that were proved useless generations ago.

More often, however, the legislatures and particularly the courts do furnish commendable models of timely intervention and decisiveness. In the present era, epidemic with indecision, American society still looks to its judges and expects them to serve as living examples of prudence and resolution. The maxim they are supposed to demonstrate—a very ancient one—says: Hear the evidence, take counsel, deliberate, reach your decision, and then go forward with an easy heart; he who forever afflicts himself with doubt defrauds himself of the day and of life.

Imprint of Control over Official Force

We have already had occasion to comment on the egregious irresponsibility of certain moral precepts proclaimed outside the law. Anyone acting in a private and unofficial capacity can command the world to conform immediately to the specifications of his personal Utopia, and when it refuses—as it invariably does—can send society and all the men, women, and children in it to the fire of eternal perdition. (However, it is necessary to report that even in this respect they do not oblige him.)

In contrast to this irresponsibility, there is the characteristic responsibility that judges develop from their habitual control over the exercise of official force. Law implies some measure of available compulsion, compulsion to be unleashed at the behest of the judges. Being constantly reminded, as they are, of their accountability to their profession, to the superior courts, to the electorate, to the whole contemporary community, and at last to the judgment of posterity, the representative judges try rather consistently to adjust moral standards to levels that society can aspire to attain. With full allowance made for an incorrigible minority of arrogant and corrupt judges, this is still a very impressive service to the good-in-law.

Unfortunately, we have to note the other side of the account. The moral level may be lowered (1) by judges who are Philistine in their own standards and assume that most other men are like them, and (2) by judges who themselves are of notably superior metal but assume that most other men are unlike them. By virtue of either of these attitudes, Philistine or "minimum standards" may be introduced into the law.

Summary of Institutional Imprints

We have been pointing out some significant ways in which the good may be modified when it makes its appearance as the good-in-law. The indications can be summarized as follows:

Where the notion of good seems excessively:	*The good-in-law can supply:*	*But in law there is risk of:*
Abstract	Projection by virtue of drama	Contest of wits between trial lawyers
Vague	Precision	Absorption with technicalities
Neutral or Irresolute	Intervention and Decisiveness	Meddlesomeness, Attribution of Artificial Guilts
Utopian	Responsibility	Philistinism

We are now ready to begin the examination of American law as a repository of moral values. In chapter I, we traced the nature of the moral constitution, the precepts of moral legislation, and the varieties of moral type. Then, in this chapter, we have turned to the good-in-law and the imprints it receives as a result of passing through the courts. Thus we have acquired the intellectual apparatus for a journey from one area of moral interest to another on the great continent of the law.

For our purposes, it is a new and unmapped continent that we propose to explore. Facing its approaches, as we now do, we need all the resolution we can muster. In Francis Bacon's words:

> . . . *even if the breath of hope which blows on us from that New Continent were fainter than it is and harder to perceive, yet the trial (if we would not bear a spirit altogether abject) must by all means be made. For there is no comparison between that which we may lose by not trying*

and by not succeeding; since by not trying we throw away the chance of an immense good; by not succeeding we only incur the loss of a little human labour. But as it is, it appears to me from what has been said, and also from what has been left unsaid, that there is hope enough and to spare, not only to make a bold man try, but also to make a sober-minded and wise man believe.

PART TWO

Moral Guides in the American Law of Rights

III

The First of Life

1. THE VALUE OF BEING ALIVE

HOLMES was a seaman on the WILLIAM BROWN, which set sail from Liverpool for Philadelphia in 1841. The ship struck an iceberg some 250 miles from Newfoundland and soon began to sink. Two boats were lowered. The captain, various members of the crew, and a passenger got into one of them and, after six days on the open sea, were picked up and brought to land. The other boat was called the "long-boat"; it was leaky and might easily be swamped. Into it Holmes jumped along with the first mate, seven other seamen, and thirty-two passengers—about twice as many as the boat could hold under the most favorable conditions of wind and weather. Just as the long-boat was about to pull away from the wreck, Holmes, hearing the agonized cries of a mother for her little daughter who had been left behind in the panic, dashed back at the risk of instant death, found the girl and carried her under his arm into the long-boat. The sailors rowed and the passengers bailed, but the over-weighted long-boat, drifting between blocks of floating ice, sank lower and lower as a steady rain fell on the sea. The wind began to freshen, the sea grew heavy, and waves splashed over the bow. Then, after the first mate had twice given the order, Holmes and the rest of the crew began to throw the male passengers overboard. Two married men and a little boy were *spared, but the fourteen remaining male passengers were cast over, and two women—devoted sisters of one of the victims—voluntarily leaped to join their brother in his death. The long-boat stayed afloat. The next morning Holmes spied a sail in the distance, exerted himself heroically to attract notice of the passing vessel, and eventually brought about the rescue of everyone left in the boat.*

When the survivors arrived in Philadelphia, the mate and most of the seamen, hearing talk of prosecution, disappeared. Holmes was put on trial for manslaughter.

In his charge to the jury as to the law, the judge stated that passengers must be saved in preference to all seamen except those who are indispensable to operating the boat. If no sea-man can possibly be dispensed with, then the victims must be chosen from among the passengers by casting lots, provided—as in this case—there is time enough to do so.

The jury found Holmes guilty but recommended mercy. He was sentenced to six months' imprisonment at hard labor, in addition to the nine months he had already spent in jail awaiting his trial.[1]

No HUMAN being has ever asked to be born and no hour passes without its toll of perfectly sane suicides. The two sisters in the Holmes case are not to be looked upon as sacrificing themselves for the benefit of their fellow-passengers or as acting in irrational panic. They no longer possessed anything of worth to yield up as a sacrifice, for without their brother whom they loved, they simply did not care to remain in this life. And so they took their departure from it quite calmly, one of them pausing only long enough to ask for a dress to put around her. If the value of being alive is to be taken for granted as self-evident, how can it be denied so often and with such irrevocable sincerity?

This question could never be resolved if our appraisal of human life were a strictly *subjective* process. From the subjective point of view, the value of being alive varies not only from man to man according to the individual's relative status and destiny; more than that, it varies within the estimation of each selfsame individual from hour to hour according to his mood, the way the sun feels on the pores of his skin, and the chemicals bubbling in his viscera.

Suddenly, life may seem precious because a member of the opposite sex has smiled and extended a compliment, or because an unexpected copper coin has been found in the pocket of an old coat. Another time it may taste like filthy grit in the mouth because a certain letter has not arrived, because a cripple has come into view, or because some cluster of strangers have burst into an unexplained fit of laughter, the proverbial "laughter of fools—like the crackling of thorns under a pot." A moment later, the incident has slipped into the past and the mood becomes neutral again. All these states may be very real to the one who experiences them, but they fluctuate too irrationally and violently to furnish any standard for moral judgment.

When we turn to *objective* examinations of the value of being alive, it would be wiser not to expect a very optimistic appraisal. Considering the sum-total of human woe, disease, and bafflement, we may wonder that a net result of positive value—however small—is ever arrived at. An objective appraisal entitled to great consideration has been preserved for us in the Babylonian Talmud, which recounts how one famous school of rabbis disputed with another famous school for two and a half years. One school held it would have been better if man had not been created, and the other school contended it was better that man had been created than if he had not been created. At the end of that period, they finally took a vote, and it was found that the majority held it would have been much better had man not been created, but that since he had been created, it is his duty to examine his past actions, or according to others, to be careful of his future actions.[2]

This estimate brings us to some very important distinctions that must be kept in view at all points in our study. They are distinctions between an *answer*, a *rule for conduct*, and a *decision*. These rabbis were giving an answer to a general question, an answer that embodied certain attitudes, empirical observations, and value judgments. They were not making either a rule for conduct or a decision, that is, either a standard for judging and punishing or a disposition of some specific human predicament to which the attitudes and evaluations developed in the *answer* might become applicable in one way or another.[3] To answer that it would have been better if man had not been created is not the same as to legislate that a man in general has the right to save his life by ending the life of someone else, or to decide that Seaman Holmes in particular was justified under all the circumstances of his own unique crisis. On the contrary, the Talmud itself rejects the plea of necessity as an excuse for taking life. Thus it is that judgments change their tenor when they are meant to be acted on in the incidents of daily living.

The objective view does not hold that under every conceivable human set of circumstances each human life has an indestructible value. As everyone knows, the law has its published list of justifiable homicides (killing in self-defense) and excusable homicides (killing by mere accident); it drafts men into the armed forces to risk death in defense of their country, and if they commit certain types of crime, it deliberately puts them to death by hanging, asphyxiation, or electrocution. To hold that my life is not worth enough objectively to justify saving it by destroying yours is not necessarily to assign a very high value to either life. When cases arise in the civil courts involving suits for money-compensation, it is notorious that more money will be awarded for an injury that, with at least the appearance of permanency, takes away one's economic earning-power than for an injury that, with indisputable permanency, takes away one's life; and in most cases where the person killed is too young an infant to have demonstrated his capacity to earn money, very little will be granted to his family by way of damages.

Interestingly enough, the United States Supreme Court and the British House of Lords, though confronting the question in connection with quite different types of litigation, both decided unanimously that to be alive is in the eyes of the law preferable to not being alive. The American opinion,[4] written by Justice Holmes, affords an example of strictly objective appraisal. A man by the name of Perovich had been convicted of murder in the first degree and was sentenced to be hanged. President Taft commuted his sentence to life-imprisonment. Perovich claimed the President had no power to do this without obtaining his consent, because the Constitution gave the President only a right to "pardon" an offense completely, to shorten the period of imprisonment, or reduce the amount of a fine, but not the right to change one form of punishment (death) to another (life-imprisonment). This contention Holmes rejected, saying: "By common understanding imprisonment for life is a less penalty than death." Just to continue in the land of the living—though with expectations as wretched as Perovich's—was held to be somewhat better than death. The appraisal was objective: Perovich the murderer could not have been jettisoned with impunity if Seaman Holmes had found him in the long-boat.

Once we grant that every human life has some value, the American courts give us very little additional information by which to ascertain the elements of that value. This vagueness—justifiable perhaps for other considerations but disappointing to our inquiry—is due to the fact that, when a person sues because he has been injured or his estate sues because he has been killed, American courts do not *separately* evaluate the loss he sustained in having his expectancy of life shortened or terminated, nor do they award separate damages for the abbreviation of this life expectancy. They usually consider the loss of expectancy as part of the general claim for damages.[5] The English do segregate this item and, doing so, have found it necessary to state officially what elements should go into evaluating the loss of an expected portion of one's life. Suppose a child is killed—deprived of his expectancy of life—at the age of two and one-half: is the judge warranted in telling the jury that, when they come to assess the damages, they may presume "that human life is, on the whole, good"? If the judge sits without a jury, may he presume so?

No—in the unanimous judgment of the House of Lords, Britain's highest court—he may not.[6] He may not make this optimistic assumption, then consult the statistical tables of mortality and life expectancy, and go on in a crude fashion to allow so many pounds sterling for each year that the child has lost. "It would be fallacious to assume, for this purpose, that all human life is continuously an enjoyable thing, so that the shortening of it calls for compensation, to be paid to the deceased's estate, on a quantitative basis. The ups and downs of life, its pains and sorrows, as well as its joys and pleasures—all that makes up 'life's fitful fever'—have to be allowed for in the estimate."

What, then, should the trier of the facts take into consideration in such a case? What view should guide him in evaluating the child's lost prospect of happiness? His view should be directed to the circumstances of the specific individual life that has been destroyed; it should be *projective*. "If the character or habits of the individual were calculated to lead him to a future of unhappiness or despondency, that would be a circumstance justifying a smaller award. It is significant that, at any rate in one case of which we were informed, the jury refused to award any damages under this [loss of expectancy of life] head at all." Nor should the test be whether the deceased person *subjectively* had the ability to appreciate that staying alive would bring him a measure of happiness: what, for instance, could an infant know on that score? It is necessary rather to estimate "what kind of future on earth the victim might have enjoyed, whether he had justly estimated that future or not." Here in this case of an extremely young victim, the high court saw so many uncertainties as to the child's future prospects, so many unsettled possibilities and lurking risks, that the award must be smaller than for some mature individual, whose prospects would have become more definite and susceptible of calculation as the years flowed by.

Prospects—what are "prospects" when we come to estimate the chances of happiness in life? Are they the "great expectations," perhaps, that former generations conceived of in terms of comfortable inheritances, well-kept lawns, and the solemn descent of social rank? Quite a few commoners filled with dreams and envies might be inclined to think so; but not the House of Lords. They knew better, and nobly said:

"I would add that, in the case of a child, as in the case of an adult, I see no reason why the proper sum to be awarded should be greater because the social position or prospects of worldly possessions are greater in one case than another. Lawyers and judges may here join hands with moralists and philosophers and declare that the degree of happiness to be attained by a human being does not depend on wealth or status." (On hearing which, the moralist, not accustomed to or altogether comfortable in such august company, may murmur: Wisdom consists in recognizing the worthlessness of the baubles *before* one holds them in his hands.)

Having announced these principles, the House of Lords then proceeded to reduce by five-sixths the sum the trial judge had awarded on the mistaken assumption "that human life is, on the whole, good." Two hundred pounds would be quite enough, and would have been excessive "if it were not that the circumstances of the infant were most favourable." The amount seems small for a whole life's expectancy, and cynics may remark that any of the high judges would willingly have paid his doctor much more to prolong his own existence for just a few months. But pounds for a life that still breathes are incommensurable with pounds for a life that can never breathe again, incommensurable in practical terms because we cannot know what horrors the dead infant was spared by its death, incommensurable in moral terms because the doctor's fee is a purchase only of his services, not of that which cannot morally be bought, or sold, or trafficked in. The House of Lords was evaluating what had been lost and was irrecoverable; the life of a living unharmed child is not in the same realm as the pound sterling.

But if a living person is incommensurable with money, is he commensurable with something else—that is, with other living humans? The United States Court in the Holmes case must have thought he was, for it announced that, if passengers or sailors, as the case may be, must be thrown into the sea in order to save the other members of the group, the terrible choice should be made by casting lots. Shall we assent to this?

The sailor, says the Court, must sacrifice himself first, unless he cannot be dispensed with. Why? Is not his life worth as much or as little as the passenger's? Of course it is, but he has burdened it with a very specific duty, and, though the circumstances of the long-boat might appear so desperate as to cancel all other social conventions and civil obligations, this one they could not cancel because it was expressly conceived and designed to yoke him in just such a plight, to bind him in conscience and in law, and to drive him open-eyed and willing to whatever course might be necessitated, including his own extinction. The power to preserve one's life is not a right where it has been put in pledge not for money or merchandise but for the lives of others, and where war, disaster at sea, or some other stroke of maleficent chance forecloses the pledge. Holmes needed no judge's summons when he scurried back to the sinking *William Brown* to rescue the little girl who had been left aboard. For—whatever the value of being alive may be—we all know perfectly well that there are many things more valuable; and while we hope both openly and secretly that we shall not be called upon to demonstrate our scheme of values at the cost of our lives, we must hold on to believing in our capacity to make ourselves do so, even if the occasion should prove so cruel as to allow time for reflection.

In the long-boat, there was such time, time—if passengers must be thrown into the sea—to select by casting lots. The judge said that would have been the only acceptable procedure, analogous in its outcome to a choice made not by man but by "destiny." Since some must be killed or all must die, let "destiny" choose among them. Some must be killed, it seemed, for the male passengers did not volunteer to lighten the boat by leaving it; on the contrary, before being thrust into the sea, they had tried by offers of bribes and by main force to stay aboard. "Women and children first" may or may not have been the maxim that governed their conduct in the initial moments of panic; they could not agree that it remained applicable after many long hours had passed and the men could take thought in their desperation.

It is rather presumptuous of us—sitting dry in our safety—to pass judgment of any kind on those poor wretches in the long-boat. May we be spared ever coming to a pass like theirs, spared the bleakness of such a choice! May we likewise be spared the duty of serving on a jury in any comparable case, or of charging a jury with the law as to what men are required to do in an ultimate crisis! If we feel free now to offer comments on the setting in which Holmes was compelled to do what he did, let us at least cling to the grace of humility and of self-doubt. Let us rather judge Holmes' judge than Holmes. It was the judge who pointed to casting lots as the single permissible solution.

In the literature of our subject, at least three different opinions have been voiced concerning the resort to lots. One is that lots must be used because no one has suggested a better alternative method of selection.[7] The second view is that matters of this kind should be left to the judgment of the jury as individual cases may arise and that it is unwise to erect any rigid legal rule to control the actions of people in such dire necessity.[8] The third view is that we should reject lots because while life remains there may be ground for hope and no one can be quite certain that a rescuing sail will not come into sight.[9] (This third view seems to deny that we can ever reach enough certainty as to our factual beliefs to be morally justified in the action we take, but Judge Cardozo, the author of this view, would probably have been among the first to repudiate such a position. Only the actual disappearance of the long-boat under the water would afford a mathematical certainty that time had run out.)

It seems to me that we are dealing here with what may be called "morals of the last days"; that is to say, such morals as men may be summoned to display when all the usual differences between man and man become irrelevant because the differences have to do with a life that continues—if not for one, then for another. The crisis in the long-boat was apocalyptic in character, the kind of crisis in which, as Jesus saw, family ties, earthly possessions, and distinctions of every conceivable kind become null and void. In a strait of this extremity, all men are reduced—or raised, as one may choose to denominate it—to members of the genus, mere congeners and nothing else. Truly and literally, all were "in the same boat," and thus none could be saved separately from the others.

I am driven to conclude that otherwise—that is, if none sacrifice themselves of free will to spare the others—they must all wait and die together. For where all have become congeners, pure and simple, no one can save himself by killing another. In such a setting and at such a price, he has no moral individuality left to save. Under the terms of the moral constitution, it will be *wholly* his self that he kills in his vain effort to preserve himself. The "morals of the last days" leave him a generic creature only; in such a setting, so remote from the differentiations of normal existence, every person in the boat embodies the entire genus. Whoever saves one, saves the whole human race; whoever kills one, kills mankind.

So, in all humility, I would put aside the talk of casting lots, not only because the crisis involves stakes too high for gambling and responsibilities too deep for destiny, but also because no one can win in such a lottery, no one can survive intact by means of the killing.

Finally, would it be permissible to suggest that this planet we live on is not entirely unlike the long-boat of the *William Brown*? By all means, provided one bears in mind that at most the metaphor can provide only a moral attitude or an answer, not a moral decision.

2. THE RIGHT TO BE YOUNG

Henry Stout was a typical boy six years of age, living with his father and mother in a small Nebraska town. One morning without informing his parents he set off with two playmates to go to the railroad depot, a mile or so away. As usual, they had no special purpose in mind. When they reached the depot, one of his friends told Henry about a turntable belonging to the railroad company, which the boys of the vicinity had played on from time to time. On various occasions, some railroad employees had seen boys playing there, and once had forbidden them to stay; but this was to be Henry's first visit. The turntable was in an open space, near two roads in a sparsely settled area not far from the depot. It was left unlocked and would revolve easily on its axis. So while the two friends began to turn it, Henry attempted to jump aboard. His foot caught in the mechanism and was crushed.

In Henry's suit for damages against the railroad company, the jury gave a verdict for the plaintiff. Despite the fact that Henry was trespassing on the railroad's property when he was injured, the United States Supreme Court sustained the verdict in his favor.[10]

There are all sorts of ways for adult society to maim its children. One of the most heinous is by child labor, which though reduced under recent legislation still continues in serious proportions in the United States and constitutes a major social evil in less prosperous countries. Child labor, with all its cruel consequences, is however only a particularly acute and conspicuous instance of the mayhem that we are concerned with here—the mayhem that results from treating children as though they were nothing more than adults in the making. At least since the time when Aristotle wrote [11] that the excellence of a child is "not a matter of his relation to his present self, but of his relation to the end [which he will attain when mature] and to the guiding authority [of the parent, which prepares him for that end]," childhood has been seen only as a process of preparation. It has been seen as a living for the sake of the future state—in much the same sense as adult life during the Middle Ages was considered only a preliminary discipline to prepare the soul for its after-existence. Over the centuries adults have slowly won the right to live in and for the satisfactions of adulthood, yet most of them continue to deny to the child his corresponding right to be young.

Of course, a child is a becoming as well as a being. Preparation for the time when he will participate in adult society is indispensable to him, and he would be sadly vulnerable without it. He must learn to adjust himself to the ways of the group, to avoid violating recognized property-rights, and to assume more and more responsibilities in his relations with others. To him some of the rules will appear arbitrary or even unjust, at least when he first meets them; but he must gradually acquire knowledge of their existence, of the punishments for infraction, and perhaps of the ways to correct whatever on maturer inspection still seems contrary to fairness. But always while he is being prepared in such ways, he lives the life of the child that he is—a life in the present which has its own course, its distinctive interests, and its precious values.

The keynote of that life is the quality of immediacy. When a child looks, he sees what he may never be able to see again because his sight is not yet obscured by associations of the past or restricted by motives pointing to the future. Suppose, for example, he looks at a bug lying on its back in a helpless condition and waving its legs about in a frantic effort to wriggle over. To him this is all a present-perfect spectacle, absorbing and fascinating as an end in itself. In later years, he may be concerned with the bug's activity as a carrier of germs. Or, if he has become a philosopher, he may consider the bug as epitomizing the tragic predicament of human life. Now, however, it is a bug that he sees, and he watches it with the intensity of an attention undeflected by outside reference. His experience is the more intense for being purely immediate. Moreover, the experience he now lives in is an irresponsible one. As yet he does not feel that he needs to account for his time or explain the usefulness of what he happens to be doing. He has the right to be young, that is, to live in lyric immediacy, intensity, and irresponsibility, to observe—not in order to serve some imperious further purpose but simply and entirely for the sake of observing. Also he has the right to tell about his experience—not in order to impart information or stimulate action but only for the sake of the telling itself.

If the adult world cannot somehow recognize that these primitive faculties represent final consummations to which the child is entitled as of right, it should at least take notice that the very same faculties constitute the core and marrow of the adult poet and the adult scientist. The child's right to be a child, to ignore the clock, and to play heedlessly with words as though they were things and with things as though they were toys—this right is both morally valid and socially fruitful. And to the extent that this right may be recognized and protected, certain new duties necessarily fall on the members of the adult world. So much is implied by the case of the railroad turntable.

I regret that the turntable case is regarded as a famous one: the outcome should have seemed anything but novel in a society that professes to value its children, and the soundness of little Henry Stout's claim should long ago have been beyond question in our law. I regret even more that a later decision [12] of the United States Supreme Court, written by Justice Holmes, sharply restricted the application of the case. In fact, in the courts of some few states, a suit identical with Henry's would be decided today in favor of the railroad. In these callous states, a young child who is seduced by the sight of a fascinating mechanism to wander over a property-line in order to see it better is put in the same class as any mature person who deliberately invades land where he knows he does not belong. Certainly this is a striking example of the Philistinism in moral standards that we resolved—in chapter 11—to expose and condemn.

What then was Justice Holmes' view and how did he restrict the rule? The opinion he wrote for the Supreme Court involved a chemical company which owned some land on the outskirts of a town in Kansas. The company decided to give up its factory there and tore it down, leaving a brick cellar which soon made an attractive pool of accumulated water. The water looked clean but was actually, as the company knew, dangerously poisoned with sulphuric acid. A husband and wife and their two sons, eight and eleven years of age, were travelling by and camped near this place. "A travelled way passed within 120 or 100 feet of it." The boys came on the company's land, saw no sign of warning because there was none to see, went into the water, were horribly burnt, and died. Speaking for the majority of the Supreme Court in a 6–3 decision, Holmes held that as a matter of law the chemical company was not liable, because "it is at least doubtful whether the water could be seen from any place where the children lawfully were and there is no evidence that it is what led them to enter the land." (Should the dead children be expected to give this evidence or should the judges try to remember how they searched and wandered and ventured when they were boys?) "It is suggested," Holmes went on, "that the roads across the place were invitations." (Were they not?) No, the Justice concluded, "A road is not an invitation to leave it elsewhere than at its end."

A few months later in another case,[13] Holmes wrote an opinion in which he upheld an adult who had gone on someone else's land for the socially approved purpose of gathering mussel shells and making them into buttons. He said the strict English rule against trespassing on land should not be followed "with regard to the large expanses of unenclosed and uncultivated land in many parts at least of this country. Over these it is customary to wander, shoot and fish at will until the owner sees fit to prohibit it. A license may be implied from the habits of the country." Thus Holmes showed that he was no servile worshiper of boundary lines; he could project himself into the position of an adult who, wandering over the line, was licensed by the *local* habits of adults. Unfortunately he could not understand that a child may be licensed by the *universal* habits of children.

The turntable case suggests still another moral value, a value which we shall meet again from time to time as we move along in this inquiry. At this point, we may call it "the moral obligation to be intelligent." The officials of the railroad company were under a moral duty to anticipate the possible temptation to children and the grave risk of injury. It would not exculpate them that, like some judges, they might fail to remember their own youthful propensities or fail to care what dangers others might court when intruding on private premises. Although in general we are not morally responsible for injuries we are powerless to prevent, the guilt even of such injuries falls on us whenever our powerlessness is the product of our own previous sloth, inertia, or defect of imagination. We are pledged as members of the human species to concern ourselves in advance with the risks to which others may be exposed by anything under our control, including our own conduct and example. And as far as children are concerned, we are irrevocably committed to the very reverse of Holmes' aphorism. We can preserve what is precious and fair in childhood only by insisting that a road is an invitation to leave it at any point, at any impulse, and for any unseen pool.

3. THE FAMILY AS MORAL ADMINISTRATION

A son and daughter, both under twenty-one years of age, filed suit (together with their mother) against their father, Dr. W——, and against a certain Mrs. T——. They asserted that Mrs. T—— had schemed to break up the W——s' happy home and family life, and had enticed Dr. W—— to leave his family and to fail to fulfill his marriage vows and paternal duties; that Mrs. T—— had obtained a divorce from her own husband and had induced Dr. W—— to institute a divorce suit against Mrs. W——; that the two had illegally represented that Mrs. T—— was Mrs. W——; and that he was squandering his money on her and her family while depriving his own son, daughter, and wife of proper support. They therefore asked the court to issue an injunction prohibiting Dr. W—— and Mrs. T—— from the continuation of this conduct.

The court held as a matter of law that, even if the children could prove the truth of their allegations, no injunction would be issued. The suit was dismissed at its inception.[14]

We are dealing here with the law's attitude toward the family, a type of social arrangement which retains some of its inherent strangeness and even absurdity despite our lifelong familiarity with it. In the estimation of idealistic philosophers, there has always been something faintly nonsensical about the family. Many of them seem to have seen in it only a prison to confine free and soaring spirits, a set of arbitrary walls where the ill-assorted are kept together and those with genuine affinities are forced apart. "There is indeed," says Santayana, "no more irrational ground for living together than that we have sprung from the same loins." [15] Plato's disposition for the guardians' offspring in his Republic is only the best known of various utopian proposals put forward in order to obviate this irrationality. For after all, why should the natural circumstance that a man and woman happen to have produced a child confer on them any knowledge or fitness to prepare the child for its social life? And when a philosopher considers that many fertilizations are not desired but dreaded, and that almost all are mere accidents, he may laugh at the family—for fear of weeping.

Certainly if we are to be guided by what I have called the "morals of the last days," the family has no strong claim to survive. Jesus, true to those morals, repudiated his family and acknowledged no brother, sister, or mother except those who did the will of his heavenly Father. So have almost all other prophets, leaders, and seers; not to mention most great artists. One might, in fact, have been able to predict exactly what would befall Napoleon because he chose to disregard their example. Where the purpose is single and the goal extreme, there can be no room aboard for the conventional loyalties and scruples of the family.

And what have the psychologists been telling us, particularly in the last two generations? Some of it we had already gleaned from our own common-sense observation, enough at any rate to make most of the balance entirely plausible. Whether or not the psychologists set out intentionally to draw an indictment against the effects of family life, the evidence they have accumulated seems mountainous in individual instances, overwhelming, and horrifying. How many millions of sons have been enslaved in their psyches by how many millions of mothers; how many daughters browbeaten, frustrated, and made into frigid, quivering neurotics! Where is there a tyranny like that of a self-pitying domestic invalid—whether pretended or real? And, turning our faces in the opposite direction, we think of the slights and cruelties that are being inflicted each passing moment by countless children on fathers and mothers who have committed the error of refusing too seldom or of living too vicariously. Moreover, we must consider the abysmal vulgarities, the neglects, the beatings, the incests, and all the other obscenities of which only a small proportion ever become known outside the precincts of the family home.

I think that in order to understand the attitudes that shape American law on the subject, it is necessary to regard the family as (a) a political, (b) an economic, and (c) a social unit. Historically, the emphasis of the law seems to have shifted from the political to the economic; only now are there instances of a possible tendency to stress the social meaning of the family. Even these instances have a strong economic coloration, because most of them relate to what we used to call "necessities of life" but, having acquired a better opinion of what human "life" should include, we now call "subsistence."

Vestiges there still are of the primitive ages when the patriarchal head of the family served as its king, judge, and priest; and despite all the centrifugal effects of modern industrialized and urbanized life, these vestiges continue to play a leading role in American law's treatment of the family. Inside the home, the father and mother have the rights of joint sovereigns and, at least in the eyes of the law, their directions and decisions are final.[16] Just as a sovereign cannot be sued for injuries inflicted on his subject (unless the sovereign consents), so parents cannot, under the law of most American states, be sued by their children for inflicting any kind of personal injury on them. The parents may lawfully exercise their sovereignty by determining many aspects of the child's education, his religious training, the nurture of his body and the inculcation of his morals; and they may resist official interference as violating the United States Constitution. And when the courts uphold a constitutional plea on the part of the parents, they habitually evade the question whether it is the right of the child (e.g., to attend a private school or the right of the parent to choose the school) that is at stake. Common sense suggests to the judges that in many cases neither the child's welfare nor its desires will coincide with the father's choice; but history replies that in our system of law, the father has been so assimilated to a sovereign that, not long since, the crime of patricide was known as "petty treason."

Let us not, however, exaggerate the importance of the "political" aspect. The law may tell the American father he is sovereign, but his children have taught him otherwise. It is well that they have: as a constitutional monarch useful on ceremonial occasions and skilled at repair jobs around the house, he has his place. If he does not attempt to rule, he will probably be permitted to reign, provided, of course, the mother of the family does not choose to do so. Whenever she does, she can readily displace him. But while her reign would generally surpass his in judgment and competence, she will be better advised to allow him the illusion of retaining some slight remnant of authority. The reason being, of course, that if she does not, it is likely some other woman will—and that consideration brings us back to our principal case, the case of the W—— family.

Among other things, the case shows that the law will not compel the sovereign either to rule or to reign, if he chooses to abdicate. He can be forced to support his family; he cannot be forced to bear its proximity. Wives and children represent enforceable legal duties of the purse, but freedom from the company of their persons can be purchased. In fact, although leaving a wife's company permanently may constitute desertion and thus give grounds for legal separation (in some states, for divorce), a child can be assigned completely, year after year, to the care of, say, a boarding-school, provided remittances are maintained in suitable amounts. And this is morally sound. For living together as a family is a precarious social expedient at best, justified mainly by the lack of any more acceptable alternative; when coerced from without, it is necessarily destined to failure and wretchedness. There are many who succeed moderately, maintaining some measure of harmony in their own households; but who except a sadist would have the law compel a child to live from day to day with a father who let it be known that the association was against his will?

The suit brought by the W—— children is particularly edifying when we consider the economic aspect of the American family. What has already been said about its political aspect would naturally lead us to expect American law to treat the family as a single economic unit, that is, as a sort of self-contained cell in the larger organism of the social economy. But that is not the case. Under the rules that we inherited from England and developed in our own courts, the law almost never recognizes any such conceptual entity as "the family." There are enforceable rights and duties between the husband and the wife or between the parent and the child; these are considered to be legal relations between one individual and another, not legal relations incident to their being members of a group entity called the "family." The conversational term may be "family law," but the term that accurately reflects the approach of our legal system is "the law of domestic relations." And this has interesting consequences.

When a society thinks of family units as its basic component integers for economic purposes, it encourages each separate group to organize itself in an authoritarian manner and to exclude or even detest outsiders. We know that there is no selfishness so pestilential as the selfishness that can be instilled, nourished, and rationalized on behalf of the pretended welfare of an exclusive group, and where the center of interest is some kind of family estate or ownership of property, everyone beyond the family circle may be treated like an object of indifference at best, at worst like an enemy and an outlaw. But, on the other hand, if the family's economic structure is organized in the way our law analyzes it—i.e., as an aggregate of rights and duties, an aggregate of relations between individuals—then there is some practical possibility of counteracting this group selfishness and separatism. In such a view, the family not being considered an organism with a tough skin of its own, moral values that begin within the family can leak through to the outer world.

Let me give an example. In the early history of Anglo-American law, the master of the household was held to be legally justified in using force to defend the members of the family and his servants against assaults, because he was entitled by law to safeguard his property right to their services. Then, as time went on, the same privilege was held by the courts to be reciprocal—the child could defend the father, the servant the employer. Up to this point, the legal rights respected by the courts were all within the economic relations of the family household; but what proved to be decisive about these rights was not the particular economic setting where they happened to arise but rather the fact that they arose out of relations. Suppose an economic relation should come into being elsewhere, for instance, a passenger is on a bus where he is assaulted. American courts would hold, in such a case, that the driver is entitled to defend the passenger. Suppose, next, that the relation is not economic at all but is the outcome of recognized social usages, as where a man escorts a lady in any public place and someone takes offensive liberties with her. Suppose, finally, that there was no pre-existing relation whatever, but that the person attacked is a stranger and all the relatedness in the case consists in one's accidentally being on the scene and being able to defend an innocent fellow-creature in a time of peril. On the very last question, American law is still in a somewhat tentative state yet clearly on its way to giving an affirmative answer. The moral principle that first gained legal recognition on the basis of economic interests within the family has been expanded step by step to include ultimately the safety of a mere passer-by.

This does not mean, of course, that our courts are naive enough to overlook the persistence of family selfishness and cupidity in general wherever money is involved, or in particular where the money is claimed by the government for taxes. The only time that our courts seem to feel really confident that the family is capable of unified action is when cooperation between members of the family will reduce their taxes. Against the claims of the government, the quarrels will be forgotten, the disloyalties forgiven, and the conflicts composed; the family picture becomes a charming one of harmony and mutual trust. When American judges have to pass on the tax consequences of a business transaction within a family (for instance, the sale of a piece of property from husband to wife or from father to son), it is hard to convince them that the substance of the transaction corresponds honestly to its form as presented to the tax authorities. And since this judicial skepticism has been produced by observing innumerable family arrangements made for no other reason than to dissemble the realities of the case, it is a sad testimony to the cohesive power of family selfishness. Does the tax collector have the only means by which brothers may be persuaded to live together in unity?

Let us then pay honor to the young children of Dr. W——. They sued for an injunction, not for money-damages. They tried, that is, to have a court compel their father to do what they considered his duty; they did not demand dollars of Mrs. T—— as compensation for the loss of his company and affection. If they had made a money demand, the outcome of the suit might have been in their favor. For, although some states which allow a husband or wife to recover damages for alienation of affections do not recognize a similar right in a child, the present trend is to uphold the child's claim provided the parent has been enticed away from home. But what the W—— children attempted in their suit puts our analysis on a much higher ethical plane. It enables us to turn away from the political aspect of the family, with its emphasis on authority, and from the economic aspect, with its emphasis on utility and self-interest, and to turn to the social aspect of the family, where we find the rudiments of moral administration and an emphasis on spontaneous assent.

In the social aspect, the family is neither a separate entity with a sovereign head nor a mere aggregation of individuals in domestic relations. It is now the former, now the latter as its function may determine. Our new social legislation may call for a grant to a "family," or living quarters for a "family," or a "family court"; whether, in the courts and social agencies, the family will be treated for a specific purpose as a self-sufficient unit or be disregarded in the interest of one or more of its members must depend on the objectives of the general program and the needs of the particular case. This is the only adequate way to appreciate the family, the moral way to safeguard all its distinctive virtues and sensibilities.

Of the myriad moral lessons that a child can learn in the school of family life, some few are underlined by the decision in the W—— case. But before we list them, we ought to mention the unique emotional matrix in which they are presented. Where could there be a more favorable background for sympathetic instruction and effortless learning than a really harmonious family home? For security is in such a home and the awareness of being loved, guidance on the one hand and the relaxation that comes from confidence on the other. In a world full of doubts and disapprovals, here may be faith, unreserved acceptance, and fond admiration to blandish away that carking distrust of oneself. Even if the child is too young yet to experience our universal need to be needed, it satisfies that need in the adults around it and doing so basks in the merited aura of its own achievement. What a setting for instruction in the maxims of moral administration!

Maxim 1. A demand seriously asserted should be seriously evaluated. This, as we saw in the W—— case, does not mean the demand need be granted; it means only that it should be considered, deliberated upon, and adjudicated or perhaps deferred—even though unprecedented, it is not to be ignored.

Maxim 2. What is not forbidden is not necessarily permitted. Refusing an injunction against Dr. W—— did not signify approval of the conduct attributed to him. On the contrary, the court pointed out a variety of other legal procedures that might be used to compel performance of his duties. If alternative practical steps are available, wise moral policy would likewise require us to consider each of them and would disapprove our assuming that just because the grievance is genuine, the remedy demanded is necessarily suitable.

Maxim 3. A crisis is not hopeless until it is fully dramatized. Unless a court by issuing an injunction should add fuel to the flame of the new attachment, there is always the possibility that the fire will burn out. When a dramatic "thou-shalt-not" is proclaimed, it works a double harm: it makes reconsideration and return more humiliating and it lends additional excitement to pursuit of the new affair. Innumerable domestic crises are survived simply because someone abstained from striking a climactic pose.

Maxim 4. In personal relations, the only things that are valuable enough to justify compulsion will generally be destroyed if we resort to it. Occasionally an American court has attempted, at some aggrieved wife's instance, to enjoin a husband from consorting with another woman. The result, we may be certain, is only scornful laughter at the expense of both court and wife. Both of them should have known what the court acknowledged in the W—— case: affection is not to be ruled by any coercive power whatever. Conscience itself can only stamp the new love as a guilty one; it cannot bid the old love to rekindle. The worth of personal ties consists mainly in their spontaneity, and if what amounts to a club must sometimes be used, it should not be left menacingly in sight but should be rushed back to the closet as quickly as possible.

For on this point Kant was right: there is no duty to love,[17] and love is not love that becomes a duty. Neither God nor man, nor we ourselves, can command our love, so far as love means only the sentiment of affection. In this sense, all the compulsions and injunctions of heaven and earth must end in futility.

But if we take "love" to mean the doing of kind, generous, and tender offices, there is indeed a duty to love. And if we take "love" to mean that the execution of those offices should be accompanied by tones and attitudes and gestures fitting to a lover, then in this sense too there is a duty to love. And we may go on to trust that according to the general course of human nature, love in its strictly emotional sense will follow as the sure result of doing these things in this way, and thus the duty we are able to command of ourselves fulfills the duty we are unable to command.

But the general course of human nature is not universal; there are many whose affections refuse to follow after their benefactions but go elsewhere, whatever the cause, and will certainly never be whipped back home. As for them, the wanderings of our own hearts should prompt us to withhold all self-righteous, definitive judgments. Frequently, the mere passage of time amends the pleadings and corrects the mistakes unless someone foolishly insists on having an immediate adjudication.

It is just because we know family affection cannot be commanded or coerced that we look upon it as a priceless gift. Where it resides, a sacred spirit takes dwelling and suffuses the hearth with happiness. If the maxims of moral administration call occasionally for submitting to restraint and repressing proof that one is right, their rewards are rich beyond the deserts of any of us. As a general rule, it is far better to establish a home than an opinion.

IV

Sexual Relationships

1. LOVE'S RIGHT OF PRIVACY

RUBY R—— ran a rooming house in a poor section of an Oklahoma town, and Frank V——, a Negro, had a rear room in an apartment house in the heart of the colored district not far away. One night, a city detective saw Ruby enter Frank's room. He called two other city detectives, who came and stood in the alley outside Frank's window, waited there half an hour, and then turned their flashlight through the window into the room. The officers broke into the room and arrested Ruby and Frank. Ruby had nothing on but her slip, Frank was in pajamas, and they were in bed together. Ruby told the officers that Frank had been nice to her, she liked him, and she could see nothing wrong with it. Frank was unmarried. Ruby had been married three times, but her first husband was dead and her second and third had divorced her. Ruby and Frank were tried and convicted for openly outraging public decency and injuring public morals, and were sentenced to be fined and imprisoned. The charge against them alleged that Ruby was a white woman but, at the trial, she testified that, although she had always lived as a white woman, she was one-eighth Negro and one-eighth Indian. The two defendants appealed from their conviction.

The appellate court set aside the conviction and released them, because whatever they had done had been done in private.

Oklahoma had no law making "fornication" a crime in and of itself.[1]

Like almost all other court reports that involve sexual conduct, the record of this case makes rather sordid reading. But we need to remind ourselves that what Ruby and Frank did in this incident was not necessarily sordid at all. The peering in, the use of the flashlight, the intrusion of the officers, and the criminal prosecution: these were foul and sordid indeed. We know they were, but we do not know anything about what the evening meant to Ruby and Frank up to the moment when the officers burst in, or what earlier, uninterrupted meetings had brought into their existences. It is not impossible that, if we did know, we should discover much loyalty and dignity, even an humble sort of beauty in their relation. It is at least probable that these times together supplied all the zest and joy they ever experienced in lives that seem to us quite drab and crepuscular. We—the community—do not know how to pass judgment on their lovemaking; and as the appellate court decided, according to the State law it is absolutely none of our affair.

In a majority of states, "fornication" even though committed in the greatest privacy is a crime by statute; in any of these states, the conviction would have been sustained. That is to say, a conviction would have been sustained if it had been obtained in the first instance, as it was in our principal case. In actual practice, the state laws against fornication are very rarely enforced unless some scandalous act is done in public or unless some officer desires an opportunity to collect blackmail. Where sexual conduct takes place in private, and where neither violence (such as rape) nor injury to a child is involved, the criminal laws relating to sex have very little systematic enforcement anywhere.[2] Most of them ought to have been repealed long ago.

Our problem here is a different and deeper one. It goes beyond the mere letter of the statute law. Even if every state were to cancel these obnoxious laws, even if what Ruby and Frank did were to be exempted from legal punishment in every jurisdiction, we should still have to ask ourselves whether it is morally permissible. We should still be concerned with the moral character of sexual relations between persons who are unmarried. Suppose, under the law, that an act done in private is not punishable; the question remains: is the doer thereof to be held blameless in the forum of morals?

I think we cannot begin to find a virtuous answer to this question unless we first achieve an understanding attitude toward the experience and meaning of sexual love. Love, like God, is everywhere with us and almost everywhere misunderstood. In the past—many Americans still live in the past in this respect—love was regarded as somehow inherently sinful, its coming was held an occasion for shame, and its magic was treated as something infernal which nevertheless might serve the useful purpose of reproduction. Our criminal statutes, of course, stand as ugly memorials to the hatred of Eros that was once so general. Now, of course, most Americans feel certain that they have become infinitely more enlightened. Now it is fashionable to regard love, not as a source of sin, but rather as a portent of various diseases. Love is what brings fixations, rejections, frustrations, complexes, inhibitions, split personalities, and a variety of other undesirable states of the psyche and the soma. Previously men thought of it as menacing the health of the soul; pathetically enough, they think of it now as shattering the health of the mind and body. Few there are, at least among the articulate, who rejoice in it freely and with grateful piety.

How anomalous! What the early Greeks perceived in their contacts with nature, what the authors of the Psalms and of the Song of Solomon expressed in their cosmology, what the true poets knew and, knowing, sang from the beginning of poetry down the course of the millennia—the ineffable power of Eros that pervades the whole universe of natural experience has been analyzed, confirmed, and explicated by every modern science of man, so that we recognize its influences more certainly and accurately than ever before, in the realms of literature, painting, sculpture, music, humor and entertainment, all the applied arts, commerce, and even in politics and government. As some of our ancestors imagined and as we may safely say we know, Eros is to the generality of human endeavors as the sunlight is to the seeds of the field; more than that, it frequently plants the seeds themselves, and then nurtures and warms them to fruition in beauty.

The demigod is, after his kind, completely anarchic and almost irrepressible. Conventions established by the community restrain him very little; all the solemn codes, the parental taboos, and the priestly fulminations of the centuries have only made his misbehaviors the more enticing. In the United States, since reliance is now placed primarily on the mores to keep him within bounds, his main concern is that he may be gradually losing the added—but superfluous—charm that love has derived traditionally from being a forbidden indulgence. As matters stand, only homosexual love retains this inverse kind of attraction and, even as to it, the mores seem to be growing less absolute in the tenor of their proscriptions.

The general populace has always sensed the overwhelming power which love exerts. That much is shown by the popular way of appraising famous men and even famous women. In the first place, it is generally admitted—though seldom with the grace of explicitness—that men who are recognized as outstanding in any single respect may become thereby entitled to flout the existing sex mores. There is no need to list instances, since they are so familiar in the history of every society, but it may be worth mentioning that the reverence of subsequent generations for Cato the Younger, one of the last exemplars of Roman republican virtue, was never diminished by what anyone who reads Plutarch can learn about Cato's marital behavior. In the second place, if the individual happens to be a poet, novelist, musician, actor or other type of professional artist—though one of very limited capacity—similar allowances will be made for his violations of the sex mores.

Now on this score at least, the mores show that they claim to be no more than mores because they grant that just as Napoleon could live with his women and Bacon with his boys in public, the adult Franks and the Rubys may do whatever they like provided they do so in private. If the mores signified that the act was evil in itself (as rape is), then the distinction between publicity and privacy would not be supportable. To condemn only what is public in it is to confess the conventionality of the prohibition and to resolve the whole question into one of good manners, esthetics, and the possible example to any children who may live in the same quarters.

Ruby deserves commendation for her candor: she was not ashamed to say she "liked it." Moreover, she testified at her trial that the reason she did not have intercourse with Frank that night was that "the officers did not give them time." Why otherwise should they forego the unique solace of their monotonous lives? Who—except perhaps the city detective, himself a Negro, who spied on them and reported their rendezvous to his two white colleagues, impelled by what somber motives one may imagine—who could be injured by what they enjoyed?

For here a moral factor operates that is relatively new in human history—that is, the great and increasing availability of contraceptives which if not perfect are at least highly dependable. This development, one of the important benefactions of modern science and technology, ought to liberate society from an age-old incubus: the doctrine—suitable perhaps to the animal world but hardly to the aspirations of our species—that love is primarily a reproductive activity, and that all its other benefits are at most only derivatively legitimate. Of this incubus we can probably consider ourselves freed. It is to be hoped that we shall not substitute, in its place, some pseudotherapeutic, orgasmic doctrine of love. Love, which quickens, inspirits, and rejoices the hearts of men, deserves a natural piety of them. It deserves to be regarded as a good so supernal that all should share in it without fear and confer its gift of compassion without hindrance.

Accordingly, an enlightened moral classification—the kind we are seeking here—will not run along the traditional boundary line fixed by legal marriage, separating the permissible intercourse within the borders of wedlock from all the outside, presumedly vile types of sexual connection. We intend to think better of marriage than certain of our ancestors did who considered it only a formal warrant for doing what must without it be an act of sin. Marriage, it will be shown in the next section, implements several very diverse purposes of contemporary society, and one of those purposes is the securing of a reasonable continuity in the life of love. For although there are many men and women who seem to feel entirely satisfied with flaring-and-flickering affairs such as Frank's and Ruby's was, American social organization expects something more responsible and continuous of the majority; and, as the statistics show, most Americans prefer a union that is lifelong in contemplated duration and monopolistic in regard to domesticity—or at least provisionally so.

2. GROUNDS FOR MARRIAGE

HARRY S—— had neither money nor a regular job, but he did have ambitions to establish himself in business. For seven years he had been keeping company with Bessie; whenever she broached the subject of marriage he would point to his circumstances and insist that he was in no position to marry. Finally, Bessie told him she had enough money to help him launch a business. A month or two later, what seemed like a desirable partnership was offered to Harry if he could contribute five or six thousand dollars to the venture. Bessie said she had eight thousand, and insisted on being married before furnishing any money. So Harry and Bessie were duly wed in a civil ceremony, but the marriage was not consummated; they returned to their respective homes. Four days later when Harry went to Bessie's home to secure the amount he needed to complete the business arrangements, he discovered that she was and always had been entirely bare of money. She told him she had hoped to borrow the cash from her aunt, but could not get it. Claiming he had been defrauded, Harry sued for the annulment of their marriage. Bessie did not attempt to oppose the suit. The New York trial court and the intermediate appellate court believed Harry's evidence, but refused to annul the marriage because Bessie's false statements did not relate to any factor which they considered essential in the legal status of marriage. Harry appealed to the Court of Appeals, the highest court of the State.

The Court of Appeals decided (4–3) that the marriage should be annulled. Harry, it said, had relied on Bessie's misrepresentation as to an existing fact (her having the necessary money) without which, as Bessie clearly understood, there would have been no marriage.[3]

Here again it is easy to dismiss the conduct on both sides of the case as vulgar, mercenary, and sordid. Even the judges who decided in Harry's favor felt a need to defend his "less than heroic" attitude. They attributed it—mistakenly I believe—to his realization that marriage would entail a responsibility to support his wife, which he could not do without the loan of her "mythical money." The judges who dissented did not think much better of Bessie's motives. They pointed out that Harry had had such ample and extended opportunity to ascertain the untruth of her statements that he had only himself to reproach for relying on them. These dissenting judges regarded the entire narrative with undisguised distaste. As they interpreted it, "the woman bought the man for $6,000."

Perhaps they were right. Perhaps Bessie did attempt to "buy" a husband—just as countless millions of Bessies have "bought" husbands in every time and country, sometimes acting directly for themselves, more often through their parents, brothers, sisters, marriage brokers, or loyal friends. In legal anthropology and sociology, the history of marriage consists of endless variations on the theme of "purchase," that is, as soon as purchase might be permitted in a given culture to replace the earlier use of rape and abduction. And the history of royal marriages—what is it but one long series of dynastic, financial, and territorial mergers? Bessie, we must remember, had waited seven years, during which she was hardly growing younger. She may have recalled that even Jacob, the great Biblical hero and patriarch, had been defrauded—and in the very person of the bride he had worked for; yet Jacob had eventually acquiesced in the deed. Bessie must have felt strongly, in her desperation, that Harry might follow Jacob's example, for surely after seven years he could not consider that money was all she could bring to a husband. And there was always the hope—however tenuous—that her aunt might relent and advance the help they needed. If the New York judges had been a bit more accustomed to Old-World settlements by way of dowry, or if perhaps the case had involved a prospective bride who said she owned a wooded park and meadow, suitable for fox-hunting and contiguous to the prospective husband's manor-house and lawns, the arrangement might have caused no revulsion.

As for Harry, it may be said with reasonable assurance that the discovery of fraud was not the authentic motive for his annulment suit. The court report of the case does not reveal his character well enough for us to analyze it; we have no right to sit in judgment on him. We do know what seven or more years of poverty and dependence can do to one's pride and self-confidence. It is not difficult to picture the exaggerated importance of Bessie's assertion to a man in such a state, the pink visions of hope with which he must have bemused himself, and the pathetic little dream in which he became a tycoon of the jewelry business. For two or three weeks, he played the role of a man of business and property; his opinions were heeded with respect; when he entered an office, people did not ignore him, they actually cared why he had come. He negotiated with them; he refused here, assented there. Then, in a single instant four days after his marriage, all this globe of elation was irreparably burst. Hereafter, whenever he showed his face, he would be mocked and insulted, never taken seriously again. What might this experience mean to all that was left in him of a man!

Of course, he had failed to investigate the existence of Bessie's "mythical" bank account; he had believed in it as one long lost and wandering in the desert believes in the sight of distant palms beside a well of water. Now that it had proved to be an empty delusion and mirage, we could scarcely expect him to surrender the final vestige of his pride by putting the blame on himself. For in truth, as he must have realized, it was at bottom not Bessie but his own dilated credulity that had brought him to humiliation.

Of course, an understanding of the highly special and individual motives that prompted Harry and Bessie is not enough. It does not enable us to see the reasoning of the four judges who granted the annulment or that of the dissenting three who would have denied it; it does not place the case in its institutional context. Harry and Bessie, probably without the slightest awareness that they were doing so, made a significant chapter in the history of a complex social institution, one with an entire corpus of legal rules and assumptions. The institution of marriage has changed its characteristics markedly in the last fifty years, and our principal case is one of the indications showing the manner in which American marriage has been evolving. The contrast between the scene at the beginning of the century and the present scene, even if confined to a small segment of the total law of marriage, will be highly interesting.

The legal assumptions of the former period were the result of two primary influences. In most aspects of Anglo-American family law, the influential models would be Biblical Jewish rules or classical Roman rules. But on the particular points that we are concerned with here, it is important to emphasize that neither Jewish nor Roman legislation determined the Anglo-American pattern.

Although both of these ancient legal systems favored the institution of marriage, cherished the family home, and punished acts of adultery, they made their regulations rational and humane by providing a liberal exit from matrimony through the door of divorce. The severest criticism we can make of the Jewish code was that it set up a double standard—not as to adultery, however, but as to freedom of divorce. The husband could divorce the wife at will, provided he performed the property provisions for her maintenance and benefit in his marriage-contract and provided he was able to resist the rabbi's stern admonitions to cling to the wife of his youth and avoid the blandishments of strange women. Hence indulgence in adultery could be regarded as inexcusable. Moreover, if the husband was guilty of some serious misconduct, he could be compelled to give his wife a certificate of divorce, thereby freeing her to find a worthier mate. (Perhaps it should be explained that Jesus' view of divorce agreed closely with the adherents of the School of Shammai—representing the *provincial* Pharisees—who generally advanced restrictive and inflexible legal doctrines; it was the more lenient view of the School of Hillel—the *urban* Pharisees—that prevailed in Jewish law.)

In the same fashion, the mature Roman law, though changing in detail from century to century, always permitted great freedom of divorce to either of the spouses. In point of fact, marriages that began in youth and lasted till death in old age seem to have been rather uncommon, at least in the early Empire. Thus it was that the Jewish and the Roman judges rarely needed to resort to any elaborate technique of annulment. Under Roman law, even where a marriage was illegal because the parties were too closely related to each other, the case would be considered rather as a criminal prosecution for incest (the dowry would be forfeited to the State) than as a civil suit for annulment. In general, the legal remedy under these systems was divorce, not annulment.

Neither in Jewish nor in Roman legislation will we find the sources we are searching for. But they are easy to identify. The institution of marriage did not exist in a social or economic vacuum fifty years ago any more than it does today. At the turn of the century, Anglo-American marriage—in the legal as well as the social sense—was a product of the Victorian era. The primary sources of its institutional maxims were (1) puritanism, whether Protestant or Roman Catholic, and (2) mercantilism.

If you weave the warp of puritanism across the woof of mercantilism, you have our earlier law of the matrimonial status.

Mercantilism, as we shall use the term, sums up four important lines of nineteenth-century thought in the English and American courts: (1) that goodwill, the reasonable expectation of future patronage, and similar incorporeal ties between one individual and another have a measurable economic price and can be owned like other commodities; (2) that anyone who maliciously interferes with this intangible kind of property becomes liable for money damages to compensate the owner; (3) that when a piece of merchandise is sold, the seller is not chargeable with foreseeing nor need he inquire about any special use to which the buyer may intend to put it; and (4) that even as to an everyday, normal use of the merchandise, the buyer should generally bear the responsibility for inspecting the article and making sure of its fitness (*caveat emptor*). In connection with marriage, of course, the function of legal puritanism consisted in identifying the specific uses that would be approved and in that manner determining what was or was not a condition of fitness.

It is time for examples. We may contrast the old Anglo-American law with the new in regard to two aspects of marriage: first, the grounds for annulment, as illustrated by the case of Harry and Bessie; and second, the various causes of action that are colloquially known as "heart-balm" suits (breach of promise to marry, alienation of affections, criminal conversation). The changes we shall see in the law are worth pondering.

The old law was consistently reluctant to grant annulments. The party who claimed to have been deceived had to take action in court very promptly after discovering the fraud and had to establish that the misrepresentation he had trusted dealt directly with the "essence" of the marital status. The general rule was that all marriages, like all purchases of merchandise, should be quite final; pleas for cancellation or annulment were regarded with the disfavor evinced by the dissenting judges in Harry's suit. People would inspect more carefully and deliberate more responsibly if they knew in advance that the transaction was irrevocable.

What frauds went to the "essence" of the marriage? Generally speaking, only a deliberate and false representation either of mental sanity or physical capacity; and virtually nothing else would do. Fraud as to character, fortune, disposition, ancestry, or elements of personal beauty was not regarded as a ground for annulment. "Physical capacity" meant capacity for the sexual intercourse necessary in marriage as a means to engendering or bearing legitimate offspring, for reproduction was considered the sole end and aim of any respectable human mating. Motives that might prompt individuals to get married were acknowledged to be innumerable, but the courts would look only to the mental and physical "essence."

How drastically all this has changed! But before we describe the new law, it is necessary to point out a causal distinction. While the *direction* of change came from outside the legal system—from radical transformations in the mores, the *tempo* of change was greatly accelerated by factors within the system. In most American states where it could exert any strong influence (New York, for example), puritanism elected to hold the line at divorce; it frequently succeeded in blocking movements to liberalize the statutory grounds of divorce. Thus, the social forces pushed all the harder against the dike of annulment, and, at various points, the dike gave way. This development is worth remembering when we consider, as we soon shall, a recent, famous annulment case in England, where divorce had in fact been liberalized to a certain extent.

A significant incident, possibly reflecting the same influences that were operating in the American courts, took place in 1926 in the Sacred Roman Rota (highest ecclesiastical court of the Roman Catholic Church).[4] In that year, the Rota granted an annulment to a woman on proof that she had been coerced by her imperious mother into an unwilling marriage. But, according to the record in the case, the wedding ceremony had been in 1895, the marriage had produced two children, civil separation was noted as of 1905, and the suit for annulment was not filed until 1925, some thirty years after the act of coercion!

Less than a decade later, the case of Harry and Bessie was decided in New York. It indicated an easy solution, at least where the "deceived" husband or wife could deny with some plausibility that sexual cohabitation had taken place. The outcome was what one might have predicted: annulment became a popular mode of exit. Secured by perjury which is no greater in quantity and much less loathsome in quality than the perjury in the run of divorces for adultery, annulments are sought and granted annually by the thousands. Why, people reason, swear to a disgusting scene of assignation and adultery for a decree of divorce, when swearing that the plaintiff consented to be wed only because the defendant promised falsely and fraudulently to take part in a religious wedding after the civil wedding, which he never intended to do—when this sort of tale may suffice for a decree of annulment? I must add that even New York respects matrimony as something more than a vehicle of adolescent mawkishness: the only fraud that the New York courts are quite certain *not* to accept as a ground for annulment is a false and fraudulent protestation of undying love.

What we have seen is the violent purgation of mercantilism out of the modern law of annulment. Because the law of divorce was meanwhile held in rigid unconformity to the needs of the people, this purgation could be achieved only by destroying, in the law of annulment, much that gave it a semblance of being rational and coherent. In any event, we are dispelling the old mercantilism, which like a boor used to say to young couples "You may expect in marriage only what we say you may expect."

Suppose, instead of deflecting legitimate claims for divorce into the channel of annulment, we had safeguarded the process of annulment by increasing the number of grounds for divorce. This is what the English did, though rather cautiously. The outcome in England has been instructive, for, in the leading English case, puritanical mercantilism was defeated.

In this case,[5] after ten years of married life, the husband sued for an annulment on the ground that the wife, being resolved not to have a child, had determinedly refused intercourse unless he would use a contraceptive device. In short, he insisted that the procreation of children was "one of the principal ends, if not the principal end, of marriage." To refuse procreation, he claimed, is to refuse consummation, which, under the English statute, would require annulment. The case reached the House of Lords. The opinion said, somewhat dryly:

"It is indisputable that the institution of marriage generally is not necessary for the procreation of children. . . . In any view of Christian marriage the essence of the matter, as it seems to me, is that the children, if there be any, should be born into a family, as that word is understood in Christendom generally, and in the case of a marriage between spouses of a particular faith that they should be brought up and nurtured in that faith. But this is not the same thing as saying that a marriage is not consummated unless children are procreated or that procreation of children is the principal end of marriage." The court added that it was "a matter of common knowledge that many young married couples agree to take contraceptive precautions in the early days of married life." The annulment was denied; and the Archbishop of Canterbury cried "Heresy!" [6]

It would be pleasant to believe that we have progressed beyond the old stud-farm philosophy (see, for example, the travesty of equine comparisons in Steele's *The Conscious Lovers*) that used to regard a lovely young woman as the present equivalent of a filly and the prospective equivalent of a foaling mare. But that is hardly true as yet. In the United States, the musty eighteenth- and nineteenth-century slander lingers on, decked out—after our national fashion—with trimmings of lachrymose sentimentality. When, in a New Jersey case,[7] it appeared that the husband insisted for financial reasons on taking contraceptive precautions, the judge announced he could hear the wife's "maternal instinct clamoring" and proceeded to award her a divorce on the ground of desertion! This sort of judicial performance would seem to require particularly long ears.

We ought to remind ourselves of the fact that almost all the Anglo-American decisions in cases concerning marriage have been made by male judges. This helps to explain why mercantile points of view continue to appear and why they are covered over with the treacle of sentimentality. The general rules of law might remain the same if the judges were female, but I think we can safely say that many individual decisions applying them would be entirely different.

For example, not many women sitting on the bench would award the custody of minor children on the assumptions the male judges usually employ. Most women know quite well that the male picture of the respective functions and talents of the two sexes is, at least in the United States, so distorted as to approach the nature of fantasy. They know that very often it is the husband not the wife who excels and revels in domesticity and household chores, who exercises sensitive taste in decoration and furnishing, and who displays the patience and inherent sweetness of temperament which little children need most of all. They know that very often it is the wife not the husband who can competently determine practical problems, earn a livelihood in the business world, and supply the necessary stamina in time of adversity or discouragement. Another fact they know is that many women who desire to be married are wholly unsuited to the adaptations and adjustments which marriage requires. Moreover, even the best suited and most successful wives—the minority whose example confers an aura of excellence on the institution—even these can count many hours and days when they feel relaxed and relieved to be away from male company, away from their husbands along with all other men, and pleasantly at ease in the society and common understanding of some other women. (One of the charms of very young children may be that, with them around, one is temporarily exempt from the psychic pulls, repulsions, and incursions of sex competition.) For only the self-importance of the male prevents his seeing that, even to the lustiest and most devoted woman, he appears at times just about as welcome as a great, lumbering Newfoundland at an afternoon tea. At such times her discreet silence or her sudden volubility may mean that she agrees wholeheartedly with Josh Billings, who said, "Newfoundland dogs are good to save children from drowning, but you must have a pond of water handy and a child, or else there will be no profit in boarding a Newfoundland."

I suggest also that with more women on the bench there would be fewer decrees of annulment. Except where a court issues its decree for the simple purpose of recording that no recognizable marriage ever took place (as, for instance, where one of the parties was completely insane at the ceremony and incapable of consenting to anything), annulment is the perpetration of a monstrous fiction, and—it must be added—a characteristically male fiction. It is characteristic of the male, when an incident or event is sufficiently disagreeable, to pretend that in point of fact it never actually happened. And if the male in question should be a clergyman, that is, if he professes by reason of his office to speak for the sole Power Who may be able to reverse the clock of time, it seems highly plausible that he should assume to eradicate the traces of time's finger and to declare that what we know very well occurred never occurred at all. Thus, our Anglo-American law of annulment may have derived some of the exaggerated reliance on this fiction from its historical antecedents in the old ecclesiastical courts. Certainly, a tough-minded, secular judge would be disposed to say—in the words of Chief Justice John Marshall—"The past cannot be recalled by the most absolute power." [8] That is one reason why women sitting as judges might be less receptive to the convenient fiction of annulment. Because—to the discomfort of the males—most women show genuine ability to accept and assimilate the past on its own terms and to remember events as they actually happened. They can understand how a past fact may be distorted in the telling, and even how it may be boldly denied; but they do not see how one can put himself at ease by a pretense of believing and simultaneously denying the very same fact.

With these observations concerning the influence of males on the bench, we can proceed to the second major illustration of mercantilism in marriage law, that is, the subject of so-called "heart-balm" suits (breach of promise to marry, alienation of affections, criminal conversation). Suits of this kind are based on the fundamental assumptions of nineteenth-century mercantilism. They presuppose (1) that intangible personal relationships—no less than solid, tangible commodities—constitute items of private property; and (2) that malicious injuries to intangible property should be compensated in dollar damages. As these assumptions entered and gradually pervaded the whole law of trade and business, they leaked out into the Anglo-American law of marriage, which still shows mercenary blotches in a number of states.

Reasoning after the manner of Philistines, our nineteenth-century courts perceived no difference between a merchant's expectation that his customers would patronize him and the same man's expectation that his wife would love and remain true to him. Intentional interference with a customer's attitude meant liability in money damages; why not likewise with a wife's attitude toward her husband, or—the next step—a husband's attitude toward his wife?

The sordidness of this line of thought is rather unusual. Surely, the judges ought to have seen that since the merchant's relation with his customers was itself an expectation of realizing money-profits, the law was only giving him from the wrong-doer what he would otherwise have obtained from the customers—i.e., dollars. The lost asset and the legal damages were commensurable; dollar expectations that had been wrongfully defeated were directed to be satisfied by means of dollar-damages. But are these the expectations involved in affection, affiancement, and marital fidelity? Can dollars make a man whole for the loss of these? They are not valuable in dollars, but literally invaluable; they are simply not to be comprehended in pecuniary scales. If his injury is compensable in dollars, then the man has really suffered no injury, at least not of this kind. He may have to hire a housekeeper as a substitute for his wife's domestic services; but if he accepts dollars as a substitute for her sexual fidelity, what do we call him?

Lawyers from France, Italy, and the other Continental countries regarded the development of Anglo-American "heart-balm" law with open contumely. They could not understand that a husband—even though English or American—would publicly salve his honor with money-damages, and rub dollars on the sore spots where the horns had grown out. And, asked these Continental lawyers, what of the courts? The Anglo-American courts had made themselves arenas for the rending of families, the destruction of established reputations, and, in view of the growing attention given to "heart-balm" suits in the yellow press, for the titillation and delight of the prurient. Wherever the "heart-balm" suits were legally maintainable, numerous particularly ugly varieties of blackmail and extortion were invited and soon were manifest.

All this has not lacked a facetious side. For example, in early-Victorian England, a linen-draper's wife, being sick and about to die, told her husband what everybody else in the household and entourage seemed to know full well but he had not suspected, to wit, that the family doctor had long been planting antlers on his forehead and had even sent him off on a solitary tour of Scotland, supposedly for the improvement of his health but actually for the more convenient care and cultivation of the aforesaid antlers. The linen-draper, far from reviling or leaving his wife, treated her as kindly during the remaining three weeks of her life as though she had disclosed an unexpected legacy. And such indeed it proved to be. Prudently he instituted suit five days before she died; and one year later he obtained a tidy verdict of £500 against the doctor.[9] Where a sudden emergency like this might befuddle less solid individuals, one can safely trust our alert and enterprising merchants—whether in England or in America—not to overlook the main chance.

Little in the history of the law is more sadly comical than the tariff of rules developed by the Anglo-American courts to guide a jury in finding the money value of an unfaithful wife, which the co-respondent must pay the husband. Good taste and a sense of professional shame forbid my elaborating them here. Suffice it to say that she was priced under two aspects: (1) the pecuniary aspect, which depended on her own property, her ability to assist in her husband's business, and her skill as a housekeeper; and (2) the consortium aspect, which depended not only on her own qualities as a wife and mother but also on how the co-respondent had acted.[10] Was she difficult or easy to obtain?—if difficult she was worth more to her husband, presumably because she had already cost the co-respondent more. If the co-respondent has used his wealth, then the jury ought to know that circumstance, said the British courts, because "if it required the use of a fortune to seduce a wife, it would indicate that she was not lightly to be won, and would therefore indicate her greater value to a husband." This seems to signify that in pounds sterling the same wife will be worth more to the same husband if only she will hold out for an ample fortune with a lover annexed. But enough of this.

Repelled and embarrassed—but seemingly more by the salacity, fraud, blackmail, and public scandal incident to "heart-balm" cases than by their inherently mercantile treatment of personal affections—several American states, including New York in 1935 and Illinois in 1943, enacted statutes abolishing and prohibiting all the various types of "heart-balm" actions. The New York statute was upheld in the courts as constitutional, but the Supreme Court of Illinois unanimously struck down the Illinois statute as violative of the constitution of that state.[11] To characterize this decision bluntly, one must say that, in the view of the highest court of Illinois, the mercantile conception of marriage is so fundamental that, even to prevent blackmail, extortion, and fraud, the legislature cannot amend or refine it. According to the Illinois court, if the law does not give a husband money as damages for the loss of his wife's affection and society, it deprives him of a sacred property-right. It is hard to dignify an outlook like this with comment, hard even to make the obvious point, ignored by the Illinois court, that the action for alienation of affections was only a nineteenth-century development in American law and that the institution of marriage was somewhat older, or the equally obvious point that marriage is at least as respectable in the major parts of the world where "heart-balm" actions are unknown as it is in Illinois.

Anatole France, speaking of the folly of masculine jealousy, has said it is all based on the idea that once a woman "gave" herself to a man, he thenceforth owned her, which, of course, is a mere play on words. So a man may "possess" a woman in the carnal sense, but surely not in the legal. The State is not able to create or transfer nor can it morally direct the payment of money in exchange for the love that arises between two individuals. The eyes meet by accident and suddenly the chemistry of rapture goes into play without anyone's understanding how or why. This is a divine boon at times, and at others it is a tragic misfortune. But—whatever it is—it can never become property, it can never be translated into sums of money. It comes from, lives in, and departs for an entirely different realm, which does not border at any point on commerce or finance.

Concerning the quality and ends of marriage, our American law is mottled and confused, not yet out of the dank forest of mercantilism, not aware yet of the moral road it is due to traverse. The social values and their corollary mores are in conspicuous movement; the old ways cannot all remain in force. We shall see more of this flux when we look at the grounds for divorce.

For the present, it seems clear that (1) despite resistances and reversals, mercantilism is receding from the American law of marriage; (2) this implies, among other things, that a man and a woman may to a larger degree than ever before determine for themselves just what their becoming married shall mean in their own scale of values and goals; (3) it also means that the puritanical emphasis on reproduction as the sole end of marriage and excuse for intercourse can no longer be maintained; and (4) it holds out the hope that, as Americans turn their gaze away from a repudiated mercantilism, more and more of them may seek in marriage the innumerable harmonies, gratifications, and fulfillments which it is capable of bringing. One thing stands certain: the bond of marriage is not in and of itself sacred; yet man and wife may together sanctify it for themselves.

3. GROUNDS FOR DIVORCE

In New Mexico, the laws provide ten different grounds for divorce, ranging from adultery all the way to incompatibility, which was added to the statutory list in 1933.

Nick and Ellis P——, residents of New Mexico, were married in 1917, had four children, and separated from each other in 1937. Nick had been a coal miner but, after suffering an injury, he left the mines and went into business. His ventures proved unsuccessful and in 1940, being insolvent, he turned over his saloon and dance hall to a banker who was one of his creditors. The banker leased the place to Mrs. Lucille W——, who hired Nick to act as bartender and manager. After a year or two, the business became very profitable.

At this point, Nick sued for a divorce on the ground of incompatibility. Ellis denied the incompatibility and opposed the suit; her main defense was that he had been living in adultery with Lucille. When the case came up for trial in 1945, it appeared that the four children of the marriage were self-supporting. It also appeared, on the basis of rather sordid details, that Nick and Ellis were completely irreconcilable. The trial judge categorically refused to give any consideration whatever to Ellis' defense that Nick had been committing adultery. He *awarded Nick a divorce on the ground of incompatibility and directed him to pay alimony to Ellis at the rate of $100 a month. Ellis appealed to the highest court in the State.*

The Supreme Court of New Mexico (4–1) affirmed[12] *the decision. Reversing its own rule laid down in previous cases, it held under the State statute that if the parties are found to be irreconcilable, the plaintiff's adultery or other misconduct does not bar his right to a divorce.*

THERE is a good deal to be learned from the legal institution of matrimony about the process by which moral decisions are arrived at. One of marriage's more obvious implications has to do with that quality of precision which, in chapter II, we noticed as a special attribute of the law. Society must needs impose some measure of order in sex relations, not only to achieve continuity and stability in the organizing of domestic life, not only to provide for children and other dependents, but most indispensably of all to preserve elementary physical peace. If marriage accomplished nothing else, it would justify itself by reducing the number of violent fights and instances of bloodshed between men who want the same woman or women who want the same man. Marriage confers precision on the sexual and domestic ties between the husband and the wife, notifies the rest of the world that they constitute a biological unit, and defines the general aspects of their duties to each other. Even so, there are many crimes of sexual passion and violence in our society; but it can hardly be doubted that without marriage the situation would be very much worse.

An equally instructive aspect of legal marriage consists in its inculcation of generosity and giving. Since the majority of marriages are contracted between young people—which is equivalent to saying, between people who are prone to be extremely selfish and have not yet been invited by experience to center their desires outside themselves—the adjustments and accommodations involved in living together can furnish a progressive education in the arts and crafts of altruism. Fortunately, this process is aided and fostered by the gratifications that the ego itself derives from it. As a woman flatters her man, restores his confidence, and allays the doubts that everlastingly eat him from within, she draws new importance to herself from the exercise of this beneficent power. And temporarily at least, he likewise may become serene, proud, and strong whenever he believes that, in her special cosmos, the things he says or does are truly consequential.

It is easy to observe the intimate causal tie between personal vanity and sexual stimulation; in point of fact, most women know that flattery is both the straightest and the surest way to a man's heart. Of course, the average woman is also quite susceptible to appeals to her vanity, but she can—if she will listen to them—depend on other women to set her right concerning herself before any genuine damage is done. If she does listen to other women, she may learn to understand her lover's compliments for what they really are. They are really courting sounds, not intended literally at all, songs and ululations of desire, not to be taken as scientific reports on the one hand or as actionable covenants on the other. Males are not so often exposed to this sort of friendly instruction in self-appraisal. Perhaps it is better for them that they are not: whatever the underlying cause may be, they apparently feel some profound need to persevere in an almost unlimited credulity. Often, therefore, it will be a waste of money for a woman to purchase a gift for the man who interests her. If he is normally credulous, any compliment, however unmerited or false, will serve the purpose handsomely; and should he exhibit an extraordinarily distrustful nature, then to breach his defense she need only puff up and exaggerate some specific quality which he knows he possesses in a minor degree. And it may be a loving kindness on her part to do so.

But these are the very familiar observations that marriage affords; they are understood as soon as they are mentioned, and the only regret attached to them is that the gracious compliments and reassurances that embellish the courtship are not repeated often enough after the wedding. Less familiar is the manner in which marriage illuminates for us the important moral process of self-commitment. In our times it is customary to discuss the problems of moral choice as though they presented themselves in some vast and formless nowhere, as though moral decisions were taken in a sort of impersonal void. Although we have learned to allow for the indirect influence of social and cultural factors on the choices that are made, we give little or no consideration to the one special causative factor that most directly shapes our individual responses. This missing factor can be called "the principle of the route."

According to the "principle of the route," a moral choice is made *only* at some presented time and place by some specific person or persons, who have previously lived lives that appear to them, at any rate, as unique. The choice is conditioned and restricted not only by previous social and external circumstances in the chooser's biography but also by his own previous commitments of a voluntary nature and by the general objectives he has thereby imposed on the course of his life. He chooses *now* and *here,* because *now* he has brought himself *here* on his way to *there.* If a previous commitment of major proportions is involved in his having come so far, he may devote great pains and much time to maneuvering past some difficult obstacle; whereas from the same spot and confronted by the same obstacle, if he does not see any connection to a larger undertaking, he will lightly back away and return home. And, of course, there are innumerable obstacles, detours, and crossroads he will never have to deal with. He can imagine, if he will, how he would try to traverse a flooded stream if one should turn up somewhere some day; but it is mathematically improbable that his imagination will anticipate the circumstances that prove decisive when the flood actually faces him. For one thing, can he possibly foresee how much or how little he will care, at that moment, to proceed?

Because of this "principle of the route," the business of embarking on a major enterprise acquires exceedingly great significance. For once one sets forth on an over-all route, all subsidiary stages and decisions are strongly influenced if not completely determined by it. If the subsidiary stages become intolerably difficult, there may be no alternative to re-examining not merely them but the original act of embarkation. Hence the "principle of the route" virtually necessitates taking precautions against flighty, capricious, or premature departure on any major route whatever.

The "principle of the route" applies to almost all the moral choices that may arise in connection with marriage. In the first place, the ceremony of marriage being, among other things, an effectual device for dramatizing and solemnizing the act of embarkation, it deters a number of unwise choices, postpones a number of premature commitments, and conveys an intimation of responsibility to certain irresponsibles. Unfortunately, the very few who are emotionally sober enough to hear the language of the wedding ritual and to understand that the covenant runs for life—these few need no such admonitions. Hence it is not the ceremony but the solemn prospect of the ceremony that can sometimes curb an impetuous impulse. When it does, it confers quite a boon on young people. Most of them continue to mature for years after their bodies are entirely ready for copulation; and, in the meantime, mere eagerness offers not a scintilla of assurance that a wise choice or commitment would be made. When they do become mature, they may make no better choices; but, at least, they will have had a reasonable chance to consider the seriousness of the undertaking.

In the second place, although dramatization seems particularly welcome and useful for a wedding, after the wedding it becomes highly injurious. In chapter 1, we made a fundamental distinction between moral judgment exercised "judicially," the way a righteous judge acquits or condemns and, on the other hand, moral judgment exercised "administratively," the way a wise and flexible manager supervises a long-term enterprise. If ever "administrative" morality is needed, it is needed in married life. It is needed because the subject-matter is ongoing, continuous, and of tomorrow as of today and yesterday. Tolerance, good humor, ductility, and an infinite capacity to forgive are worth more in this intimate continuum than all the right judgments of Rhadamanthus. When guilt is adjudged, whether justly or unjustly, the structure trembles. And when the guilt is histrionized in some act of symbolic mummery—for instance, deserting the marital home—the structure is bound to collapse.

For in a sense, every lasting marriage comprises an endless series of reconciliations, most of them picayune and unspoken, a series of occasions through which tears, mostly unwept, may gradually solder the real bond of matrimony, which will thus become the end-product of the relation. And though forgiveness is indispensable to this process, let no one assume that a man must be adjudged guilty before he can be forgiven. He may need forgiveness most of all because, without his being consulted, a dream was dreamed about him once and now he does not seem to incarnate that dream. All this requires husbands and wives to keep alert to everything that is ongoing in marriage and to abstain from dramatic trials and adjudications. It is a wise policy to start with the assumption that both spouses, having the usual traits of human beings, are sufficiently guilty in one or more of a thousand possible respects that neither has the right to sit in judgment on the other. But, of course, this is a policy that cannot succeed unless it is reciprocal, and when neither party follows it, then something like our principal case, the one between Nick and Ellis, will eventuate.

Perhaps there could be no clearer test of the reader's own attitude toward marriage and divorce than the way he or she has reacted to the New Mexico Supreme Court's decision in our principal case. The test is all the more searching because Nick waited to file his suit for divorce until there would no longer be any question of supporting his and Ellis' children and until the poor times that Ellis had borne so many years were followed by a new prosperity with Lucille, which Ellis could not hope to participate in. Nick would not have made an attractive petitioner, even if Ellis had not charged him with adultery. It is easy to be misled by his conduct into feeling revolted by his suit and dismayed that the court granted it. But the reader who really understands the moral values in marriage and divorce will applaud this New Mexico decision. It is extraordinarily wise and just. For it embodies the three basic criteria of modern and enlightened divorce law. They are: (1) divorce without courtroom drama; (2) divorce without defendant's guilt; and (3) divorce despite plaintiff's guilt.

As we noted in chapter II, one of the attributes of legal procedure is its powerful capacity to dramatize human disputes and conflicts. Usually, this attribute works to advantage, because the very theatricality of the process summons our powers of imaginative projection and thereby stirs our moral constitutions into action. We comprehend a conflict with our heads and hearts, as the tedious and winding developments of many months are compressed into a few hours of courtroom testimony, as irrelevancies and digressions are cut from the narrative, and as the sight and hearing of the man on the witness-stand—his mannerisms and gestures and the tone of his speech—re-enact for us the experiences that have brought him there.

But these advantages of the court trial, indispensable as they are, serve only one main objective: finding out what a litigant *deserves* in connection with some *particular* transaction. If the transaction instead of being particular, involves his whole personality and domestic life, and the most intimate subtleties of his private relationships, then the trial in court—with its foreshortening of time, its lopping-off of details that appear irrelevant only to the outsider, and its inflaming of partisanship and animosity—the trial becomes an inadequate if not an actively harmful procedure. And if it is not the judging of desert that we are concerned with but the resolving, as wisely as may be, of an unsuccessful marriage, then again the forensic method of procedure is bound to be inappropriate. You can bring the parties into a trial court, but you cannot bring their broken marriage there. In court appear only the symptoms—a slap, a brutal drunkenness, or an adultery, which the testimony dramatizes beyond all sensible proportions, while the effective causes of the failure remain hidden outside.

Hence, what we need is not at all the traditional trial or anything resembling it. We need sympathetic, patient, and sophisticated efforts at reconciling the parties and restoring their marriage. These efforts, if they are to have any chance of success, must be dissociated from the setting of forensic drama and from all charges and imputations of guilt. It is very encouraging to observe that conference and reconciliation procedures, as legally required preliminary steps in suits for divorce, are appearing here and there in the United States. The experience of the judges who use these procedures, like the experience of most family lawyers, has been favorable in a gratifying ratio of cases, particularly where the skills of social workers, psychologists, and marriage-counselors were called on to assist the judge. But there are marriages, many of them, shattered beyond all human possibility of repair. For example, Nick and Ellis had been going their separate ways for five years before he filed suit.

In the irreparable cases—which are to be identified as such in the course of the judge's informal investigations and interviews—the New Mexico statute authorizes a divorce decree on the ground of "incompatibility," which the New Mexico court wisely held to mean "irreconcilability." Just as a marriage requires the consent of both, so too a reconciliation requires that both desire to try the relation once more. Just as either party could have prevented the marriage, so either may prevent the reconciliation. That the two are in fact irreconcilable is the center of the moral situation and, under the laws of New Mexico and like-minded states, of the legal situation as well. If in a specific case irreconcilability is a proved and established fact, what kind of opinion must one have of marriage to insist on anything further as a condition to divorce—to insist, for example, that the defendant's course of conduct be paraded to demonstrate that it had caused the irreconcilability?

There is a story of Plutarch's (he liked it well enough to tell it twice) about a Roman whose friends were reproaching him for divorcing his wife. They called his attention to her charms and attractions, her chastity, and the extent of her private wealth. Whereupon he only held out his shoe and said, "Now, this is new and fine to look at, but nobody knows where it pinches me!" And, by way of comment and advice, Plutarch added:

> *A wife ought not to trust to her dowry or her family or her beauty, but to things which touch her husband more vitally, namely, her congenial disposition and companionability, her capacity for making everyday life neither tiresome nor harassing, but harmonious, cheerful, and agreeable. For as doctors are more afraid of fevers that spring from obscure sources and grow worse gradually than of those that come from obvious and sudden causes, so the petty and constant daily squabbles of husband and wife, which the world knows nothing about, are what set them widest apart and spoil their life together . . .*

We may say further: Is it necessarily the shoe's fault that it pinches? Surely, once it is clear that the two will never accord with each other, we can separate the shoe from the foot without laying blame on either. For in any marriage that deserves the name, each spouse must always play foot to the other's shoe and shoe to the other's foot. If the fit should prove a bad one, then, as we know, responsibility can often be traced to parental or societal shoemakers. But we still have to separate the two—unless (*absit omen!*) we were to consider marriage like the unholy Red Shoes in the ballet-fable: once put on, they will never, never come off, and one dances in them till exhaustion arrives, then despair, and finally death.

Suppose the law in every state should be changed to conform to these two maxims, that is, the maxim of divorce without courtroom drama and that of divorce without defendant's guilt: what would be done about alimony, and the custody of the children? Usually, these matters are now disposed of by an agreement between the parties, which the judge examines and, if it seems acceptable, confirms. If the issue of defendant's guilt were legally excluded from consideration, such agreements would probably be arrived at more often, because the atmosphere of the hearings would not be charged with hateful and acrimonious tensions. But if no agreement could be reached in a particular case, the judge, under this system, would feel entirely free to fix the alimony by what is needed to support the dependents instead of what is needed to satisfy vindictiveness or punish guilt. Custody likewise would be awarded with an eye single to the best interests of the children; it would no longer be employed to put a permanent stigma on one or the other of their parents.

Should anyone be so blind as to infer that this kind of divorce system condones the committing of adultery or similar wrongs, his moral myopia ought to win our compassionate sympathy. Perhaps as he becomes better accustomed to the new legislation, he can be made to see its civilized respect for the dignity of the marriage bond and its melancholy wisdom that classifies adultery as only one and by no means invariably the most telling symptom of matrimonial inadequacy. Ultimately he too may come to believe that marriage should not be used as a legal prison for the ill-assorted nor divorce as a legal weapon of revenge.

But there is a third maxim to be found in our principal case: the maxim that divorce should be granted despite the plaintiff's guilt. Nick, it will be remembered, was accused of adultery, and the court held that the accusation, even if substantiated, constituted no legal bar to his suit. This is the latest trend in American courts, appearing as yet in only a very few states. It sets aside the doctrine which the ecclesiastical courts had established in medieval times and which every Anglo-American secular jurisdiction took over from them. The overwhelming majority still recognize the "defense of recrimination," that is, if the defendant, no matter how guilty, can show the plaintiff is guilty too, no divorce will be granted to either. (Some of these states use a modified "recrimination" rule that is called "comparative rectitude"; they make an exception and allow the divorce if the plaintiff's marital offense seems trivial in comparison with the heinousness of defendant's.)

It is hardly necessary to argue that the "doctrine of recrimination" offends our common sense and insults the institution of marriage. If any marriage whatever should be recognized as a complete failure justifying judicial severance, it is obviously the marriage in which both parties have misconducted themselves in the respects defined by statute. Each party rightly claims a divorce; therefore, under the droll logic of this doctrine, neither gets one. The law which sends them out of court still tied each to the other displays either a strange conception of matrimony or an uncomfortably quaint sense of humor.

What lies behind the "doctrine of recrimination"? Merely the fond, sentimental, and hopelessly mistaken belief that one of the parties to a divorce litigation can be genuinely innocent. Because of the distorting effects of courtroom dramatization, the divorce suit has been regarded as a sort of apocalyptic conflict between a wronged spouse and a wrongdoer spouse; the more one blackens the latter, the more the former will glow and be vindicated in resplendent purity. This is the kind of folly that inquisitions of matrimonial guilt lead to. Innocent, indeed! There never was a husband or wife altogether fit, in the forum of conscience, to throw the first stone.

In America, divorce is no longer interpreted as a bitter abandonment of the marital state, but, more often than not, as an opportunity, by re-entering it, to try again for domestic happiness. We are a nation of congenital optimists, kept awake at night by the brawls and obscenities of the couple next door, but quite oblivious of all this in the daytime when we see the same people smiling and preening themselves in their new clothes on their way to a wedding-anniversary celebration.

Perhaps we are not wrong. There is a vernal impulse in love

that simply defies summer droughts and the withering cold of winter. Marriage at its best would seem to be well worth some incidental suffering, and if in the end there is nothing to find but the suffering and nothing to show but the scars, the search itself may rise to the rank of piety; for search is a ritual of spring.

V

The Conduct of Business

1. HONESTY WITHOUT POLICY

On an April day, Al B—— and Mrs. E—— came into the fur salon of a Los Angeles store. (Mrs. E—— was apparently unmarried at the time.) A store employee showed them a mink coat priced at $5,000. B—— said he would like to buy it for Mrs. E—— but refused to pay more than $4,000 for it. Then, without B——'s knowledge, Mrs. E—— induced the store to pretend to sell him the coat for $4,000, agreeing to pay the difference herself. Accordingly, the store made out and presented a sales slip for $4,000; B—— signed it; the coat was handed over to him; and he turned it over to her, saying that he gave it to her. She put on the coat and they left the store together.

The next morning, Mrs. E—— paid $1,000 to the store and left the coat with it for monogramming. That very afternoon, B—— notified the store that he had revoked his gift to Mrs. E—— and that he would pay the agreed price ($4,000) only if the coat was delivered to him. Since Mrs. E—— also demanded delivery of the coat, the store brought an action to have their conflicting claims decided and to require B—— to pay $4,000 as he had agreed. B—— pleaded that he had been defrauded.

The highest court of California held (4–2) that B—— had in fact been defrauded and was entitled to rescind the entire transaction. The majority of the court considered it decisive *that B—— would not have made the purchase except for the store's intentional misrepresentation to him. The dissenting Justices contended that B—— had received from the store and delivered to Mrs. E—— the very same article he had bargained for, and that whatever disappointment he had suffered did not arise from his expectations of the store but from his expectations of Mrs. E——.*[1]

WRITING at the height of the Victorian era, W. E. H. Lecky set down some important observations on the general subject of veracity and its role in industrial countries.[2] He wisely distinguished three different planes for the exercise of veracity, which he styled (1) industrial, (2) political, and (3) philosophical; and he maintained that "The promotion of industrial veracity is probably the single form in which the growth of manufactures exercises a favourable influence upon morals." For in an industrial society, Lecky asserted:

> Veracity becomes the first virtue in the moral type, and no character is regarded with any kind of approbation in which it is wanting. It is made more than any other the test distinguishing a good from a bad man. We accordingly find that even where the impositions of trade are very numerous, the supreme excellence of veracity is cordially admitted in theory, and it is one of the first virtues that every man aspiring to moral excellence endeavours to cultivate. This constitutes probably the chief moral superiority of nations pervaded by a strong industrial spirit over nations like the Italians, the Spaniards, or the Irish, among whom that spirit is wanting. The usual characteristic of the latter nations is a certain laxity or instability of character, a proneness to exaggeration, a want of truth-

> *fulness in little things, an infidelity to engagements from which an Englishman, educated in the habits of industrial life, readily infers a complete absence of moral principle. But a larger philosophy and a deeper experience dispel his error. He finds that where the industrial spirit has not penetrated, truthfulness rarely occupies in the popular mind the same relative position in the catalogue of virtues. It is not reckoned among the fundamentals of morality, and it is possible and even common to find in these nations—what would be scarcely possible in an industrial society—men who are habitually dishonest and untruthful in small things, and whose lives are nevertheless influenced by a deep religious feeling, and adorned by the consistent practice of some of the most difficult and most painful virtues. Trust in Providence, content and resignation in extreme poverty and suffering, the most genuine amiability and the most sincere readiness to assist their brethren, an adherence to their religious opinions which no persecutions and no bribes can shake, a capacity for heroic, transcendent, and prolonged self-sacrifice, may be found in some nations in men who are habitual liars and habitual cheats.*

I quote this passage, not because I find any warrant for its disparaging reference to commercial standards among the Italians, Spanish, or Irish (Lecky, by the way, was an Irishman), but because it conveys an important monition for the stage we have reached in our study. It cautions us that commercial or pecuniary honesty, indispensable as it is, relates only to the petty concerns of moral life and very often does not deserve to rank with the grander honesties of political enterprise, of artistic pursuit, or of religious consecration. We shall be preoccupied in this chapter with the kind of honesty that merchants can be expected to exhibit and that we ought to prize in dealing with them. But let us remember that an honest merchant or an honest customer is only a fragment of an honest man—frequently, for lack of the higher honesties, a very unsatisfactory fragment.

Lecky further reminds us how very little connection there may be between the mercantile conception of honesty and the traits of character of a gifted religious mystic—the kind of individual who is an aristocrat by grace of spiritual excellence. I think he might have illustrated his point more amply by turning to the theatre, literature, music, and similar creative undertakings where the grand honesties are apt to manifest themselves. One of the reasons why an artist's business methods are so often the despair of merchants and bankers (not to mention the artist's wife) is his responsiveness to a higher plane of integrity, which sometimes makes him feel sincerely indifferent to the lower one. On occasion it may turn out to be a great boon for contemporary society and for posterity that he develops a certain insouciance, that he borrows without caring whether he will ever repay or agrees to commissions which he suspects he will never execute. Nevertheless, we cannot consider him or his conduct a whit less dishonest on the commercial level. Artists, even the most talented of them, are not professionally exonerated from the decent duties of the market place. In the life of morality, their function is not to ridicule or erode the standard we have styled "petty honesty" but simply to disclose its very real limitations.

Returning once more to the passage from Lecky, we are likely to be troubled by the compliments, qualified as they are, which he pays to the practice of commercial veracity in modern industrial societies. The statistics of governments and business bureaus, the grist of the court reports, and our own unpleasant experiences combine to make us wonder whether any moral improvement whatever has attended the progress of industrialization. The Bible is replete with strictures against false weights and crooked scales and fraudulent measurements; they are denounced for abominations in the eyes of the Lord. The Book of Ecclesiasticus in the Apocrypha bluntly comments: "A merchant shall hardly keep himself from doing wrong; and an huckster shall not be freed from sin. . . . As a nail sticketh fast between the joinings of the stones; so doth sin stick close between buying and selling." Do we have any reason to believe that these statements have become obsolete?

I think not. I think Lecky's complimentary remarks relate mainly to the business community's professed faith and—except where unremitting official supervision insures honest methods—they relate hardly at all to the practical application of the faith. If there has really appeared anything that could be called a spontaneous improvement in mercantile practices, I suggest (and think Lecky would agree) that the explanation is not moral but economic: the capital investment in equipment for industrialized mass-production is so great that fewer businessmen dare take the risk of losing their customers' confidence in the articles they manufacture. The itinerant merchant of the past, if detected in fraud, could move to a different territory. Even today, the sale of a defective mink coat would probably alienate only a single customer and her coterie; but production of an immense mass of identical items for a nationwide market requires some minimum of quality that, while not necessarily treating the customers fairly, at least keeps most of them quiescent. Because of sound economic considerations such as this, a slight advance in the level of commercial deportment would seem plausible.

It is interesting to observe how wholeheartedly our legal system detests the use of fraud. In the demonology of Anglo-American law, the three archfiends are force, fraud, and malice.

Nevertheless, one may sometimes resort to force (as in self-defense) and sometimes indulge in malicious exercise of one's personal rights without running afoul of the law. Fraud, on the other hand, is always forbidden, always unforgivable in the courts. "Fraud," the courts habitually say, "vitiates everything." Why does it? Morally speaking, what is so especially diabolical about fraud?

In the moral sense, fraud is a particularly hideous evil because it combines the essential features of both force and malice. Fraud resembles force inasmuch as it seeks to subdue one person's will and, through it, his actions to the will of another. It resembles malice inasmuch as it destroys the bonds of social benevolence. Treacherously and by stealth it goes about its work.

These traits are repellent enough, in all conscience, but they do not complete the picture of fraud or deceit as presented in a law court. Fraud, as defined by law, has such a supremely ugly mien because it appears in court with a smirk of at least temporary success. The plea of fraud, according to the common law's lexicon, requires that someone actually credited and relied on the false representation. A mere attempt to deceive is not enough in the traditional law; there must be proof of a successful deception and an accomplished injury. Taking cognizance of the pit of prevarication only when some victim has set his foot on the false cover, has fallen in, and has suffered a hurt, the law has come to abhor deceit with an intense and distinctive hatred. For at the sight of a successful fraud, the fear that sleeps uneasily in every man's mind begins to stir, the primordial fear that, despite all promises and firm assurances of civilized society, he can trust no one and must pass through life unsheltered in the midst of wolves.

If reliance and disappointed expectations are considered indispensable to a charge of deceit, with what kind of expectations is the law willing to concern itself? This is, of course, the central question involved in our principal case. The majority of the Supreme Court of California disagreed with the dissenting Justices on the precise question whether Al B——'s disappointment was of a kind that the courts would dignify with legal consequences. We shall shortly take up their disagreement, but first it is worth while to note the area in which, without explicitly saying so, the majority and minority agreed with each other.

They agreed, as all courts do, that a man *can* have sufficiently clear knowledge of a matter of fact to become obligated to make a sincere statement to the person he deals with. The law of fraud refuses to surrender to any doctrine of extreme skepticism about what men can and cannot know. It admits that skepticism is warranted as to matters of opinion (it is not a fraud merely to puff up the attractive qualities of one's merchandise). But when the matter is one of fact (for example, whether a coat is made of mink or of muskrat dyed to resemble mink), then the judges will never be found simpering like Pontius Pilate and saying "What is truth?"

Secondly, they all agree that when it comes to representing facts of which the speaker or writer holds himself out as having special knowledge, there arises a legal duty to exercise reasonable care, or, as we have put it from time to time in this book, to act intelligently. No one has a moral or legal right to assert negligently and heedlessly as a fact that which he has not troubled to investigate or confirm, when he can foresee that someone will rely on his careless statement at the risk of injury.

At certain points, the courts have limited the legal liability of a negligent speaker or writer of commercial data. Fearing to bankrupt him by allowing too many claims to be asserted against him, they have generally granted damages only to those parties who have contracted directly with him in connection with the information. For example, a negligent public accountant would ordinarily be held liable only to the corporation which engaged him to prepare its balance sheet, not to outsiders who were shown the balance sheet and relied on it. But the law tends gradually to do away with these restrictions; and even now if the accountant's negligence in a particular case should seem gross and reckless, the courts will consider it tantamount to fraud and will hold him liable to outsiders as well.[3] There should be no moral shield in one's own sloth and stupidity.

Of course, since B—— had transacted his business directly with the store and since it had deceived him not negligently but quite intentionally, his claim appeared to present a typical instance of commercial fraud. Why then did two Justices dissent from the decision in his favor and insist that the store had not defrauded him at all? Their reasoning is strong and tough-minded. They argue in effect: B—— got exactly what he wanted; he loved Mrs. E——, at least for the day, and wanted her to possess that specific coat; her (secret) contribution merely enabled him to fulfill his wish; he changed his mind about giving her the coat only because, as his lawyer said at the trial, "on the very evening of this gift Mr. B—— became confronted with the reality that the young lady wasn't telling him the truth about things."

Obviously, the court would not listen to what was alleged to have happened that unhappy evening away from the store, and we too have discretion enough to respect the privacies of the situation. The real question in the case is whether B—— had obtained what he expected from the *store*. Facing that question, the dissenting Justices erred, in my opinion, because they failed to allow for B——'s "non-economic motives"—as the majority opinion discreetly called them without, however, saying what the "non-economic motives" were. Perhaps we could offer a conjecture or two.

I suggest that B—— may have had in him something of the medieval troubadour, or at least of the poetic dreamer who serves and worships at Aphrodite's altar. Where another man might fling up to his beloved on her balcony a rose or a song or a poem, B—— would fling her a mink coat. What a beautiful and appropriate symbol of the warmth that filled his bosom! This gay gesture of his, so delicate in feeling and taste, recaptures the charm of the age of chivalrous romance.

If B—— was really this kind of gallant cavalier, did not the store disappoint his expectations? Surely, if I hire a band to serenade my love, I do not expect her to pay the musicians overtime charges because the performance takes place at night. If I hire a poet to write a poem expressing my passion, the twelve lines I pay for should tell it all, and the poet is a scoundrel who charges her for two more lines on the ground that nothing less than a sonnet will do. B—— likewise did not want to give the lady of his dreams only four-fifths of a mink coat. Can it then be said that he received what the store agreed to give him?

My second conjecture converts B—— into an experienced and successful denizen of the market place. Let us conceive him as a clever businessman, adept at negotiating and bargaining and understandably proud of his prowess. If that is the case, surely one of his legitimate expectations in the transaction with the store has been grievously disappointed. I mean his expectation that, when the store billed him $4,000 for a $5,000 coat, he had purchased a bargain. Ever since business began, this has been one of the attendant satisfactions that make business a pleasure for those to whom it is a pleasure. In the wise sayings of the Book of Proverbs, we read, " 'It is bad, it is bad,' saith the buyer; But when he is gone his way, then he boasteth." This right to boast the purchaser buys along with the merchandise, and it is injurious—not to say cruel—to strip him of it. So when B—— learned that the store had not really yielded to his bargaining as it led him to believe, he may have suffered very keenly.

In any event, the outcome in B——'s case is a good one. It shows that into their business arrangements men may mix whatever dreams they as individuals happen to be capable of. Into the package at the store may go considerably more than an article of merchandise, because the buyer may buy much that the seller cannot possibly sell.

We have now reached the two dominant moral questions in the topic of commercial honesty. The first of these is whether the traditional common law is a correct moral guide—insofar as it passes by false statements unless someone has been damaged by relying on them.

This question need not delay us long. The answer is obviously negative. When the courts are asked to award money-damages, they are justified in insisting on proof that the attempt to deceive did in fact inflict some harm which deserves compensation. When the courts are asked to set aside an agreement or a conveyance of property, they are justified in requiring proof that the fraud complained of did in fact induce the complainant to agree or to convey. Their function has nothing to do with determining the defendant's general desert, but only his desert in a particular transaction.

Consequently, though a man is a chronic swindler who constantly tries to defraud people, he is nevertheless entitled to enforce any specific agreement he has made honestly and without taint. His attempts to deceive do not outlaw him. And this is desirable in morals as well as in law, for otherwise every one of us would be in peril of losing our property and personal rights just because a court might decide that on some unconnected occasion we had said an untruth.

On the other hand, it would be absurd to employ these considerations, stemming as they do from the limited function of the court in a civil litigation, throughout the whole province of the law. If a commercial lie is uttered under such circumstances that it may inflict harm on a large group or on the entire public, the utterance itself is a legal wrong, whether or not anyone relies on it. In these situations, the danger is too great to permit official toleration. Assume the case of a false prospectus issued to the public by a stockbroker, or a false labelling of medicines sold by a drug-manufacturer. The law may enjoin the continuation of the wrong, may take away the wrongdoer's license to conduct his business, and may put him behind bars—without proof of public reliance or injury. In the same fashion, a man who testifies to a falsehood when he is under oath is guilty of the crime of perjury though in fact no one believes him, because he has jeopardized the very machinery of justice. But even these species of wrongdoers are not completely outlawed; they retain all their rights that are untainted.

Here we have, as I see it, the correct guide for a moral assessment of veracity. Someone's reliance on a falsehood can only increase the moral guilt involved; it does not create the guilt. A man who knowingly tells an untruth does a moral wrong though no one actually believes him. Yet, however much others may hate him for a liar, they must avoid rejecting the remainder of his humanity.

Our ultimate moral question in this topic is: Why should one be honest? The best way, I think, to answer this question is to distinguish and describe the three varieties of business honesty.

First, there is compulsory or policed honesty. This is the honesty of those who assume, sensibly enough, that dishonest people are quite likely to get caught sooner or later; that without a certain proportion of honest actions one cannot have the sort of reputation which is indispensable for commercial credit, advancement, community esteem, and business success; and that honest dealing will probably be reciprocated, to one's pro rata share of the mutual advantage. Though we may not admire honesty that has to be imposed or compensated, we shall in all probability never cease to need it—because even in the hearts of the best of us it enforces the moral way when the higher honesties fail.

Second, there is congenital or voluntary honesty. Here we have the honesty that rises from its own roots and, flourishing, bears incidental benefits and fruits. This is the honesty we expect in the superior, more integral man. He appreciates the individual esteems and the social solidarities that honesty may produce, yet he cherishes it cheerfully and devotedly in seasons when it seems to be sterile. On rare occasions, he may wonder whether it has ceased to yield its fruit and, if so, whether temporary barrenness is a token of decay and approaching death; but then he squares his shoulders and dismisses the thought as unworthy. Since the harvest has always been a fitful one, he knows that prosperity cannot finally confirm the worth of honesty, nor adversity discredit it.

Third, we come to righteous honesty—the sort displayed by men whose moral processes are severely judicial (as distinguished from administrative). Here we have the categorical honesty of the prophetic type. It could be styled "the honesty of the burning bush." According to the Bible, the bush Moses came upon in the wilderness was aflame with an unremitting fire but was not consumed. The fire gave no necessary light, benefited no one with its warmth, nor did it destroy anything; it burned only because it burned. The burning bush typifies prophetic veracity, which cares nothing for consequences whether beneficial or harmful and proceeds with its mission as heedless of a blessing as of a curse. Even to good people this may prove a very uncomfortable sort of honesty. In point of fact, it has been the historic function of the moral prophet to discomfort first of all the good people who are around him.

There is a story of Bishop Jeremy Taylor's that might serve to symbolize this sort of intense, uncompromising self-dedication. He relates: "St. Lewis the King sent Ivo Bishop of Chartres on an embassy, and he told, that he met a grave and stately matron on the way with a censer of fire in one hand and a vessel of water in the other; and observing her to have a melancholy, religious, and phantastic deportment and look, he asked her what those symbols meant, and what she meant to do with her fire and water; she answered, my purpose is with the fire to burn paradise, and with my water to quench the flames of hell, that men may serve God purely for the love of God." [4]

The world being what it is, we are fortunate indeed when a business transaction displays any one of the three honesties. The compulsory kind we are entitled to require of all men. Of our friends and intimate associates we may, if we are so disposed, require spontaneous or voluntary honesty. The honesty of the burning bush we have the moral right to require only of ourselves.

2. PROPERTY AND OPPRESSION

ACCORDING *to the complaint he filed in court, Edward C. Tuttle had for many years been a successful and popular barber in the Minnesota village where he lived. He had maintained his family comfortably and had actually saved $800 a year, which in 1909 when his case was litigated could certainly be called "a considerable sum." But somehow he incurred the enmity of Cassius B——, a rich local banker. B——, Tuttle-*

pleaded, decided to drive him out of business and, to that end, opened up and furnished a second barber shop in the village, hired a barber to run it, and used his wealth and prominence to divert Tuttle's customers to B——'s shop. Tuttle alleged that B—— took these steps maliciously to destroy Tuttle's business, and that, far from trying to serve any business purpose of his own, B—— had started the new shop without regard to any loss it might entail. Therefore Tuttle sued for damages.

B—— contended that even if these allegations were proved, he would not be liable, because, however ill his motives might be, he had only exercised the right everyone has to enter into competition in a lawful trade.

The highest court of Minnesota decided (3–2) that, if Tuttle could prove the truth of his pleading, B—— should be held liable for damages. B——'s alleged conduct was not competition but a brutal "application of force." [5]

CONTRITION taken neat at reasonable intervals (there is no way of moderating the individual dose) provides an indispensable moral corrective. Hence, just as every lawyer should read periodically Plato's comments on the legal profession in the *Theaetetus*, so every rich person, regardless of his merits, should expose himself from time to time to what Aristotle said concerning the wealthy:

> The type of character produced by Wealth lies on the surface for all to see. Wealthy men are insolent and arrogant; their possession of wealth affects their understanding; they feel as if they had every good thing that exists; wealth becomes a sort of standard of value for everything else, and therefore they imagine there is nothing it cannot buy. They are luxurious and ostentatious; luxurious, because of

the luxury in which they live and the prosperity which they display; ostentatious and vulgar, because, like other people's, their minds are regularly occupied with the object of their love and admiration, and also because they think that other people's idea of happiness is the same as their own. It is indeed quite natural that they should be affected thus; for if you have money, there are always plenty of people who come begging from you. Hence the saying of Simonides about wise men and rich men, in answer to Hiero's wife, who asked him whether it was better to grow rich or wise. "Why, rich," he said; "for I see the wise men spending their days at the rich men's doors." Rich men also consider themselves worthy to hold public office; for they consider they already have the things that give a claim to office. In a word, the type of character produced by wealth is that of a prosperous fool. There is indeed one difference between the type of the newly-enriched and those who have long been rich: the newly-enriched have all the bad qualities mentioned in an exaggerated and worse form—to be newly-enriched means, so to speak, no education in riches.[6]

Among classic writers, Aristotle's is only one of several traditional attitudes toward the consequences of wealth. In the kind of appraisal he arrived at, not much stress is laid on moral criteria; at most they exercise a secondary influence. If our observations, like his, lead to the conclusion that rich people are generally pompous, arrogant, and ostentatious, the judgment we pass is primarily of a cultural or esthetic nature. Though it may be important in determining whether we care to associate with them, it tells us very little about the strictly moral meaning of economic disparities, for bad taste does not of itself denote moral evil.

Wealth often makes its possessor feel a sort of sentimental

unease. Curiously enough even the rigorous Kant once allowed this sentiment to leak out.[7] Wealthy men and women who face the simple truth know right well that their advantages have been brought about almost entirely by accident. The accident of birth is, of course, ridiculously capricious; the accidents of economic life are scarcely less so; and every day of a man's prosperity depends on the happening of innumerable chance factors, any one of which can make his desert irrelevant and his acumen powerless. When this is perceived, a vague, sentimental desire to succor the poor may evince itself, motivated at times by inner intimations of guilt that come from possessing advantages one did not earn, at other times inspired by a secret hope that in practicing generosity and altruism one may possibly placate fortune's malice.

Certainly, this sentimental attitude, despite its imperfections, is greatly to be preferred to the imbecile conceit of many millionaires. We are all familiar with the type of rich Philistine; in the United States his name is legion. He confidently believes that, at least in his case, God—Who seems to him to err very strangely in the choice of other privileged persons but never when it comes to selecting the underprivileged—God has duly appraised his deserts and has allotted his receipts fittingly. He sees in his prosperity not simply the product but also the divine certificate of his merit.

I imagine he and his ilk must provide considerable entertainment in heaven. For while God practices pragmatism—as indeed He practices every other known and unknown philosophy—we may be certain He is far too experienced a pragmatist to consecrate the play of chance or to confuse material goods with moral worth. It is equally obvious that men's taking pride in possessions and estates would never pass unrebuked unless God had a sense of humor, which, being His, must needs be a perfect one.

The third and I believe the strongest moral tradition on the subject of wealth has focused on the poor rather than on the rich. It is less concerned with the esthetic unattractiveness of rich men and the chance sources of their advantages than with impacts which may be felt and suffered by their less fortunate neighbors. So it turns to the wealthy, not to improve their culture or to assuage their guilt, but to enforce various responsibilities that arise concomitantly with the acquisition of goods. All property, it holds, is a species of power; every power involves corresponding responsibilities. Ownership of property does not of itself present the moral issue. The issue arises because the mode of use, the failure to use, or the misuse of power may work an oppression.

From its ancient beginnings until quite recently, this tradition was wont to concentrate on the kind of behavior that Tuttle, the barber, complained of: that is, the expelling of a poor man or one of modest means from a possession necessary to his livelihood. Occasionally, there was no sign of malice in the oppressive behavior but only of selfishness and greed (e.g., Isaiah excoriated those who join field to field until no space is left for the poor); more often, however, some vicious impulse appeared as the motive (the incident of Uriah the Hittite or of Naboth's vineyard). Even in the latter instances of oppression, the victims were injured only in order to take something away from them; whereas nothing that we know of actuated the banker in our principal case except enmity and the impulse to destroy.

Nature has an ingenious arrangement to assist us toward goodness. By this arrangement, if anyone persistently entertains malicious motives and desires, he punishes himself in a number of vulnerable places—most directly in the nerves and tissues of the stomach and viscera. Long, probably, before he can harm the person he hates, he will begin to inflict harm on himself.

From the somatic condition, this process works its way into every other interest where hatred has been harbored; for example, B——, completely contrary to his established instincts as a banker, found himself committed to a senseless loss of money in a barber-shop for which there was no economic justification. Vindictiveness is by nature more misleading than passionate love, for love being blind to the real sees the ideal, while hatred, eschewing both, glares at its own ugly reflection. In business as in politics, the prudent man who values his health and his money will remember Disraeli's advice: "Next to knowing when to seize an opportunity, the most important thing in life is to know when to forego an advantage."

Our principal case, though completely sound in law and morals as far as it goes, can only serve to introduce the more complex and sophisticated moral problems that have emerged in the United States since World War I. Oppressions in this modern period are not characteristically the result of malice or personal spite, nor is it easy to identify the oppressor with a specific, isolated monad, like banker B——, free in his own volition to exert or relax the economic power. In appearance at least things have changed. Malice is no longer very important because, in this new period, the major forces that may injure any individual in the mass of people seem to have lost their personal identity. While the dangers from economic oppression have grown more ominous, the oppressors themselves have been made to look as though they had neither faces nor human names, nor any local situs of responsibility.

In the moral life of the individual property-owner these great changes on the surface of things have left ugly marks. Only too anxious to find a release from the inhibitions which past customs and moral restraints used to attach to his powers, he can argue now that whatever he does is done quite impersonally, that he acts only as an implement of delocalized forces, and that, though he personally deprecates the oppressive impact of, say, charging his tenants iniquitous rents, not he but some nationwide economic movement without a face or a conscience has brought it all about. What, he asks, can we expect him to do? If he should limit his charges or profits, the "others," who he knows have no human sympathies, certainly would not limit theirs; and since the general business condition—whether of inflation or of depression—is obviously not of his making, he feels scarcely obliged to forego the opportunities it offers him.

Moreover, he argues, his self-restraint would be inconsequential in stemming the economic tide. Why, then, should he make what in effect would be gifts to his tenants or debtors? Surely, if charity is in order (Americans are a very charitable people insofar as "charity" means giving money to incorporated humane causes), he has probably made a generous list of donations, though perhaps not so generous as the amounts deducted therefor on his income tax return. But no one has the right to suppose that he is in business for charity's sake. Finally, if these arguments do not suffice, he can put the blame on the state or federal government. Why does it not regulate the prices or the rents? It possesses the power to keep those greedy and conscienceless "others" under control; hence it alone, he claims, is morally responsible for the oppressions resulting from an unregulated market.

When we review these answers which the self-interest of the man of property uses to stifle his sense of doing wrong, we find ourselves at a solemn place in our progress. The place is solemn because the contentions and excuses of the property-owner compel us to face one of our deepest and most pervasive moral predicaments as human beings. The predicament crops up everywhere in our moral careers. Since it is the direct corollary of our own finite natures and finite capacities, we can never get away from it. Again and again each of us is confronted with the question: Have I a moral duty to do the righteous act which I am reasonably assured will be ineffectual?

Let us assume that the questioner is an exceptionally honorable and sensitive property-owner, one who puts the question not to defend his profits but with complete sincerity and a genuine desire to perform his moral obligations. The law, we are supposing, imposes no limit on the rents he can charge. What then is his duty?

In the first place, I think he ought to be assured that his private ownership of property is *per se* neither moral nor immoral in any general sense. Private ownership is a civic institution, involving an extensive variety of economic and political relations, which derive their moral coloration from the extent of the powers they confer on individuals over other individuals and over the community, the degree of diffusion of the ownerships and powers, and the manner in which the powers are actually used. A moral beneficence at one time and place, it may become a moral iniquity elsewhere or at another time. Certainly, in contemporary America private ownership, appropriately regulated by law, produces significant moral goods and benefits that are well worth preserving. Unless a more morally advantageous way of administering the country's material goods should present itself in the course of future economic changes, a private owner need feel no moral guilt by reason of merely owning.

In the second place, although the business market is not esthetically attractive, it does serve a restraining purpose under usual conditions, i.e., under conditions which, if not technically "normal," at least manifest gradual adjustments up and down in the price structure. This "usual" market acts as a (fairly long) leash on the cupidity of property-owners. Of course, it will not work with economic monopolies; they always require official regulation or fragmentation. But in activities where aggressive competition must be met, the charging of market prices for honest merchandise should generally furnish some assurance against oppressiveness.

Now we come to our critical case. Suppose the market leash breaks, either in a time of extreme inflation because goods are so scarce that every owner becomes a monopolist of what he owns, or in a time of extreme depression because every creditor becomes a monopolist of what he claims to be paid. In the former case, there is no other vendor available to sell the needed merchandise; in the latter, there is no other investor available to lend the needed credit; in both cases, the disappearance of the usual market is nationwide, impersonal, and spiteless.

When the leash breaks on a well-trained dog, he stands still beside his master and quietly waits until it is repaired or some alternative control is devised. The leash is not his only incentive to restraint; discipline and the desire to abide by taught standards will hold him for a fair time at least, though sooner or later he will probably need the leash again. If on the other hand there was never anything to his previous good behavior but the tensile strength of the leash, then when it breaks he will scamper away, wild, anarchic, and defiant in his suddenly-discovered liberty and likely to travel far and destroy much before hunger brings him skulking home. And the lawless example of other dogs likewise freed of their leashes can inspire him to behave like a cur—or a wolf.

I do not think we can salve our consciences by pleading that self-restraint will have no practical consequences in leashless periods. We do not know how great the cumulative effect of a single demonstration may become, how many may notice and respond to an exhibition of mercantile discipline. Nor do we know the impact our recommendation backed by our example may have on legislators and other officials charged with the restoration of economic order. If our efforts should prove completely futile in these respects, they would nevertheless justify themselves by inspiring public esteem and gratitude. And if even these should fail, then to abstain from acts of economic oppression would still be utterly desirable for its own sake and as a testimonial to the proposition that it is better to stand quietly beside Master Conscience than to hunt with the wolves and slink with the multitude of curs. Experience never gives anyone a general and absolute warrant to despair of righteousness or even of righteousness' direct, practical benefits. For just as the morally educated man doubts—with good reason—that right will *always* produce an external reward and wrong an external punishment, he likewise refuses to believe that in any *specific* instance the doing of right will necessarily go unrewarded and the doing of wrong will necessarily go unpunished.

As fai as American law is concerned, the prime question has been: While awaiting the arrival of a new leash in the form of a more balanced market, can the government hold back economic oppression during an emergency? This question has presented grave difficulties, since our Constitution explicitly forbids the states to impair the obligation of contracts and forbids both the Federal Government and the states to deprive anyone of his property without due process of law.

Immediately after World War I, as after World War II, there was a severely inflationary housing shortage in the great urban centers of the United States, due in large part to wartime cessation of residential building. Congress enacted for the District of Columbia and the New York legislature enacted for New York City laws that temporarily fixed maximum rents to be charged for apartments and permitted a tenant to retain his apartment after the expiration of his lease on paying the legal rent. The Supreme Court (5–4) held these statutes constitutional, Justice Holmes writing the majority opinions.[8]

At the opposite extreme, the deflationary conditions of the early 1930's threatened to bring about the foreclosure of mortgages on a calamitous proportion of private homes in all sections of the country. Minnesota in 1933 enacted a law which compelled mortgagees to postpone foreclosure during a limited, emergency period as long as the home-owner should pay the reasonable rental value of his property as fixed by the State court. The Supreme Court (5–4) held this statute constitutional, Chief Justice Hughes writing the majority opinion at the very peak of his judicial form.[9]

It is safe to say that under these and other wise decisions of the Supreme Court (one shudders to think how close they were) American governments have the needed constitutional power to restrain oppressive use of property during emergency periods of extreme inflation or deflation. The reasoning of the decisions is very instructive. As far as Holmes was concerned, the central question had little to do with morals. In fact, in his view, "it is unjust to pursue such profits from a national misfortune with sweeping denunciations." Tax the profits, he said in effect, or regulate them as you regulate the return on money by your "more debatable usury laws"; the public interest furnishes justification enough. So he thought; but clearly his analysis will not suffice for our purposes, which of course are quite different from his. Since, as he would insist, the legislature is the judge of the public interest, no moral duty of restraint would arise until it acted and even then the moral duty would meekly follow the provisions of the statute.

In the Minnesota mortgage moratorium case, Hughes wrote the kind of detached, cool, and overpoweringly rational opinion that was typical of him. At one point however a glimpse of warm reality—legally far in the background—broke through, almost in spite of the Chief Justice and all his objectivity. He somehow could not help mentioning that the owners of mortgages on Minnesota lands were "predominantly corporations, such as insurance companies, banks, and investment and mortgage companies. These, and such individual mortgagees as are small investors are not seeking homes or the opportunity to engage in farming. Their chief concern is the reasonable protection of their investment security." So, Hughes said, Minnesota has given them a fair economic equivalent of what they bargained for; let the little mortgagor (the mortgage in this case was about $4,000) keep his home until the storm subsides. Contracts should be kept literally, he held, but not at the price of destroying government itself, "by virtue of which contractual relations are worth while." Thus, a widespread economic oppression of individuals may equal, in the law, a threat to the existence of the government. When we reach such a pass, all our best impulses—moral, legal, and political—unite to resist the oppression.

But there was one factor that Hughes chose not to mention, although it was called to his notice. The mortgage moratorium case had come to the United States Supreme Court on appeal from the Supreme Court of Minnesota. In the Minnesota court, one of the state justices, dissenting from the decision that the statute was constitutional, pointed out that these large corporations, banks, and insurance companies that held mortgages on Minnesota properties were themselves mainly trustees for the savings of "little" people, farmers and retired farmers, women and children.[10] What of them? It is all very well to prevent oppression of the home-owner, but suppose what seems like oppression is asserted on behalf of other individuals, themselves probably in need of protection or at least of the assurance they contracted for. Suppose the manager of the corporation holding the mortgage is duty-bound to consider these people who have confided their savings to him. Can he then give thought to the impact of his policies on anyone else? This—

the problem of loyalties—we shall consider in the section that follows.

3. THE RADIUS OF LOYALTY

In 1902 Walter S——, a real estate operator, obtained a lease of the old Hotel Bristol in New York City for twenty years at $55,000 per annum. Having agreed to make elaborate alterations to improve the building, he secured one-half of the money he needed from Morton M——, a woolen merchant. S—— and M—— agreed that they would divide the profits and the losses between them, but S—— alone was to manage the joint enterprise. Thus M——'s participation remained unknown to the landlord. After some early losses, the hotel yielded them a rich annual return.

About four months before the lease was due to expire in 1922, the landlord, who at that time owned four additional buildings adjoining the hotel, proposed that S—— take a long-term lease on all five plots (including the hotel), demolish the buildings, and construct one huge edifice on the combined tract. S—— said nothing about this to M——. About three weeks later, the landlord and S—— signed a new lease, covering the five plots and specifying yearly rentals of $350,000 to $475,-000. Soon thereafter, as the hotel lease was nearing its expiration date, M—— learned about the new arrangement and claimed he was entitled to a half interest in it. When this was refused, M—— instituted a suit in which he asked the court to enforce his interest.

The highest court of the State of New York decided (4–3) that M—— was legally entitled to a one-half interest in the new transaction. It held that although S—— had had no con-

scious purpose of defrauding M——, he had violated a duty of loyalty to him. As managing coadventurer, S—— was bound at the very least to tell M—— promptly about the landlord's proposal so that M—— might, if he chose, compete for the advantages involved in it. Having failed to perform this duty, S—— must treat M—— as jointly interested in the extension of their enterprise.[11]

It was Chief Judge Benjamin N. Cardozo, our national paragon as infuser of moral ideals into rules of law, who wrote the majority opinion in this celebrated case. The opinion has exerted a powerful and lasting influence in the courts of New York and other states. However, its chief interest for our purposes does not consist so much in what it tells trustees about their duties as in what it reveals about Cardozo's very special excellence. One of the qualities of a great judge stands out clearly in this opinion: he showed by what he wrote that he fully understood S——, the man *against* whom he was deciding.

He understood how M—— must have looked in S——'s eyes in the spring of 1922. True, M—— had put some money at risk back in 1902; for that investment he had been richly repaid year after year. He had received his full share of the profits, though S——, who had furnished an equal amount of money, had also contributed the time, effort, and acumen that made the enterprise a success. The seemingly interminable commitment to share with M—— was finally drawing to a close. It was not a question of gratitude; S—— had probably learned by 1922 not to expect gratitude from M—— or any other investor; emancipation after twenty years of sharing would be enough for him. But now came M——, who in his ignorance of real estate operations would doubtless have lost his entire stake had it not been for S——; he came, this Old Man of the

Mountain, and shamelessly demanded his one-half share in an entirely new and different enterprise, an enterprise which was not only many times the size of the one he had been asked to join in 1902 but was actually scheduled to continue, at S——'s option, for the next eighty years! In short, M—— was conducting himself like a businessman.

In the eyes of a lesser judge these considerations might have proved decisive; but Cardozo understood that a determination in favor of M—— would not necessarily imply admiration for him or disparagement of S——'s abilities as a manager. On the contrary, Cardozo reasoned, it was precisely because S—— had used these abilities of his and had taken the reins of management that he must be subjected by law to the duties of a trustee. And the judge went on:

> *Joint adventurers, like copartners, owe to one another, while the enterprise continues, the duty of the finest loyalty. Many forms of conduct permissible in a workaday world for those acting at arm's length, are forbidden to those bound by fiduciary ties. A trustee is held to something stricter than the morals of the market place. Not honesty alone, but the punctilio of an honor the most sensitive, is then the standard of behavior.*

Here we have, at least by way of implication, what might be styled the ideal maxim of business conduct under our present system of property tenure. At one point or another heretofore, we have had occasion to insist that the possession of economic power should be associated with moral responsibilities; now we see that the standard must rise still higher. Responsibility though indispensable is not enough. To attain the ideal level of economic conduct, those who wield power on behalf of others must voluntarily accept certain disabilities, certain disqualifications from doing what would normally be permitted to them.

Loyalty then exacts more than the fulfillment of responsibility; it requires the manager to identify himself with his coadventurers by renouncing some of his own selfish interests and some of his usual economic freedom.

Even if we choose to overlook for a moment the inveterate selfishness that most human beings begin with, that competition in the business world pays a premium for, and that the deference of sycophantic employees constantly exacerbates—even if we overlook this ugly and ubiquitous selfishness, the ideal relationship between manager and coadventurer still seems exceedingly difficult to reach. For in the contemporary American scene with its close-knit industrial organization and its manifold financial interdependencies, ours is not merely, as some seem to think, the age of managers; it is, perhaps more significantly, the age of the coadventurers.

S—— at least knew exactly who M—— was; the managers of many nation-wide industrial enterprises are by no means so fortunately certain. Who is the M—— of which account must be taken? Is it the security-holders only, or they plus the company's labor force, or these plus the distributors, customers, and consumers, or all of them plus some interest of international policy which may or may not have been articulated officially? Loyalty is indeed a beautiful moral quality, if only one knows to whom to be loyal.

To make matters worse, the exit that was available to S—— may often be closed to other managers. S——, as we know, could have resolved his personal dilemma by making a timely and full disclosure to M——. This would have sufficed because M—— would then have had a fair chance to compete for the new opportunity that had come out of the joint enterprise. Fully informed, M—— would have been free to act as his interests, judgment, and resources indicated. But on the larger canvas of corporate industry, that is very often not the case.

Often all that disclosure can possibly accomplish is a demonstration of the manager's candor, because the coadventurers have no conceivable capacity to compete with him or to find an adequate alternative answer to their needs. As an example (not unprecedented at that)—if the directors of an oil company proposed to sell aviation fuel to some unfriendly and menacing nation, they could hardly expect that merely disclosing their sales would cancel their moral responsibility.

The problem of assessing loyalties is therefore one of the most acute in modern economic life, and very few powerful managers seem to meet it with wisdom. Clearly, no one who has read the previous chapters of this book will look here for a naive, simplistic formula to dispose of the problem, or a neatly logical hierarchy of ascending and descending loyalties. When two moralists argue and contend with each other on such questions as, say, whether loyalty to country comes first or loyalty to family, we may well remark (as the philosopher Demonax did once, according to Lucian), "Doesn't it seem to you, friends, that one of these fellows is milking a he-goat and the other is holding a sieve for him?"

The most valuable moral lesson that the law can teach concerning loyalty is the lesson of relations. We are familiar with the way the duty of loyalty arises out of relations between individuals, but we are likely to overlook the converse principle: the principle that the relation, being finite, confines and defines the duty of loyalty. The duty always remains a function of the relation. Hence S——'s special duty of loyalty was not owed to the undifferentiated person M—— with his myriad diversified interests, but solely to M—— as participant in the joint enterprise. By the same token, there can never arise in anyone's moral life an indefinite, unlimited duty of loyalty to any other creature or institution. Loyalty—however light or intense it may be—always has reference to a defined and specific relation; for example, everyone understands the full difference between the phrase "an unfaithful trustee" and the phrase "an unfaithful wife."

It is precisely this finiteness of loyalty that makes it practically effective on the one hand and morally defensible on the other. In the world of business affairs allegiance is valuable between partner and partner, manager and stockholder, employer and employee insofar as it operates within the bounds of their relation. It becomes destructive when for reasons that may be tyrannical or merely sentimental, it insists on transcending the relational boundaries and pushing into areas where other claims are rightly paramount. The manager of a clothing concern who, prompted by loyalty, insists that his wife wear only the company's products is liable to find other women very smartly accoutred; and the clerk in a banking house who, similarly motivated, puts his savings uncritically into securities issued by his employer is liable to free himself of financial problems in a way he scarcely contemplated. Sentimental fondness of this sort can addle loyalty's brains.

This same finiteness in the duty of loyalty serves to maintain its moral worth. S—— owed an allegiance to M——, an allegiance which was all the stronger by virtue of being bound on every side. One of the firm limits on that allegiance was that M—— could not have required S—— to do on his behalf any act that M—— had no moral right to do for his own account. S—— as trustee had neither the duty nor the right to steal in order to benefit his trust. Nor, by like token, would he ever be justified in using the trust property in such a manner as to oppress the poor or the weak. In the Minnesota mortgage-moratorium case where the managers of the insurance companies and other depositaries seemed to face a choice between oppressing the home-owners and breaking faith with their own depositors, the supposed dilemma was a false one. It is not a breach of faith to abstain from acts of oppression; on the contrary, the trustee's promise to avoid using the trust fund to oppress others should be considered one of the fundamental and unalterable terms of every trust.[12]

Loyalty—even on the level of commercial affairs—bears a special beauty of its own to which men are irresistibly drawn. For the example of a faithful trustee reminds us that rapaciousness and insensibility do not necessarily make up the final sum of human character. Perhaps even in the conduct of the market place we receive intimations from time to time of a loyalty with an unlimited radius.

VI

Business with Government

1. GOVERNMENT UNOFFICIAL AND OFFICIAL

UNDER the provisions of the federal Railway Labor Act * the labor union selected by a majority of a craft or class of railroad workers has the exclusive right to represent the entire craft in collective bargaining with the railroad companies. Accordingly, the locomotive firemen were represented by a union called the Brotherhood of Firemen. The majority of the firemen employed by the Louisville & Nashville Railroad were white, but a substantial minority were Negroes. The Brotherhood was composed of white firemen only, because it refused to accept Negroes as members. In 1940 it demanded that the railroad company change the existing collective bargaining agreement so that ultimately all Negroes would be excluded from employment as firemen. Yielding to the demand, the railroad company entered into new agreements which sharply restricted both the employment and the seniority rights of Negro firemen. Neither the railroad nor the union gave the Negroes any notice or opportunity to be heard concerning these provisions.

Performance of the new agreements began promptly. Bester

* Throughout this book, statutory law is summarized in the version which the court applied to the circumstances of the specific case. Allowance should be made for the possibility that the statute has been changed by some later enactment.

William Steele, a Negro who had a good job as fireman on passenger trains, was replaced by a Brotherhood member junior to him, and was assigned much harder and less remunerative work on a switch engine. Protests and appeals to the railroad and the union were ignored. Consequently Steele sued for an injunction against the performance of the new agreements and for money damages from the Brotherhood.

The United States Supreme Court held unanimously that Steele was entitled to an injunction and an award of damages. When Congress gave the union legal power to act as bargaining representative, it impliedly obligated the union to protect the interests of all members of the craft equally. The union could lawfully agree to classifications and discriminations among craft members based on competence, skill, and other relevant factors, even though some members might be affected unfavorably. But, said Chief Justice Stone for the Court, "Here the discriminations based on race alone are obviously irrelevant and invidious." [1]

ONE OF the most intriguing tales in *The Thousand and One Nights* has to do with a man in Baghdad who, having lost his wealth, had nothing left but a home and a garden. He dreamed that his fortune was in Cairo and resolved to go there. After suffering considerable hardships and privations, he finally reached Cairo, only to be arrested as a penniless vagrant. Brought before the local judge, he related his dream. The judge laughed at him, explained how foolish it was to put faith in dreams, and—by way of illustration—mentioned that he himself had dreamed three times that his fortune was under a certain distinctive type of fountain in a garden in Baghdad. The judge's description fitted perfectly the fountain in the corner of the poor man's own garden. Admonished and released, he wended his way back to Baghdad, dug beneath his fountain, and unearthed a magnificent treasure. And as he rubbed his hands in glee, he probably mused, "The very things we search for so ardently lie close at home waiting for us, but unless we journey abroad we never learn to recognize them."

So it is with government, which—as chapter III showed in some detail—appears in a more or less complete microcosmic form within the family-home. We human beings deal with government and its responsibilities from the moment of birth; from that moment, we are engaged, whether we intend it or not, in regulating the conduct of others and in being regulated by them. We are continually regulated through the sensibilities of our emotions and passions, which lead some of us to a life of dignified service, others to a weak and debasing servitude. In America at least, we can govern others quite effectively by providing them with examples in our overt behavior. Through it we legislate, we *enact* honesty or dishonesty, kindness or selfishness—all without using a single word.

For some reason, Americans seem to be peculiarly responsive to a moral maxim when it is illustrated by conduct they can observe. Perhaps this is only an instance of the national tendency toward pragmatism, which would test a man's beliefs by what he does rather than by what he protests; it may be due to a plethora of tedious hypocritical preachings; or perhaps, just because speech is relatively free and untrammeled in America, the spoken word appears too easy, too cheap in and of itself to purchase a complete credence. Whatever the cause may be, Americans have an emphatic way of subordinating words to deeds when they grade moral influences; so much so, in point of fact, that a man whose behavior displays exceptional rectitude is certain to attract an exaggerated notice, even though he insists quite sincerely that he has no intention of reflecting on anyone else. Once he has impelled people by his example, they are likely to continue moving, whether the direction in which they proceed is toward resentment or toward approval and emulation. At any rate, the audience is rarely an indifferent one; it reacts and responds. And therein may reside—paradoxically enough—one of the American people's most promising traits. For it is the self-same desire to copy and imitate that drains the color and individuality out of the people and simultaneously compensates them by making them egregiously susceptible to concrete examples of moral excellence. If these observations are correct, the American enjoys a special opportunity, a more cogent one perhaps than he would find in other, less conformist societies, to convert his personal conduct into a sort of unofficial government.

All these forms of regulation between persons and groups we may call unofficial government pure and simple. They have their own authorities and orders. (Jeremy Bentham went so far as to say that the request of a husband to his wife, if uttered in "the harsh form of a command," was an instance of "law";[2] but then we have to allow for the time when he lived and the expectation of wifely obedience.) They are purely and simply unofficial inasmuch as the official government does not become involved in their doings; at very most, we can say that, by failing to interfere or prohibit, it affords a tacit acquiescence in the unofficial regulations. But the difficulty is that unofficial government does not generally remain pure and simple. It calls on official government for assistance in accomplishing its objectives; often it seeks to enlist the coercive arm of official government. This is what the labor unions did in the field of collective bargaining between industrial employers and organized employees. At their instance, the official force was loaned to the unions, and because of the way one of them—the Brotherhood of Firemen—used it, Bester William Steele was compelled to appeal from unofficial government backed by official government to official government itself, represented by the United States Supreme Court.

In sustaining Steele's rights, Chief Justice Stone presented two distinct principles, both of which are significant for our purposes. With one of them we are already familiar, having just examined it in the preceding chapter. It is the principle of loyalty, which requires any member of a group who exercises power on behalf of the group to safeguard the interests of all coadventurers and to abstain from turning the power to his own exclusive advantage. Probably this principle would have been entirely sufficient to dispose of the case, in view of the Brotherhood's record of patent disloyalty to the Negro firemen. But the Chief Justice did not confine himself to the matter of loyalty. He went on to establish a second principle which was to prove most fortunate in a later case.

The union involved in the later case [3] was the Brotherhood of Trainmen, which was made up of white brakemen only. For many years, the Negro workers had done the same work as the white brakemen, but they were paid less, were given some slight additional duties, and were designated as "train porters." The so-called "train porters" formed and supported their own union. Then in 1946 the Brotherhood of Trainmen forced the St. Louis-San Francisco Railway to agree to discharge all "train porters" and to fill their jobs with white men, who under the agreement would do less work but get more pay. When Simon Howard, a Negro who had served the railroad nearly forty years, presented his case to the Supreme Court, he was met by the answer: "We of the Brotherhood owe you no duty of loyalty. Your own union represents you under the statute, hence you cannot look to us for protection." With this three Justices agreed. Indeed, it would be a highly plausible position if one assumes that the principle of loyalty was the sole basis for the outcome in Steele's case.

Since in point of fact it was not, Howard prevailed (6–3). Where loyalty alone might or might not have served the purpose, Chief Justice Stone's second principle became decisively applicable and vindicated Howard's claim.

This second principle may be called "constitutional infusion." If we return to the holding in Steele's case, we are reminded that Congress had said nothing in the Railway Labor Act either to permit or to forbid racial discriminations by unions. The Supreme Court held that Congress intended to forbid racial discriminations. How does one arrive at that inference?

One begins with the United States Constitution, which in effect forbids both the federal and the state governments to discriminate on racial grounds. (Concurring in the Steele case, Justice Frank Murphy remarked, "The Constitution . . . abhors racism.") But, as the Supreme Court has held on many occasions, the Constitution does not prohibit acts of racial discrimination by *private individuals,* and under our present legal rules a labor union is a mere association of private individuals.[4]

Nevertheless, these private associations did receive certain specific powers under the Railway Labor Act, which armed them with the coercive force of official government. If in conferring these powers Congress had explicitly authorized the associations to use them for racial discrimination, then said Stone, the statute would have been open to a grave claim that it was unconstitutional; therefore the Court must infer that Congress intended to confer no such authority. Why unconstitutional? Because an unofficial government which wields power granted by official government must conform to the same maxim of racial equality for those under its protection as any official legislature in the United States. The moral standards of the Constitution are infused along with the official power; they seep down from the Constitution's explicit phrases, through the silent implications of the Act of Congress, and into the clauses and provisions of every collective bargaining agreement.

The principle of "constitutional infusion," however, is not without limits. It does not mean that the union must act in conformity with official standards when it is not engaged in exercising official power. The Supreme Court has employed the principle with careful restraint. Racial bigotry in the United States being such a virulent disease, the Justices appear to have considered caution not only wise but necessary.

Their caution occasionally seems unacceptable. For example, in Steele's case, Chief Justice Stone—perhaps in order to achieve unanimity among the Justices—remarked by way of dictum that the union had the right to determine the eligibility of its members (which was of course a polite way of saying that it could continue to exclude Negroes from membership). True, the Chief Justice firmly insisted that the union give the Negroes a chance to be heard whenever their interests were involved in a contract negotiation; but this only provides the hat-in-hand kind of status that Americans would have none of in 1776; moreover it fosters the growth of separate unions for whites and Negroes, like those we noticed in Simon Howard's case.

Be that as it may, we may pause here long enough for a sardonic smile—directed at those who talk about legal rules as furnishing nothing more than "minimum moral standards." If the rules in the Steele and Howard cases (not to mention many others in this book) amount only to moral minima, one can still wish that the unions and the balance of our society would find their way up to that "minimum" plane. A "minimum" which so many fail to achieve would appear relatively elevated.

We may also note the indelible proposition that no class or stratum in our society holds a monopoly on moral virtues and vices, neither rich nor poor, male nor female, young nor old. The incidental manifestations may vary, they are almost bound to, because each group confronts a moral issue under the circumstances that accord with its distinctive course of life; the superficial deportment may differ—where, for instance, the rich and the powerful (including leaders of labor unions) are prone to exhibit arrogance, the poor may resort to meanness or to violence, and the middle class to a deaf and callous complacency; nevertheless, whether one looks into a hovel, a house, or a mansion, there is much the same probability of finding the strongest preying on the strong, the strong preying on the weak, and the weak abusing the helpless, all living by what the sages of ancient India were accustomed to call "the Law of the Fish." "The Law of the Fish" is not confined to employers and industrial capitalists; it has its full, ample, and sufficient quota of followers everywhere, without exception. We need to keep this bitter fact in mind, for otherwise our natural sympathies will lead us, by dint of understanding the offenses of the poor, to exonerating them. Nor should we fail to notice the wrongdoings of the middle class, which, just because they appear so very dull and normal in their grayness, are quite likely to escape detection.

The middle class has its favorite instruments of unofficial government. Chief among them is the so-called "private" contract. A private contract may be regarded as a species of government with the consent of the governed; those who accept the agreement thereby take allegiance to an unofficial government with a very specific and limited jurisdiction and a temporary duration.

In the first half of the twentieth century restrictive covenants became a popular type of respectable, middle-class contract. All the owners of land in a particular district would agree together that none of them would ever sell his holding except to a member of the "Caucasian race." These restrictive covenants went along with title to the land; they were to bind not only the original signers but also their remotest successors in ownership; and so it was to be on and on until the end of time, or at least until time accidentally or advisedly ran out of Caucasians.

Are covenants of this kind permissible under the United States Constitution? When the question came before the Supreme Court in 1948, it answered as we would have expected it to.[5] The mere making of a racially restrictive covenant, it said in effect, is unofficial government pure and simple; the Constitution does not interfere with private, unofficial conduct, morally wrongful though it may be. The moment, however, anyone asks a court to enforce such a covenant by enjoining some proposed sale to a non-Caucasian, he invokes the official government, to which the constitutional inhibitions do apply. Just as *official* power could not be availed of by the Brotherhood to enforce racism in employment, it could not be used by the land-owners to enforce racism in respect to residence.

Now, if we should put aside the specific phrases of the Constitution and the historic influence of legal precedents, would we be able to find any independent *moral* reason for distinguishing between unofficial and official government? Obviously, unofficial racial discrimination cannot stand for a moment in the forum of conscience; it violates the most elementary tenets of the moral constitution. If such is the case, that is, if discrimination by private individuals or associations constitutes an offense in morals, then the question necessarily arises whether American law has really illuminated our topic at all. In law, the distinction between the unofficial and the official seems valid enough. Has it, though, any pedagogic value for moral purposes?

I think it has, on two significant counts. In the first place, the Supreme Court's laissez-faire attitude toward unofficial discrimination reminds us that morals, like law, actually needs areas of anarchistic behavior in order to maintain its discipline. Humanity being what it is and behaving as it does, an effective ethical regime must reserve some intervals and recesses for conduct which is morally neutral. It must even allow for the types of reprehensible conduct which will cost more in moral terms to repress than to tolerate. If we see a man seething with insecurity, fear, and malice, it may be kinder to accept his bigoted curses than, by blocking them, to drive him to a worse offense. And when we cannot block them without inflicting a disproportionate hurt on him, we would do better to let him vent his bile, to reason with him, or to cure the causes of his unhappiness, than waste our heaviest sanctions and punishments on a trivial provocation. A dog that barks may or may not bite; he probably will if he sees that force is the only implement you have mastered.

But when the scene shifts from the unofficial realm to the official, suddenly all these mitigations and extenuations become irrelevant and we have not a shred of grace to extend. Why have we none? Because an *official* act of bigotry implicates every adult member of the political community.

If we lived under a despotic form of government, we might be able to escape this burden of vicarious involvement. Though probably chargeable with the regime's actions in general, we could hardly be held for any specific and particular wrong it might commit. In a democratic commonwealth, however, the case is very clear. The constituted officers are rightly assumed to express the standards of the entire national community, and of every individual in it—unless he raises his voice in protest. Legal and political representation brings a measure of moral responsibility to the represented, which we may not relish but can hardly avoid.

In fine, the great number and variety of unofficial governments can provide special scope for experimentation in flexibility, indulgence, and non-intervention. Official government performs a different function. Since it purports to bind and commit all of us to its conduct, it should not be excused if it defiles us.

2. CHEATING ON TAXES

A FEDERAL STATUTE provided that any alien who had more than once been sentenced to more than a year of imprisonment because of conviction of "a crime involving moral turpitude" would be deported from the United States. In February, 1938, Alberto B——, an alien, pleaded guilty to concealing liquor with intent to defraud the government of whiskey taxes, and in May, 1938, he pleaded guilty to conspiring with others to violate the revenue laws. On each charge he was sentenced to imprisonment for a year and a day. B—— claimed he could not be deported because his crimes did not involve "moral turpitude." When this contention failed in the trial court, he appealed to the United States Court of Appeals. There he argued that the Court should follow the rule it had established for an earlier case in 1929—during the Prohibition era. In the previous case, the Court had held that selling whiskey in violation of the Prohibition laws was not such "moral turpitude" as to justify deportation.[6]

The Court of Appeals held (2–1) that B—— should be deported. Two very distinguished judges (Augustus N. Hand and Robert P. Patterson) considered that B—— had attempted to defraud the Government of taxes and that fraud is an unmistakable badge of moral turpitude. In their view, the earlier case did not apply, because what it involved was not "any specific intent to defraud the government but only a general purpose to disregard the prohibition laws." Prohibition had been repealed long before B—— committed his offenses.

Judge Learned Hand, who is justly celebrated as a judicial sage, expressed his dissent. He said "I could wish that it was commonly thought more morally shameful than it is to evade taxes; but it is certainly true that people who in private affairs are altogether right-minded, see nothing more than a venial peccadillo in smuggling, or in escaping excises on liquor . . . we must try to appraise the moral repugnance of the ordinary man towards the conduct in question; not what an ideal citizen would feel." [7]

To certain of our reflective readers, B——'s case may prove the most rewarding to be found in this book. It deserves exceptionally careful rumination. For if the majority and dissenting opinions are taken together, they recapitulate and exemplify in the clearest possible fashion the two maxims which are immanent in any intelligent moral decision. The first: What men ought to do cannot be determined by what they actually do (else, why any laws or moral precepts whatever?). The second: What men ought to do cannot be determined without regard to what they actually do (else, how can laws or moral precepts be made fit for mundane men?).

Now, at the risk of knocking some paint off the papier-mâché figment of the model American citizen, it is necessary to recognize that one of his characteristic practices has always been and still is to cheat the government on taxes whenever he feels it safe to do so. In point of fact, he has exhibited considerable native ingenuity—though probably less than the citizens or subjects of certain other countries—in discovering ways and means to make the cheating reasonably safe for himself. Over and above the various subtle and legally permissible maneuvers which are euphemistically called "tax-avoidance," there is, as Judge Learned Hand acknowledged, a firmly established American custom of tax evasion. In small, medium, and large amounts at each passing hour, this kind of chicane is practiced by citizens of all ranks and of every level of repute. In colonial times, the so-called "best people" were wont to defraud King George of his legitimate revenues long before political grievances came along to cloak their dishonesty with the excuse that they were only doing their patriotic duty; and so it has been generation by generation ever since. (Some who read here may notice—speaking quite privately—how relieved and pleased they are to be told that theirs is a time-honored American custom.)

There is no blinking the history of the subject. Excise taxes, the kind that B—— failed to pay, have met with popular resistance down the centuries. They were the traditional revenue-raising devices of Europe's absolute despots; they were imposed on necessities of life and increased the sufferings of the poor; they fell due very frequently and thus every minute transaction involved an irritant; and since as a general rule the excises were levied to implement the sovereign's economic and political program, they were bound to meet resistance whenever the program turned unpopular. Smuggling became a not-disreputable part of the folk mores in America and everywhere else. Even a professional smuggler—like Jean Lafitte—was welcomed beside Andrew Jackson at the Battle of New Orleans in the War of 1812. At the other end of the country during the same war, two-thirds of the enemy's army in Canada were sustained by consuming beef smuggled across the Vermont border. Probably the worthy farmer of that state reasoned to himself the way many an American reasons today when he fills out his income tax return; probably he felt that he was under obligation to his family to do the things he did.

Of course, if someone is caught and his cheating is exposed, much public indignation may ensue and eloquent denunciations are heard; but in every such scandal there are many who fulminate so indignantly because they too have cheated and now discover for the first time a feeling of self-righteousness. They may feel self-righteous because someone was caught while they were not, or because the dollar amount of his fraud makes theirs seem unimportant, almost minikin. For this also they abhor him, for he seems to tell them mockingly that their former restraint was needless and that they really should have treated themselves more generously.

But this upsurge of popular excitement soon subsides and little remains beyond the tincture of envy in it. Hence, unless the defendant happens to be a notorious gangster, federal judges generally mete out very short sentences for defrauding the Government of taxes; they apparently assume, along with most of the American community, that a single embezzlement of private funds equals in heinousness five to ten frauds on the federal revenue. And then so many tax prosecutions can be compromised by paying money only, and so many more are put aside and allowed to lapse, for reasons proper or improper. Finally, there are uncounted frauds that simply never come to light at all. Well and heartily may a perjurious taxpayer say, in the words that Juvenal supplied for the perjurer of his time: "The wrath of the gods may be great, but it assuredly is slow; if then they charge themselves with punishing all the guilty, when will they come to me? And besides I may perchance find the god placable; he is wont to forgive things like this. Many commit the same crime and fare differently: one man gets a gibbet, another a crown, as the reward of crime." [8] In American tax prosecutions, there is no fear of anything remotely like the gibbet.

To complete the picture, we must pay tribute to American inventiveness in concocting balms and unguents for abrasions of the taxpayer's conscience. The variety is admirable; there is a specific salve for every type of citizen. For example, if your political party happens to be in office, you recount to yourself the manifold services you are rendering to it and through it to the nation; why not leave taxes to the others? If your party is out of office, you ask why you should exacerbate the follies of the administration by providing funds for imbeciles to squander. If you are conservative, you oppose change by keeping your money where it is. If a progressive, you remind yourself that tomorrow new demands will inevitably be made on your purse. If opulent, you have proved you know how to use your money better than any politician can use it for you. If poor, you need it more than the Government does. If married, you must take care of your family; if single, you have no one else to take care of you. And so the theme flows on and on through inexhaustible variations.

Nevertheless, there is an area of exception where none of these excuses will be received. According to the American estimate, nonchalance stops where "professionalism" begins. In this view, what stamped B——'s acts with moral turpitude was not that he had cheated the government but that he had virtually made a business of doing so. He had lost his amateur status and with it his expectation of indulgence. In the popular American judgment, which exhibits on this score an acumen we cannot but admire, everybody slips from time to time because everybody has his share of the impulses, foibles, and flaws that characterize human nature; no one, however, is licensed either to make a livelihood, as a vendor of narcotics does, by trading on the weaknesses of others or, as a bootlegger does, by converting the casual peccadillo of tax fraud into a systematic business. The ordinary man commits retail cheats on the revenue in order to retain what he has; B—— was committing wholesale cheats in order to enrich himself.

For all the record shows, it is conceivable that later on B—— reformed his ways and redeemed his life by coming forward and serving the United States in World War II. The court's decision which affirmed the order for his deportation to Italy was handed down during the historic summer of 1940, at a time when execution of the order would hardly have been feasible. But, whatever may have happened in the intervening years, there is nothing to justify equating the offenses he had committed with the ordinary tax-cheating of the average amateur. On this score, Judge Learned Hand appears to have been in error.

We come now to the very pith and marrow of our problem. Why, in point of fact, ought one to practice honesty in paying taxes to the Government? Americans are by no means alone in being rather myopic to this duty; nor does the United States *as yet* suffer from cheating in such major proportions as some other countries. For example, the Government of the Soviet Union has never been able, despite all its propaganda and coercion, to keep pilfering and fraud within limits that would be relatively harmless to its economic program, and the regimes of Western Europe find that they have to carry on their various socialized enterprises in a state of chronic fiscal anemia induced or aggravated by popular dishonesty. Taxes, which to the economist and political scientist represent a levy on the gross national production of goods and services, represent to the ordinary citizen something very much less abstract; they mean a taking away of some of his personal goods or some of his personal services. And whether the government collects by demanding part of his harvest in kind or in money equivalent, it is hard to convince him that his moral obligation is not to protect his own but honestly and cooperatively to assist those who are taking from him.

It is so hard, in fact, that only through requiring the major sources of distribution or payment (vendors, employers, corporate disbursing agents, etc.) actually to collect or withhold the tax money from the citizen and remit it to the Treasury for his account, has the contemporary federal revenue system maintained any semblance of efficacy. Yet this device too inspires a practice of dishonesty: innumerable small merchants simply pocket and retain a generous share of the excise taxes they have collected on the Treasury's behalf. As a general rule, should one of these small merchants eventually expand the size of his business, he will become more public-spirited in this respect because he will begin to maintain systematic inventory and sales records; it does not take long to find that loose, informal procedures which facilitate him in cheating the government may likewise facilitate some of his employees in cheating him.

Now, although the American mores seem to countenance defrauding the government of taxes (except by "professionals"), they assuredly do not countenance what we have written here. We have depicted the perpetration of tax-fraud as a general and usual practice in American life; and by doing so we have violated the established mores. According to the mores, the American who cheats his government must be described as an aberrant exception quite unrepresentative of his fellow-citizens and of his community. The tradition insists that he is an exception not merely in being caught but also in being dishonest. For if he were not considered abnormal in respect of dishonesty, if cheating on taxes were acknowledged to be frequent and general, if in effect nearly everybody else swindled the government, what possible scruple could remain to deter a single one of us?

The dilemma is particularly difficult to Americans, for having long since surrendered our manners to conformism, we now bid fair to do the same with our morals. Americans have customarily avoided discomfort from tax scandals by simply denying the facts; in the very face of the objective realities, they still reiterate that tax-cheating is not a general American phenomenon. But this attitude cannot endure very much longer, because the high tax rates of the present and the progressive socializations of the proximate future will inevitably compel recognition of the distasteful truth. Perhaps, if we understood just why those average Americans who would not think of cheating their neighbors and customers will nevertheless cheat their government, we should fear the truth less. If we understood the workings of their moral processes, we might gain courage enough to put the traditional hypocrisy aside.

Let us begin on an elementary level. Our average American of the honester sort, having picked up a loaf of bread in a grocery-store, has laid his coin on the counter in payment. Although he sees that the grocer is occupied with other customers, he feels not the slightest temptation to cheat by taking his coin back. At the door of the shop, there stands a telephone booth. He enters the booth and makes a call by means of the coin-operated instrument. Having completed the conversation, he almost instinctively sticks his finger into the receptacle provided for return of coins on uncompleted connections, finds that the telephone company's mechanism operating faultily has returned his payment, takes the coin, puts it in his pocket, and leaves the store with a gratified smile and a quiet conscience.

The three factors that dull his moral perception in regard to the telephone company—they apply with even greater force to the government—are size, impersonality, and compulsion. He can easily project himself into the grocer's shoes; the grocer is a man like himself with rent to pay and a family to feed. But who except a child at play or a megalomaniac can imaginatively perform the functions of a telephone company, much less those of a modern government? The sheer size staggers our imagination and forbids us in the name of common sense to look upon the enormous corporation or the still greater government as another, interchangeable self. What, after all, is this overpoweringly huge entity? If in essence it is all the stockholders or all the citizens, then how could the loss of a single coin be divided among them with any consequence that would justify consideration? If it is some abstraction apart from these individuals, then what harm has been done to any human interest? Our average American would conclude, if he ever thought about the subject, that only a machine had been outwitted.

Every manager of a large corporation knows the influence of size and impersonality on employees' and customers' behavior, the dissipations of supplies, the incessant peculations, the strange relaxation of ordinary decencies and scruples. What, moreover, is the history of all the armies and navies that the world ever bore but an unrelieved narrative of theft, plunder, and titanic waste? As soon as the owner becomes too large or too impersonal to permit an imaginative interchange with him, even very honest men may act as though they were blind to his rights. And these factors, serious in themselves, are intensified when the entity is an identified source of compulsion: the telephone company with its legalized monopoly coerces one to deal with it alone and slams the gates of individual choice; still worse, the government does not even inquire whether one desires the manifold services for which it sends its imperious bill. How can conscience possibly liken the government to a corner grocer?

We are about to show that it can. But by way of summary let us first note these three basic observations: (1) So many taxpayers will always be disposed to cheat that only the justified fear of detection and imprisonment will insure fair remittances from them and prevent them from shifting their tax obligations to honest men's shoulders. (2) We should not judge what American taxpayers ought to do merely by observing what they actually do. (3) But on the other hand if we should adopt a rule of moral rigor and completely fail to take into account the things taxpayers do in the way of amateur tax-cheating, we should wind up by inflicting Draconic measures on the citizenry, alienating them from their government, and exacerbating the very evils we set out to reduce. For millennia, the civilized world has endeavored to mark off and separate *meum* from *tuum* and has met with very indifferent success. Now appears a mendicant new aspiration that the mass of men accord the same measure of respect to *nostrum.* It is not impossible that ultimately they will learn to do so, at least if the official personnel improve a great deal in quality and intelligence. But, as matters stand, it will be a long time before any Secretary of the Treasury can recommend dismantling the federal penitentiaries.

These observations made, we are at last prepared to state the reasons why men ought to practice honesty in paying taxes. They are reasons furnished by political, social, and individual morals, and taken together, they leave no doubt that defrauding the United States Government of taxes is "a crime involving moral turpitude."

The political standard rests on something firmer than patriotic impulse. Patriotism if exhibited on an appropriate occasion, in a humanistic manner, and for a country whose history and conduct deserve it, is a highly estimable sentiment; yet it does not seem to preclude the coexistence of other sentiments, such as rapacity and greed. Who is more patriotic than the man who risks his life in time of war, or who sends his son to fight for the homeland? Nevertheless, we know that such men have not infrequently cheated the government in various ways and have employed their patriotic sacrifices to rationalize their dishonesties. In the political morality of tax-payment, there is something far removed from military patriotism, something that stems rather from the status of a free citizen in a free polity. When the American Revolution preached "No taxation without representation," it must have implied that representation gives taxation a claim on political conscience; representation means that the obligation to pay taxes is, in political morals, self-assumed, voluntary, not impersonal, not imposed from without, but as to each citizen binding upon conscience because essentially autonomous.

Social morality reaches the same conclusion via a different route. It reasons that taxes are the price each of us pays for his participating share in civilized society and for enjoying the immeasurable benefits of community existence. For what are we, what does any one of us have without the community? If there is any possession a man can be said to enjoy when he is severed from the community, certainly it is not the wages, the property, the sales, the accrual of dividends and interest that bring about liability for taxes. The community fashions his wealth, whatever it may be; he can only assemble and manage it. The community protects whatever he has or hopes to have. He takes the loaf of bread from the community just as he takes it from the corner grocer. Honesty, reciprocity, and social virtue know no distinction between the grocer and the community except that on occasion they may speak more urgently for the equities of the latter.

Finally, there is the voice of individual honor, which needs no cue from political democracy or social solidarity to speak its part. It appeals to a man's personal pride and self-esteem, regarding them as quite sufficient in themselves to prevent his sliding down the declivity of fraud. The American who heeds this voice does not defraud the government simply because he does not defraud. Unlike the others, he prizes his integrity more than some oblong pieces of officially printed paper.

3. THE CITIZEN'S ALLEGIANCE

GRACE MARSH and Arthur Tucker, members of the religious sect called "Jehovah's Witnesses," considered themselves ordained to promulgate the doctrines of that sect by distributing its booklets and magazines. Every Saturday afternoon, Grace Marsh would stand on the sidewalk and display the magazines to passers-by. Arthur Tucker would call on people from door to door, present his religious views, and distribute the magazines to those who were willing to receive them. Grace and Arthur conducted themselves in an orderly manner. It was the peculiar legal status of the respective localities where they operated that eventually involved them in trouble with the police.

Grace's station was on the only business block in an Alabama company town. The very sidewalk on which she would stand and the street she would face belonged to the company that owned the entire town. She was warned several times that she could not distribute the magazines without a company permit and was told that no permit would be issued to her. When she refused to leave, she was arrested and convicted under an Alabama law which makes it a crime to enter or remain on the premises of another after being warned not to do so.

Arthur's endeavors took him to a village located in Texas. The United States Government owned the entire village and used it to provide housing for workers in national defense projects. The village manager, appointed by the appropriate federal agency, ordered Arthur to cease all religious activities in the village. Arthur refused. The manager ordered him to leave the village. On the ground that the manager had no right to suppress the exercise of religion, he again refused. He was arrested and convicted under a Texas law which makes it an offense for a peddler to remain on any premises after the owner or possessor has told him to leave.

On appeal, the United States Supreme Court (5–3) reversed and set aside both convictions as unconstitutional. Legal title to the town, the streets, and the sidewalks is not decisive, said Justice Hugo Black for the Court. Regardless of technical ownership, the public has a paramount interest in keeping the channels of communication free and open. The people who live in towns such as these must, like all other citizens, "make decisions which affect the welfare of community and nation. To act as good citizens they must be informed . . . their information must be uncensored." [9]

Justice Black's reasoning in these cases is incandescent. There have been many other occasions when the Supreme Court has vindicated an individual who claimed that his freedom of speech or religion had been infringed, so the actual outcome of the Marsh and Tucker litigations was not their extraordinary feature. They are remarkable rather because of the reasons assigned for the outcome. Justice Black made it clear that in reversing the convictions of the Jehovah's Witnesses the Court meant to uphold the basic rights of *the people they addressed.*

From the lawyer's point of view this was a bold departure. The residents of the company town in Alabama and of the federal project in Texas did not in any legal sense appear before the Supreme Court. They voiced no claim of violated rights. No one spoke to the Court on their behalf (except perhaps the States' attorneys, who contended that the Jehovah's Witnesses should *not* be allowed to address them). Nevertheless the Court said that it was they whose rights were at stake, whose access to information must not be cut off, and whose status must be upheld as citizens capable of intelligent political determinations. So reasoning, the Court threw an edifying light on what an American citizen undertakes when he pledges allegiance to his country and its flag.

The primitive form of allegiance, which obtains in despotic as well as in democratic societies and consists in rendering goods and services to the government and physical obedience to the laws, we need not comment on here because we have considered some of its moral incidents in the preceding section. As soon as a government evolves to the plane where its citizens are consulted before a decision of state is put into effect, they assume a higher level of allegiance. This is the level of self-equipment and participation, the former becoming a moral obligation consequentially with the latter. In opening the door to public discussion, the governors assume that discussion will generally lead to wiser decisions and that active and critical participation will enrich the commonwealth by enhancing the quality of the citizens. Because in a substantial degree it accepted these assumptions, the Athens of the Enlightenment became "the school of Hellas" and the world's cultural preceptor. Pericles boasted:

> *Our public men have, besides politics, their private affairs to attend to, and our ordinary citizens, though occupied with the pursuits of industry, are still fair judges of public matters; for, unlike any other nation, regarding him who takes no part in these duties not as unambitious but as useless, we Athenians are able to judge at all events if we cannot originate, and instead of looking on discussion as a stumbling-block in the way of action, we think it an indispensable preliminary to any wise action at all.*[10]

In the feudal states of ancient and medieval times, all who held noble rank were required to equip themselves with provisions, horses, and armor for the service and defense of the state. Correspondingly, in democratic countries the citizen-peers are under obligation to bring informed and practiced minds to the performance of their civic functions. And there is no possibility of their reporting for duty with a political upbringing unless the courts sustain their constitutional right of access to information and ideological variety. Had the technicalities of property titles prevailed in the circumstances of the Marsh and Tucker cases, countless residents of company towns would never have an opportunity to become equipped for allegiance.

Yet when self-equipment and political participation are fully allowed for, the citizens may manifest their allegiance in still another mode, one that Pericles was not very likely to emphasize. To the founders of the United States this mode appeared almost paramount, and throughout the nation's history it has been closely associated with our finest political figures. It may be called "allegiance through principled recalcitrance."

In the fall of 1774 the Continental Congress prepared an "Address to the People of Quebec" and asked that they join in resisting the policies of the British ministry. Perhaps because the authors of the "Address" were familiar with Pericles' description of the virtues of Athenian democracy, they proceeded to set forth the advantages of their own institutions to the end that Quebec might be persuaded to participate in a common effort. For the culminating item in this proud list they chose none other than their enjoyment of freedom of the press, "whereby," they said, "oppressive officers are shamed or intimidated into more honourable and just modes of conducting affairs." [11] In other words, a good scheme of government must welcome free exchange of information and opinion, because that freedom furnishes the implements to restrain and discipline the governors.

It is not only because the governors must periodically account to the people and stand for re-election that the distinction between the lasting government and the temporary governors has remained fundamental in American political philosophy. Americans constantly invoke the distinction in order to continue thinking well of their government. The checks and balances in the Constitution were inspired by serious misgivings as to how human beings behave themselves when they become vested with great authority over their neighbors, and the historical experience of the American people has not removed the misgivings. Bitter personal criticisms and invective furnish the dominant motif of our political literature, relieved here and there by the American talent for good-natured ridicule of government officials. It would strain the imagination to visualize an America in which criticism of the governors had been effectually suppressed.

Recalcitrance sometimes calls for physical courage. The growth of constitutional liberties in the Anglo-Saxon legal systems is a narrative full of attempted oppression and bloody resistance, which each new generation studies with legitimate pride. The difficulty is that cultivated and sensitive individuals —the kind who prize free expression—are generally unprepared in terms of experience and temperament for the ordeals which may follow from asserting their liberties. The superior type of citizen has been trained all his life to obey laws and policemen not only because confinement in jail is painful, not only because his social stratum considers it shameful, but primarily out of a sense of allegiance to majority rule and to the majority's official instrumentalities. Such a citizen reasons that while the principle of majority rule does not signify that the majority is always right, it does mean that the majority is entitled to have its way even when it is mistaken. The very cultural preparation that enables an individual to understand the ideal of free expression may hamper him in summoning his psychological resources to incur the risk of confinement and police brutality. Nevertheless, some do find these resources; some do demonstrate, to the advantage of the entire community, that under the Constitution there are areas in which the majority is not entitled to have its way even when it is right. All this requires a personal valor which cannot be conscripted by any external authority but must come somehow from within.

The Supreme Court has adopted Thomas Jefferson's view that constitutional freedom of speech and religion protects opinions only and does not exempt overt actions from government control. But the actions involved may be of more than one kind: on the one hand, an action may affirmatively and aggressively violate an official statute; on the other hand, it may consist merely in failure or refusal to take some step, such as paying taxes, which the government has required of its citizens. When in the latter part of the nineteenth century the Mormons practiced polygamy under the claim of freedom of religion, the Supreme Court rejected their defense and held them criminally liable, because entering into a polygamous marriage constitutes an affirmative, active violation of the law.[12]

By the same token, the act of plotting to overthrow the government by resort to brute force cannot share the immunity which the Constitution guarantees to mere advocacy of political change and like appeals to men's rational capacities. Occasionally even a passive show of resistance has led to incarceration. When Henry Thoreau, disavowing the United States' toleration of slavery and its war with Mexico, refused to pay taxes to the officials of his state, he was put in jail. Against his wishes, his friends paid the tax on his behalf and obtained his release. Men who have forgotten the burning issues of that day will always honor Thoreau, because he ranked his principles above his personal liberty—which may suggest the difference between the skulking conspirator and the candid patriot.

What of the allegiance of pacifists? On this score the record of American law, though sadly spotted, shows an occasional sign of improvement. One such sign was furnished by a recent decision of the Supreme Court. Three times beginning in 1928 the Supreme Court had permitted an alien to be denied naturalization because on humanitarian or religious grounds he would not swear to defend the United States against its enemies by bearing arms. Finally in 1946, the dissenting opinions which Justice Holmes and Chief Justice Hughes had written gained the support of the Court's majority.[13] The Court then held that pacifistic allegiance to the cosmic value of human life is not incompatible with assuming allegiance to the United States.

Ultimately, the highest allegiance to the United States is that which transcends the country's boundaries and comprehends the realms of being where the power of national government cannot reach. One of these realms takes in all members of the human genus and the needs and griefs with which they pursue their troubled search for illumination of the spirit. Deferring to this realm, the Supreme Court again dramatically overruled one of its previous decisions and held that a school board could not require children of Jehovah's Witnesses to salute the American flag, which they regarded as an idolatrous image.[14]

The other realm to which allegiance calls the American is the immediate and independent domain of nature, which acknowledges no human police, not even of an international government, but abides in a free sufficiency of its own. It was this allegiance to which Henry Thoreau turned, saying:

> *I was put into jail as I was going to the shoemaker's to get a shoe which was mended. When I was let out the next*

morning, I proceeded to finish my errand, and, having put on my mended shoe, joined a huckleberry party, who were impatient to put themselves under my conduct; and in half an hour—for the horse was soon tackled—was in the midst of a huckleberry field, on one of our highest hills, two miles off, and then the State was nowhere to be seen.[15]

VII

The Enlargement of Personality

1. THE QUANDARY OF THE GOOD SAMARITAN

THE International Railway Co. operates a small electric railway between Buffalo and Niagara Falls. At one point on the line the tracks cross high above those of the New York Central. A gradual incline on a trestle brings the tracks to the necessary height, then they make a sharp turn and pass over a high bridge.

Arthur Wagner and his cousin Herbert boarded a car at a station near the bottom of the trestle. The car was so crowded that they had to stand on the platform. The platform was provided with doors, which the conductor failed to close. The car moved ahead on the incline and, when it turned the curve, gave a violent lurch. Herbert Wagner was thrown off close to the point where the trestle changed to the bridge. Someone cried "Man overboard!" The car proceeded across the bridge and then stopped. The scene was all in darkness.

Arthur Wagner got off the car and walked back some distance until he arrived at the bridge where he expected to find Herbert's body. Several other persons instead of following him climbed down under the trestle and found the body under the bridge. As they stood there, Arthur's body struck the ground beside them. He had reached the bridge, had found his cousin's hat, had missed his footing in the darkness, and had fallen. Though severely injured, Arthur was not killed by his fall.

Arthur Wagner sued the International Railway Co. When his case was tried, the trial judge held that he could not recover damages unless he could prove both that the conductor had invited him to go on the bridge and that the conductor had followed with a lantern. On this ruling, Arthur lost his case in the trial court and appealed to the highest court of the State of New York.

On behalf of a unanimous Court of Appeals Judge Cardozo reversed the judgment of the trial court. He said "Danger invites rescue. The cry of distress is the summons to relief. The law does not ignore these reactions of the mind in tracing conduct to its consequences. It recognizes them as normal. It places their effects within the range of the natural and probable. The wrong that imperils life is a wrong to the imperilled victim; it is a wrong also to his rescuer." Moreover, Arthur's case was not defeated by the mere fact that the circumstances gave him an adequate chance to deliberate and to weigh the risks he was assuming. The railway company claimed that even if it could be made liable where the rescuer's actions were "instinctive," it could not be held where the rescuer had time to reflect and make his own choice. But Judge Cardozo ruled, "The law does not discriminate between the rescuer oblivious of peril and the one who counts the cost. It is enough that the act, whether impulsive or deliberate, is the child of the occasion." [1]

EMERGENCIES do the work of moral revelation. Suddenly and without forewarning, the rhythm a man is accustomed to in his daily life will break into a wild clangor like an alarm bell, beat out a frantic summons to action, and then—just as quickly—subside to its normal, regular tempo. When the emergency has passed, he is likely to know something entirely new about his latent capacities or incapacities. He may discover, with gratification or shame, what kind of moral being he has made of himself and what care he really feels for the other human selves that move about him. Thus, as we shall see, the Wagner case puts questions to each of us which are penetrating to the point of embarrassment.

Not everyone will experience this embarrassment, for a question is "penetrating" only when the mind to which it is posed has some depth. Shallow minds may be inclined to wonder how the rest of us can find anything complex in our present subject. To their way of thinking, Jesus disposed of the whole matter by relating the story of the Good Samaritan [2] who "had compassion" on the man who "fell among thieves" and rescued and succored him. What more is there?

Without stirring up a hornets' nest of theological and exegetical debate, one may safely reply that the Good Samaritan passage (which, by the way, appears only in the Gospel according to St. Luke) makes a fine beginning to our analysis but certainly cannot end it. Jesus' supposititious case—anyone who reads the Gospel will see that, if Jesus spoke as he is reported, he did not recount an actual incident or even tell one of his beautiful parables but merely followed the time-honored custom of lawyers by posing a supposititious case to the lawyer who had questioned him—this case leaves many problems open and unresolved. For example, we are told that the Good Samaritan rescued the man because he saw his plight and compassionated him. Suppose then a person does not happen to feel compassion; is there nevertheless a moral duty to rescue? Suppose the rescue will involve one in grave personal danger; suppose further that the danger may emanate from the apparent victim himself, who has assumed his position in order to ensnare and entrap. Suppose the victim's plight is genuine enough but it has been brought about by his own wrongdoing. These are specimens of the unanswered questions.

Before we turn to the law, let us take some other instances from the store of literature. For although in logic even the best literary insights can never serve to demonstrate a valid answer, they can throw light on the depth of our problem and on the directions which a sophisticated inquiry might adopt. Once we have sensed the limitations of the facts supposed in Jesus' Good Samaritan case, almost inevitably we find ourselves turning to a work which illuminates the very opposite point of view. And that, of course, will be Cervantes' *Don Quixote*, a book which from start to finish can be regarded as a magnificent travesty on the foibles of Good Samaritanism.

There is no need to labor the point: the very word "quixotic" epitomizes the kind of helper whose good intentions do not compensate either for his imprudence or for his officious interference in other people's concerns. For example, there is a place in Cervantes' book where Don Quixote, who always hates to see men restrained of their liberty, proceeds to assault the official guards who are conducting a chain-gang of convicted rogues to the galleys. In the mêlée, the convicts break free, beat up Don Quixote, strip him of what little he has, and roam the countryside terrorizing, robbing, ravaging.[3] To this kind of requital for kind intentions we have a parallel in our modern technological context: so very many American autoists have been assaulted, raped, or robbed by strangers whom they met on the road and stopped to assist that, in a number of states, the mere act of standing on a highway in order to solicit a ride has been made a punishable offense.[4]

If the success of a Good Samaritan is uncertain, there may also be room for doubt concerning his inner motives. For even while he compassionates the victim, he may despise and detest him. This fact seems strange—the antitheses that split the human breast often seem strange; but it is manifest that pitiable men do resent gestures of pity and do eschew the help that pity may inspire—not always, as we imagine, out of pride, but quite frequently because they sense the nexus between pity and contempt or abhorrence, between commiseration and the black impulse to annihilate.

There is a dreadful incident in Dostoyevsky's *Crime and Punishment.*[5] The protagonist, Raskolnikov, walking along the avenue, has come across a poor girl who is hopelessly drunk. Obviously, she has been put in that state by someone, attacked, abused, and then set adrift. A lecherous dandy has also noticed her condition and lurks nearby to make use of her as soon as she can be taken alone. Raskolnikov endeavors to chase him away and, when a policeman happens on the scene, explains the girl's peril in the most urgent and frenetic terms. The policeman, sincere in his concern, tries to escort her safely home. Then, like a flash, a complete revulsion of feeling sweeps through Raskolnikov. He shouts to the policeman to leave the girl alone, and let the dandy amuse himself. "What is it to you?" Raskolnikov calls out. And he laughs.

It is worth noting that the law and its personnel have a way of cropping up conspicuously in these fictional episodes of Good Samaritanism. Don Quixote chose to interfere with the force of law, Raskolnikov summoned its aid, and we are about to see law again play a significant role in our final example out of literature. This final incident is especially apt for a transition from the insights of novelists to those of judges, because its author was Henry Fielding, himself a member of the bar and later a distinguished magistrate.

At a certain point in his novel *Joseph Andrews,* Fielding was apparently inspired with the notion of portraying the Good Samaritan story as it might actually unfold in a setting of his own time. By confronting a typical group of travelers with a man in distress and reporting their various comments and reactions he could neatly display a full gamut of moral qualities and expose the bitter comedy of human existence.[6] So he has the hero, Joseph Andrews, set upon by thieves, stripped by them of all his possessions—even of his clothing—and left bleeding and naked in a ditch beside the highway. Then a stagecoach comes by, the postillion hears Joseph's groans, the coach is halted, Joseph's condition is observed and reported to the passengers, he pleads for their assistance—and thus our scene is laid.

At the outset absolutely no one in the coach expresses compassion for the helpless Joseph. The coachman refuses to take him unless his fare is paid, the lady cries that his nakedness will offend her modesty, the old gentleman fears to be robbed; every inclination is for passing him by. However, it happens that one of the unsympathetic passengers is a young lawyer, a very cautious lawyer at that. He warns the others that if Joseph should die, they might be proved to have been last in his company and might be called to account for his death. This warning having been repeated, the coachman finally becomes afraid on his own account, the fear opens the door to compassionate feelings, and he agrees to take Joseph in. But here arises another dilemma: since Joseph is naked, he refuses to enter the coach unless someone will furnish him with covering enough to spare the lady's exceedingly dubious modesty.

This time again everyone—from the old man to the lady's footman—refuses. And so Joseph would have been left to perish after all, "unless the postillion (a lad who hath been since transported for robbing a hen-roost) had voluntarily stripped off a great-coat, his only garment, at the same time swearing a great oath (for which he was rebuked by the passengers), 'that he would rather ride in his shirt all his life than suffer a fellow-creature to lie in so miserable a condition.'" Thus it is that Joseph finds succor at last, or at least a conveyance to some place of succor. And the American reader, as he huddles in the coach at the side of the injured Joseph, is bound to entertain a special hope. He is bound to hope that when the postillion lad was "since transported" by the English authorities, they sent him to an American colony and to a new world of many fine greatcoats, not to mention many fat hens out of his own proper hen-roost.

Fielding, however, had some different reflections. Considerably later in his chronicle,[7] he underscored the seriousness of this little episode by returning to it and analyzing it as an arch-specimen of his method. Perhaps just because he was a lawyer himself, Fielding felt impelled to comment most harshly on the lawyer in the stagecoach interlude, whom he regarded as the incarnate type of self-centeredness, meanness, and indifference to one's fellow-creatures. It is easy to share this antipathy of Fielding's; the lawyer's motives were manifestly far less than noble. Yet, notwithstanding all this, I make bold to suggest that Fielding may have missed one of the principal points of his own episode. He seems to have passed it unobserved and left it by the roadside.

The point in question is that the lawyer's remonstrance did in fact cause Joseph's rescue and that without it he would have been incontinently abandoned. It alone saved Joseph. Granted that the remonstrance might have deserved admiration if it had been actuated by worthier motives, the fact remains that what Joseph required at this particular juncture was not a moral example but a means of conveyance. The lawyer's exclusively prudential motives could hardly reduce Joseph's gain in being admitted to the coach. And as for the other passengers and the coachman, how handsome was their conduct? At first it was only an unenlightened selfishness; later, when the lawyer had infected them with his own fear of prosecution, it became a more enlightened selfishness.

All in all, assume the world is made up in large part of postillions who are generous enough but cannot provide one with a place in the coach and of passengers who, however reluctantly, provide a place because they fear the penalties of law: then, at least when any Joseph pictures himself shivering and bleeding beside the road, he will heartily commend the law as one of the episode's implicit heroes. And he may be disposed to infer that in certain important respects the fear of the law is the beginning of virtue.

If we leave the realm of fiction and turn to the American decisions on the subject, we find the law in a steady movement toward requiring acts of Good Samaritanism. As yet, the movement has not proceeded very far but all the changes that have occurred recently are in the same direction. For generations, Anglo-American judges were accustomed to say that the law imposed no duty to rescue mere strangers and that a man could not be held legally responsible for callous inaction, however reprehensible he might appear in the judgment of conscience. These holdings were bitterly criticized and, to the extent they still remain in our law, are now attributed by expert commentators to nineteenth-century laissez-faire and individualism in economics and morals.[8] The explanation is somewhat incomplete. For although excessive individualism has been one of the influences shaping this attitude of the courts, there are other factors to be reckoned with, factors which deserve mention here because their significance is moral as well as legal. It is shocking to read that a good swimmer incurs no legal liability by standing on the beach and smoking a cigarette while he watches someone drown; but just what the law should do about him is not always obvious.

In cases such as this, if the person in peril is a complete stranger to the passer-by, then American courts are unwilling to hold the latter liable for damages unless he had something to do with creating the state of peril. But they do gradually move the law forward by whittling away at the concept of "stranger." Step by step, they have discovered one relation after another between the passer-by and the victim or between the passer-by and the peril which will justify them in imposing a legal duty to assist and to rescue. For example, no matter how careful one may be in exercising control over a piece of machinery, if a "stranger" happens to become entangled in it, there arises an affirmative duty to halt the machine. But if halting the machine would require the operator to incur a grievous injury to himself, that is beyond the limits of his legal duty. In other words, the law's tendency is to compel men to act like good neighbors and to leave heroism to individual option.

In juristic writings, there is considerable preoccupation with the question: *whose* is the duty to rescue? Suppose that not one but fifty good swimmers happen to be on shore and callously watch the man drowning. If so, shall we hold them all liable to his estate for money-damages and send them all to jail for a criminal offense? Some legal commentators would penalize all; some would penalize none; some would give one answer on damages and a different answer on imprisonment. This diversity of views should not be interpreted to mean that the moral duty is obscure; on the contrary, each onlooker's moral duty seems perfectly clear. The obscure matter is whether this is the kind of moral duty to which it is socially expedient to annex a legal sanction; and, believing as I do that instances of such wholesale callousness at the very scene of dramatic peril are extremely infrequent among Americans, and that the penalties imposed would be divided so fine as to lose any deterrent effect, I care little which rule the law adopts to meet these far-fetched suppositions of the scholars.

To see the moral issue with any degree of clearness, it is necessary to put aside the customary indulgences in sentimentalism and hypocrisy and look at what really takes place in our society. Civilization must come a very long way out of the forests of barbarism before the Good Samaritan problem can become a serious topic in social discourse; in point of fact, the discipline of law and order must progress to a highly advanced degree before it can lead a helpless person to expect that others who notice his condition will be so humane as to pass on their way instead of killing him and plundering his possessions. If the force of law can protect the helpless from further aggression, that would itself be no small accomplishment, and we should only hope to see the force of international law achieve as much within its sphere of operation. In this respect, it is easy for middle-class Americans to be misled by the very efficacy of the civilized policing they are accustomed to; the law makes them feel secure enough from personal aggression that they forget the wolves around them and demand that their sheep dog act more like a solicitous veterinarian. Perhaps he should; nevertheless, statistics and case-histories of violent crime indicate that our society still needs canine teeth on guard to protect it—not against the passive indifference of the passer-by but against the active assault of the robbers, rapists, and murderers.

Moreover, let us not flatter ourselves that we are entirely different from Raskolnikov. We are human beings, that is to say, limited and finite in all things including our respective reservoirs of compassion. Like olives from Italian groves, we may yield a fine sympathetic oil at the first pressing, a somewhat inferior and cruder product when the pressing is repeated, and eventually nothing that could possibly serve as a balm or emollient. If we find ourselves prating about compassion for men's suffering in general, it is quite likely because at the moment we do not experience any suffering in particular; for at all times the sum of human suffering that lies immediately about each of us surpasses and overwhelms our capacity to share.

So it was that even Jesus, the paragon of compassion, wisely gave himself a healthful respite from the troubles of the poor and welcomed the precious ointment of spikenard which an adoring woman poured over his head. "Ye have the poor with you always," he said. In this saying Jesus admonished against the kind of obsessive and frenzied anxiety about misfortune that—as we saw—took possession of Raskolnikov and drove him to a revulsion in mockery and sadism. We should on occasion exhibit mercy to ourselves in order that we may exhibit it to others.

Among other things, mercy requires that we make allowance for the reactions of sudden hysteria and panic which sometimes —despite our most humane intentions—force us to flee like a stampeded herd from the place where misfortune has struck. This irrational impulse is in fact so powerful that the law in most states has had to counter it by forbidding the motorist to leave the scene of an accident in which his car has been involved. If he leaves, he will be prosecuted though he had not the slightest responsibility for causing the accident. He may know he is innocent and that he has been wronged in the collision; nevertheless, under the law, he may no longer consider the others involved as "strangers" to him. Regardless of fault, the misfortune has, for a limited time and purpose, made neighbors of them, and so he must subdue his natural impulse and remain until the officials arrive and take charge.

Granted that flight is natural, is it the only natural impulse for the observer in a calamitous situation? If it were, then human existence would never have risen from the level of its pre-social condition, which was—to use Thomas Hobbes' famous words— "solitary, poor, nasty, brutish, and short." [9] Our society is still uncivilized in many regards; many existences still are wholly "solitary, poor, nasty, brutish, and short," and many others still are so in part. Yet fear is not the only emotion we acknowledge nor is flight our invariable recourse in moments of peril. There is also some firmer stuff in the human compound, stuff sufficiently apparent and efficacious that when the case of Arthur Wagner came before Judge Cardozo—instead of saying, "Danger invites escape"—he said on the contrary, "Danger invites rescue. The cry of distress is the summons to relief. The law does not ignore these reactions of the mind in tracing conduct to its consequences. It recognizes them as normal."

In other words, rescue was considered such a "normal" human reaction to someone else's state of danger that the railroad company which negligently caused Herbert Wagner's danger became liable for the injuries Arthur Wagner suffered in attempting to rescue him. It was such a "normal" reaction that Arthur Wagner could recover damages whether he acted "instinctively" or had an opportunity to reflect as he hurried in search of Herbert. Finally, the reaction was so "normal" that, although in previous reported cases the injured rescuer had been the father or mother of an endangered child and had done what one would expect of a father or mother, Arthur Wagner could recover for injuries sustained in trying to save Herbert, who was only his cousin.

Suppose, then, Arthur had endeavored to rescue not Herbert, "his kinsman and companion," but some utter stranger. The answer is clear: the jury could still award damages to him if under all the circumstances his attempt was not condemnable in reason. Of course, in such a case he could not excuse any excess of impetuosity by pointing to family ties between himself and the victim of the accident; but if he proceeded reasonably under the circumstances of the emergency he faced, then he could recover for his injuries. Or, to paraphrase Judge Cardozo, if our conduct is proportioned to the emergency, any human being whom we see in jeopardy may be treated as our "kinsman and companion."

In the light of this Wagner case and what it says about the naturalness of softened and opened hearts, we are at last ready to delineate the moral duties involved in Good Samaritanism. Without Judge Cardozo's holding and his estimate of normal human conduct, we might scarcely have ventured to do so. For we have seen that the matter is far from simple and that it deserves very careful reflection. In this instance, the law has at very least provided us with confidence and trust.

I think we can now appreciate the full intrinsic value of Jesus' supposititious case, which may account for its universal popularity and even for the fondness with which it has been mistaken for an actual incident. In this passage (too characteristic of Jesus' principles to permit caviling over its literal authenticity) Jesus depicted the workings of the moral constitution with sublime accuracy and realism.

First, the victim in his narrative is described only as "a certain man." No further identification is given because none would have been appropriate. The person in need of succor is to be conceived in purely *generic* terms. He stands for mankind in its prototypical predicament. Jesus' story implies that man as a species inherits—not corruption or sin by any means—but need, dependence, and primordial distress. Generically he lies naked in his woe appealing for succor.

Second, the duty to provide assistance is of the clearest and highest. It is so clear because the person in need stands for the whole human species, unlimited and unqualified by personal attributes of identification. Thus, to save him is to save the whole human race. The duty is so high because by executing it one most closely emulates God's functional relation toward man, i. e., one acts toward the species as He is conceived to act.

Third, being ourselves individuals as well as representatives of the species, we may not lend succor so indiscriminately as God does, or if we do we may suffer for it. Hence we are under an additional burden of duties—the duty to abstain from quixotic or officious interferences and the duty to guard our own safety from those who would trap us by fraudulent appeals. The desert of the victim is not material; the genuineness of his plight certainly is. As we draw close to him, prudence dictates that we examine his sincerity and ascertain whether he does in actuality represent the distressful state of our species. But prudence can ask no more than that, and if it insinuates that we pass him by without a glance, it must not be heeded. The chance of saving the whole species is worth a magnanimous risk.

Then, there is the tragic postscript to Jesus' story that the Wagner case appends. It would be foolish optimism to disregard what happened to Arthur Wagner. He did not rescue his cousin; he only injured himself. And herein too there is a truthful commentary on the consequences and outcomes of morally righteous conduct. For the rescuer all too often fails of his rescue and injures or kills himself in the effort. There can be no guarantee of success. Some will be saved, others will be lost. The only guarantee we have—the only one we are entitled to—is that attempts of this kind glorify our existences which without them would be like grass and like dust.

One more word is needed—concerning organized society and the law. In our century, the community has provided many institutions and services—some official, some unofficial—in order to prevent individual distress or to succor it when it arises. We admire and cherish these institutional symbols of social solidarity and compassion. If they have not been dwelt upon here in analyzing the problem of Good Samaritanism, it is only because the availability of organized community facilities does not alter the nature of our problem. Institutions may effectually reduce the number of victims we will meet on the highway, but when we meet one, we cannot assign our moral duty to an institution and pass him by. For no institution can make us whole if we lose an opportunity to rescue, in him, the entire human race.

2. THE ARTIST AND HIS WORKS

In 1948 Dmitry Shostakovich, Aram Khachaturian, Sergei Prokofieff, and Nicolai Miaskovsky sued Twentieth Century-Fox Film Corporation in New York for an injunction. The film company had just produced a picture ("The Iron Curtain") which was based on disclosures of Soviet espionage in Canada. In the "credit lines" preliminary to the picture, there was a statement that the music had been taken from selected works of these four renowned Soviet composers. In the picture itself the music was used exclusively for background purposes; the characters and the plot had no possible connection with the plaintiffs. All of the music was concededly "in the public domain" and not entitled to copyright protection. Nevertheless, the plaintiffs claimed that this use of their compositions should be enjoined because the picture was openly hostile to the political ideology they avowed as citizens of the Soviet Union.

The plaintiffs' application for an injunction was denied by the New York court of first instance. On appeal the decision was affirmed.[10]

It is quite possible that if Shostakovich and the others had brought their suit in one of the countries of Western Europe or of Latin America, they would have prevailed. According to the law of these countries, an artist has, in relation to his works, a certain so-called "moral right" which is completely independent of technical copyright. The publisher or purchaser may own the copyright but the artist always retains the "moral right"; he cannot part with it or contract it away. The "moral right" is regarded as an aspect of his creative personality and will be protected by the courts even though there is no claim of injury to his reputation or his pecuniary interests.

Recently, one of the divisions of UNESCO endeavored to define this rather amorphous "moral right," at least so far as literary authors are concerned. The conclusions were that *regardless of copyrights and contracts* (1) an author's work should be made public only with his consent, (2) his name should always be associated with his work, and (3) he has the right to require that the artistic integrity of the work be preserved. Under proposition (3), the UNESCO report would forbid all alterations and abridgments without the author's consent as well as any presentation of the work in "a form obviously inappropriate to it." For example, the work could not be inserted in an anthology if the author "does not wish his work to appear in the company of that of the other authors represented." [11] By analogy, this doctrine might be extended to prohibit the use of a Soviet composer's music in an anti-Soviet film—"a form obviously inappropriate to it."

While the Continental legal systems have emphasized the sanctity of the artist's personality and the inseverable bond between him and his works, the English and American courts have preferred to focus on the community's interest, which they consider primary and paramount. They agree unreservedly that the author has the right either to withhold his work or to publish it and, until he does decide to publish, everyone else is prohibited by law from using it in any manner. But, they hold, once he publishes, his only legal rights in the work are those comprised in his agreement with the publisher and in the copyright statute. If someone should libel him by distorting the work, he may sue for libel; if someone should maliciously use the work in a way that is calculated and intended to injure him (for example, if Shostakovich's music had been used in "The Iron Curtain" with the deliberate purpose of harming him) he has a grievance which the courts will repair. But where the use neither violates a copyright nor stems from personal malice, the Anglo-American courts generally will not interfere. Their view is that the artist's copyright privileges are accorded not for his benefit but for the public's, that he is rewarded by the grant of a legal monopoly on his work to the end that he may be induced to produce and publish for the general good, and that the monopoly should not be extended beyond bounds which experience has shown are actually necessary as inducements. And deep beneath this rationalization, there lies a very sincere anxiety that if authors and artists should be permitted to assert "moral rights" in the courts, there would be no discernible limit to the aesthetic subtleties, dialectics, and controversies in which the judges would find themselves entangled. The more a judge knows about the arts and particularly about artists, the more he will dread this kind of controversy.

Take for example the dilemma presented in another New York case,[12] where the overtones were religious rather than political in nature. In 1937 a Protestant church held a competition for the design of a mural to be placed on an inner wall of the edifice. Some twenty artists competed; the committee unanimously selected the sketches of Alfred D. Crimi, a well-known artist. A contract having been signed, Mr. Crimi executed the work and received $6,800. His mural was done in fresco, which meant that as the wet plaster on which he applied his pigments gradually dried, the color became part of the plaster, that is, part of the wall of the church. In 1938 when the mural was dedicated, the congregation seemed pleased and proud but some parishioners felt that the artist had represented Jesus with too much of his chest bare. In 1946 the church was redecorated and, without any notice to Mr. Crimi, the mural was painted over.

Although it was perhaps because of Mr. Crimi's own oversight that his contract contained no provision against obliteration of the mural, we can readily understand why he felt incensed enough to bring a lawsuit. Nor is it difficult to comprehend the congregation's decision, the aesthetic tastes and sensibilities of religious congregations being what they usually are. Of course, someone who took the essential teachings of the church to heart may have suggested consulting with the artist before covering up his work, but if so, others who believed that artists labor only for money-hire had succeeded in dismissing the suggestion.

Under the circumstances, the one thing the New York court would not be induced to do was to utter any hint or intimation of a judgment on the merits of the aesthetic and iconographic controversy. If the court would not decide this, the fundamental issue between the parties, then who should? Certainly not the artist: even if he were inconceivably immune from bias, he was not compelled—as the congregants were—to look at the mural on every call to worship. If the artist considered his mural fit to endure forever, he should not have painted it in a private structure owned by others, nor should he have used a technique that effectively incorporated it into their real property. Better that his sensibilities be offended than that the congregation feel rancor instead of reverence within their house of prayer. And far preferable almost any kind of legal solution that would avoid submitting aesthetic controversies to the average English or American judge.

These are factors that have shaped the Anglo-American law of the subject and have made it different at least in emphasis from the systems of Western Europe and Latin America. But the difference should not be exaggerated, it does not amount to a polar opposition. Both systems—the Anglo-American with its emphasis on the artist's utility to the social community and the Continental with its emphasis on the artist's individual rights of personality—both are opposed to the philosophy of Soviet law, which regards the artist as a servant of the political organism, that is, of the State. Both would reject the Soviet's subordination of artistic achievement to the ephemeral tactics and changing objectives of a State bureaucracy; both would recoil from the ideological orthodoxy and the abject servility with which some Soviet artists pay for professional advancement.

At a certain point, however, the two Western systems do begin to differ. The Anglo-Americans are solicitous of the artist's special pecuniary interests but otherwise regard him like any other member of the social community. The Continental jurists show rather more concern for his rights of personality; to them he may be more than a person, he may become a personage. As an empirical matter, the Anglo-Americans tend to compensate him better in terms of money, which leads him to suspect that he lacks social esteem, while the Continental societies stint on money and balance the account with generous grants of fame and dignity. Thus, in America he is likely to appear far too humble about his métier, on the continent of Europe far too venal, and everywhere as discontented as he is unsure of what he should seek in order to content himself.

I do not know how one can be an artist without caring to excess about the reactions and judgments of other persons. When an artist (Thoreau for example) protests an attitude of indifference, he only exposes his hypersensibility all the more nakedly. For whatever else art may be, it is always an attempt to assert something over against a felt otherness, for some moment and in some corner to transcend one's status as object and to become a subject and a compelling will. And where is one to find the certification that this has really taken place, that the word has become flesh, or the clay has become animated with spiritual form, or the music has snatched reverberations from the spheres, where is any genuine assurance to be had except in the responses of observers and recipients? One must be gifted with sensitivity even to attempt the creation of art and cursed with sensitivity to ascertain whether the issue is failure or success.

There are two times when it is fitting for an artist to voice his contempt for fame: when he does not possess it, and when he does possess it. When he has not won fame, he can see rather clearly what a useless substance it is, how insatiable the most famous personalities remain for more and headier supplies of it, how insecure they seem to feel concerning its measure, solidity, and endurance, what foolish posturings and silly affectations it appears to inspire in them, how fortuitous its advent is and how capricious its departure, and what corrosive ingratitudes, treacheries, and self-betrayals may be comprised within its price. The artist without fame could swear fame was worthless and worse than worthless—if he were only certain that he also did not lust for it.

"If any one sees that he seeks honour too eagerly," Spinoza said, "let him think of the right use of it, to what end it should be sought, and by what means it may be acquired: and not of its abuse and vanity and the inconstancy of men, or of other things of this kind, of which no one ever thinks save from an unhealthy mind. . . . Thus those who are badly received by their sweethearts think of nothing save the fickleness, deception, and the other often related faults of womankind, all of which, however, they immediately forget as soon as they are received again." [13]

Well spoken, Spinoza! but how long are they permitted to

forget these somber things? For if fame appears to be of somewhat doubtful virtue in the eyes of the unknown artist, he whom she has visited and embraced knows her through and through for the lubricous jade she is. Before one takes her, she is all vanity; once one has her, all futility. Fame is: a sound in a few or a few thousand mouths; one's name recognized while one's thought is ignored; misapprehensions grosser and more offensive than the most malevolent insults; the sour envy and backbiting of companions and even of strangers who do not enjoy similar privileges or, enjoying them, fear to see them shared; and—crowning misfortune—the recurrent discovery of individuals who have never heard of one's reputation and if they had heard would not care a straw for it. Fame has a bangle at hand to aid in her fraud; it is the seductive illusion that posterity will display more intelligent taste and discrimination than one's contemporaries—an illusion which in most cases posterity can be trusted to refute.

In the twentieth century, American society has finally given fame her quietus. The philosophers and the poets had persistently abused and denigrated her, but for some reason or other—perhaps because (like myself) they took such pains to attach their names to their books,[14] no one paid much heed to what they said on the subject. Then, in our own time and perhaps unintentionally, the hollowness of fame was made so very manifest that sensible men may at last avoid being misled. The revelation took place rather suddenly—American "public relations" experts discovered that fame need no longer be courted or sought after, much less earned; like other commodities, fame could be fabricated! It could be either mass-produced or styled to individual taste, developed slowly or instantaneously, and delivered in a size commensurate with the quoted price. Philosophers had often insisted that fame amounted only to the repeated sight or sound of a name, but even they could hardly have anticipated how adept our era would prove with the apparatus of mechanized repetition. Nowadays, almost anyone can hire a claque with robot pens, robot voices, and pairs of robot hands to beat a multiple and tireless applause.

Consequently, although its pecuniary advantages may prove very substantial, fame can hardly be ranked today as one of the moral goods. The factitious in it is so indistinguishable from the spontaneous that, at least during the artist's years of productivity, it can bring no assurance to him or anyone else that his endeavors have succeeded. Once he has retired or—better yet for the purpose—has died, the jealousy of his rivals may abate, so too may the enthusiasm of his admirers, and a calmer but not necessarily wiser judgment may be able to emerge. But in the period of his youth and artistic prime when fame is likely to hold itself out as an active incentive to creation, under present social conditions it is much closer to mere notoriety than to the "good name" which men have traditionally prized as one of the rewards of a useful career.

A "good name" was always worth earning and having, and it still is. It stands for the judgment of those relatively few (by no means always the accepted experts) who are truly acquainted with the man and his works, who are equipped to understand them at least in part, and who feel sufficiently concerned with the experiences and gratifications they have received from him not to care about altars that are being built and decorated and ripped down in the market place. They make the only audience he will ever intentionally address unless he really prefers to be beguiled; their approval provides fare opulent enough to satisfy any intelligent man's vanity.

We may insist on the hollowness of fame without denying that vanity and self-conceit are among the most cogent forces in human society and specifically in the province of artistic creation. No male artist, whatever his age or eminence, fails to respond throughout his being to an apt compliment, preferably one from a pretty girl (but then any girl who gives a compliment is very likely to seem pretty at the time). The community gains tangible benefits for itself when it glorifies its men of art and fulfills the fitting demands of their vanity. Yet if the artist is genuinely perceptive, he will not let compliments and praise lull him into forgetting that the material source from which he has extracted everything in his creation is—none other than the *community*.

In this respect the process of artistic creation appears to resemble the process of moral legislation. The artist like the moral legislator offers back to the community only the substance of what he has already taken from it. True, the substance has been shaped, colored, animated, and orchestrated all in accord with his unique genius and inspiration; true, if it deserves to rank as an authentic creation, the work will bear the stamp of the man who moulded it. But nothing, not even form or afflatus, comes created out of nothing, and the utmost that any artist can assert is that he has sired a work of art in the matrix of the communal culture. He may choose to keep the offspring in his own private custody and, if he does, the community will acquiesce because it is confident of its unlimited fertility. But if, as seems more probable, he should decide to send the offspring forth, i.e., make it public, then he must expect it to have a destiny of its own which will, in the usual manner of emancipated children, proceed quite independently of paternal control. After the sale or the publication, though the work he engendered is still said to be "his," that does not mean that he possesses or owns it. The law will safeguard him in his title of exclusive paternity; by forbidding infringement of copyright, it will secure his offspring's earnings for him during a period of many years; but in other respects, under our system, the whole community is free to enjoy the work without hindrance.

Since what the artist sees in himself as sacred personality he usually sees in his fellow-artists as mere pretense and vanity, it is quite possible that a consensus of artists would prefer the Anglo-American to the Continental doctrine on this subject. It is possible, for example, that their fellow composers would suggest to Shostakovich, Khachaturian, Prokofieff, and Miaskovsky that the grievance they presented to the New York court was too trivial to mention: just consider what their illustrious predecessor, P. I. Tschaikowsky, had done with *La Marseillaise* in his 1812 *Overture?*

In final analysis, the intelligent artist should resolve to find his main and magistral gratification in honest craftsmanship and the integrity of his creative process—not in the product apart from the process but in the product as the less than perfect outcome of the process. The artist's work can be better than his works, truer, finer, and cleaner of self-interest. He knows that when he succeeds even in part, the community may hail him as joyously as the ancients used to hail Persephone when after bleak wintry months in the underworld she would return with the promise of spring and renewed life. But shall it be accounted to Persephone for a personal merit that she did not eat more of the pomegranate seeds?

3. THE EXPERIENCE OF MAGNANIMITY

In 1931 Charles E——, a chauffeur living in Duluth, Minnesota, took out a life insurance policy for $1,000 with the F—— Life Insurance Company. The contract provided that double indemnity would be paid in case of death by accident, but also provided that the double indemnity benefit would end automatically if Charles E—— should enter military service in time of war. He named his wife Anna as beneficiary of the policy.

In February, 1941, Charles, who had joined the National Guard, was inducted into the army. For a short time, he sent money to Anna for her support. Later the Government granted her an allotment, which she continued to receive until December, 1947. Meanwhile she heard nothing further from her husband, but she kept up the premium payments on the policy. When the allotment ended, Anna obtained the help of an attorney in trying to locate Charles. The attorney ascertained that Charles had been discharged from the army in 1943 and had met his death by accidental means in Texas in December, 1945. The fatal accident had not been connected in any way with his period of military service. Accordingly, on January 12, 1948, Anna wrote to the insurance company and claimed double indemnity. The company began an investigation immediately and received two successive reports which showed that Charles had been in military service. On February 3, 1948 the claim was approved for double indemnity by three authorized officials of the company, and on February 20 the company sent its check to a Duluth bank to pay Anna the double indemnity and return to her the premiums she had paid after Charles' death. Three days later, the insurance company telegraphed the bank to countermand the check and to pay Anna only $1,000, the face amount of the policy, plus the unearned premiums.

Anna sued the insurance company. The company claimed the double indemnity agreement had been cancelled automatically when Charles entered military service. The trial judge instructed the jury that if the insurance company had been informed of the military service and had purposely disregarded it, Anna was entitled to recover. The jury having found in Anna's favor, the company appealed.

The highest court of Minnesota unanimously awarded Anna

the double indemnity because the insurance company had waived the military service forfeiture and would not be permitted to revoke its waiver.[15]

WE ENJOY the description of a virtuous act, saying to ourselves in all probability that it gives us hope; we also enjoy the description of a vicious act, saying to ourselves with a sad sort of pleasure that it gives us truth. As long as we are only readers, these are the passages that will hold our attention, move our emotions, and send us on to utter judgments about the brightnesses or the ugly splotches in human nature. But when we lay our reading aside and return to the small routine of our daily lives, there grows in us a subconscious awareness that neither virtue nor vice is so conspicuous as the authors and artists might lead us to expect. From our rising in the morning to our going to bed at night, the most persistent trait we encounter is mere pettiness, smallness of spirit, parvanimity.

In some ways it seems more harmful even than consciousness of vice. When feelings of guilt rise inside us, they exert an expulsive force, they push to break out of us, they impel us to sigh or exclaim or confess: all of which demonstrates something alive and striving. But pettiness can pile up a humid, ignoble, oppressive mass that weighs us down, defeats our minds and feelings, and saps the strength of our capacities. Manhood recedes as we watch the members of the crowd struggling with one another for the first place in an inconsequential queue, raging over a few paltry minutes in a meaningless day, or consuming themselves in the chase for a handful of paper money. Most people will insist on their "rights" with the same fierce intensity whether life is at stake or only the undivided attention of a butcher at a meat counter. As we know, elaborate systems of economic and political theory have been constructed on the assumption that behavior like this makes up the representative social norm, i.e., that no one anywhere ever yields an advantage, no one accepts a penny less or pays a penny more than he must. While the systems are sometimes adjusted to allow for ostentatious waste in the society or for the effects of personal improvidence and corruption, to propose making an allowance for acts of spontaneous magnanimity would be considered quite unscientific and naive.

Yet if parvanimity be the norm, surely magnanimity is the super-norm in every society. Sometimes group pressures bring it about, sometimes they approach so close to coercing it that a skeptical observer might say there is nothing voluntary or autonomous in obeying the super-norm. But since under identical group pressures, individuals do differ as to degree of magnanimity and since some act magnanimously when there is no group pressure in operation, we are justified in seeking individual as well as social explanations for especially generous behavior. And if the skeptic should pause to consider how much immediate satisfaction he himself has derived on occasion from this or that move of magnanimity, he would concede that others may possibly enjoy similar experiences.

For one thing, there is a distinct sense of augmented power that comes directly from a magnanimous deed and, like other accesses of power, inspires a pervasive euphoria. One feels, as it were, elevated, literally buoyant. And the reason for this delightful sensation is not far to seek: it is that a magnanimous act constitutes an assertion of command over destiny. It masters destiny by proclaiming in the teeth of prescribed, accepted, and usual consequences that these need not ensue, that one has willed they shall not and therefore they do not. If it does nothing else, a magnanimous impulse rips a hole right through the seemingly ineluctable net of cause and effect. It is like working a miracle.

Though the law, as we shall see, takes a somewhat less subjective view of magnanimity, it is surely no stranger to the application of super-norms. Beginning with the discussion of moral legislation in the first chapter of this book, we have noticed again and again that the moral norm or standard is not singular but plural, i.e., that what is incumbent on certain moral types in a society is not necessarily incumbent on the others. The law too, though it claims to be no respecter of persons, has developed a similar scheme of plural, multi-level norms. There are legal norms for ordinary people in ordinary situations and super-norms for extraordinary people and for extraordinary situations. The law casts its light on two major problems: (1) how does one become subject to the super-norm? and (2) what are the moral consequences of complying with the super-norm?

There are so many techniques for the legal enforcement of super-norms that we shall have to content ourselves with a few representative specimens. For example, the Jewish rabbi-judges would employ a doctrine called "beyond the line of the law" (*lifnim mi-shurat ha-din*). According to the doctrine, the judge would apply the technical rule for the ordinary run of cases, but if the party who happened to be in the more advantageous position could be persuaded to accept the higher, more generous super-norm, this would become the law governing his case. And the judge had various communal sanctions available to assist him in the process of persuasion should the situation become urgent enough. This doctrine of magnanimity "beyond the line of the law" may have been part of what Jesus had in mind when he told his followers, "If any man sue thee at the law, and take away thy coat, let him have thy cloak also."

Sometimes in American law we achieve magnanimity in a covert and irregular fashion. In many states, for instance, the strict letter of the law makes contributory negligence a complete defense without regard to its degree. This means that a man struck by a negligently driven automobile has no claim whatever if he contributed to the accident by even a slight lack of carefulness. But since the rule would work harshly in extreme cases, our juries will often disregard it when they think the driver's negligence was much greater than the negligence of the man he injured. They apply, in effect, a more magnanimous rule than the law avows.

As the law's avowed super-norms are more instructive for our purposes, it will be interesting to list five different categories and notice how they rise from material and economic levels to a rather lofty moral plane. I suppose the first and most ordinary way to secure a super-norm is to pay for it. If I leave my goods with you and pay you for your promise to keep them safely, you will generally be held to a higher standard of care than in the case of a merely courteous accommodation. Your burden in the transaction increases with your benefit from it. Second, if you know I am about to rely on your assurance (say, by losing the chance to take other available precautions to protect my goods), then you too must regard it as a serious obligation, though originally it may have been nothing but a casual gesture. The norm becomes higher either when you have taken a benefit or when you know someone else may suffer an injury. Third, the norm rises when your relation to me is so confidential that it gives you a special power and me a special vulnerability. Examples are the relations between husband and wife, parent and child, trustee and beneficiary, and lawyer and client. In relations like these, conduct that would ordinarily be permissible may become an illegal abuse of confidence.

The fourth category of legal super-norms arises out of special circumstances that have put me at your mercy because you alone can supply what I need. When these circumstances arise, you are not permitted to follow the ways of the market place and squeeze the final drop of profit out of my necessity; you are required, on the contrary, to exercise restraint, honor, and self-discipline. Of course, this is the familiar standard which the law applies to innkeepers and public utilities, but I think its moral meaning comes out more sharply in a dramatic situation like the following:

The ship *Richmond* left its home port on Long Island in 1846 and, after a ramble of three years on the Pacific in pursuit of whales, sailed into a thick fog near Bering Straits. In the fog, it ran upon rocks about half a mile from shore. It could not be extricated. "The coast was barren; the few inhabitants, savages and thieves. This ocean is navigable for only about two months in the year; during the remainder of the year it is sealed up with ice. The winter was expected to commence within fifteen or twenty days, at the farthest. The nearest port of safety . . . was at the Sandwich [Hawaiian] Islands, five thousand miles distant." The home port was over twenty thousand miles away.

At this juncture, along came the ship *Elizabeth Frith* and two other whalers. They rescued the crew, bought the *Richmond's* whale oil at a bargain price to which the *Richmond's* captain readily agreed, and carried crew and cargo first to the Hawaiian Islands and then back to the United States. Whereupon the *Richmond's* owners repudiated the agreement of sale. The dispute having finally reached the United States Supreme Court, it held in favor of the owners.[16] The rescuers were entitled to fair compensation for saving the cargo (computed at one-half the value of the oil); they were also entitled to charge freight after they had conveyed the cargo to the nearest port, the Hawaiian Islands; but they were not permitted to take advantage of another's calamity by driving an unfair bargain with him. Thus, in effect, there is a super-norm to protect not only the specially vulnerable but also the sorely wounded.

Most of the super-norms we have been considering are, to a greater or lesser extent, involuntary and imposed. As a general proposition, a man can accept or decline a post of trusteeship, but if he accepts the trust, the super-norm comes along with it. So too with the innkeeper and the public utility company; and so too with the elaborate body of regulations imposed by law on insurance companies, such as the F—— Life Insurance Company in our principal case. But there was no *general* regulation or rule of law to require payment of double indemnity under a contract which made an explicit exception for military service. The exception in the contract was a valid, binding provision. The F—— Life Insurance Company had not been paid anything to disregard the clause; it had made no representation on which anyone had placed reliance; nor did the company stand in a confidential relationship to Anna E——, the beneficiary. Why then was it not permitted to insist on the letter of its contract?

The reason is of the highest moral significance. It is that when the company, with full knowledge of the fact that Charles E—— had been in military service, decided nevertheless to pay double indemnity on his policy and openly manifested that purpose, it performed an act of magnanimity. Unless some extraneous legal policy or moral consideration forbids, an act of magnanimity possesses and exerts legislative power over the person who performs it. It enacts a super-norm which locks him tight. The doctor, the engineer, the laboratory scientist—each is obliged to a certain type of expertness because he has held himself out as possessed of a superior skill; each is bound in law and morals to rise to the level of his general pretensions. By like token, the doer of a magnanimous act holds himself out (if not to the world, at least in conscience) as fit for the level of the super-norm. In the immediate case he will not be allowed to sink below the law he has shaped *for himself*.

If he enacts this law often enough, it will bind him in all cases, it will become his familiar and obligatory norm. And even if the super-norm should be attained only once, it will leave an ineradicable vision of that which he can reach and below which there must remain a sense of falling short.

Our topic has a corollary for readers who are interested in a better understanding of the Bible. For millennia, men have been haunted by the mysterious statement that God created man "in His own image." While innumerable interpretations have been assigned to the phrase, they are likely to leave us unsatisfied because they generally assume a much greater knowledge of God's own nature than the intelligent among us will pretend to have. The analysis we have just made suggests an interpretation which would be immune from this sort of implied presumptuousness. For without venturing beyond the very words of the text or saying anything whatever about His other attributes, we can assert confidently that the Bible describes God here as creator of man. "In His image" then would mean that He created him (at least in the partial and imperfect sense of an "image") to be somehow a creator of *himself*. Within limits every man can create himself by means of the supreme uplift in a magnanimous act.

He can, if he will, create a morally elevated being in himself; but—let us not be beguiled—there are other, different possibilities which are realized more often than not. Perhaps the euphemism we usually apply to a loose and promiscuous woman will fit the remainder of us: take us all in all, we are none of us much better than we ought to be.

VIII

The Last of Life

1. PARTIAL DISABILITY

In Pennsylvania (as in many other states), an injured plaintiff's contributory negligence bars completely his right to recover damages from a negligent defendant. In other words, he loses his ENTIRE claim if his failure to exercise reasonable care for his own safety was a substantial factor in causing his injury. For our present purposes, although this rule of law may be highly debatable, it will be put to use—without approval or disapproval—as a serviceable postulate.

Joseph H. S—— made his living as a house to house salesman in a certain neighborhood of Philadelphia. Though he was nearly blind, he had become somewhat familiar with the section and managed to go about alone. Guiding himself by the sky line of the buildings, he would follow the sidewalk by making out the lines of poles, trees, and hedges on either side of it. On a bright July day, while walking carefully on the sidewalk, he came to a place, where Peter Sn——, a plumber, was installing a sewer connection between the street and one of the houses. The workmen had torn up part of the cement walk and had dug a deep trench straight across from the curb to the building line. They had thrown the excavated soil up on the sides of the trench, making a pile about two feet high on the side which Joseph was approaching. On the far side of the trench *they had placed a barricade, but on this side there was nothing but the heap of excavated material. Of course, Joseph did not see it. He stepped on the loose material; it slipped under his foot; he lost his balance, fell into the trench, and was injured.*

Joseph sued Peter Sn—— for damages. The trial jury awarded Joseph a verdict of $500 but, Peter having appealed to the Superior Court of Pennsylvania, the verdict was set aside and Joseph's suit was dismissed on the ground that he had been contributorily negligent as a matter of law in not employing a cane. When Joseph took the case to the state's highest court, he lost again by a unanimous decision. The court said that "he was bound to take precautions which one not so afflicted need not take. In the exercise of due care for his own safety it was his duty to use one of the common, well-known compensatory devices for the blind, such as a cane, a 'seeing-eye' dog, or a companion." [1]

When we approach a subject like partial disability, we need to reason together at some length. For it is specifically the function of reason to discipline our moral sentiment while rebuking and dispelling any tendency to indulge in sentimentality. Most of us have a bad conscience in regard to disabled persons; we see their rights and duties only in dim outline, through a sentimental fog which veils them in the same sort of condescending pity we feel for helpless infants. The more we know about the past history of the subject, the more difficult it is to put aside our regrets and achieve a rational valuation.

Herodotus describes an Asiatic tribe that regularly sacrificed their elderly people along with their cattle, boiled the flesh and feasted on it. There was also a nomadic Indian nation, he says, who killed and ate not only the aged but anyone else who betrayed signs of illness. Even in Herodotus' time there were

Indian nations who abstained from all forms of flesh; among these, a sick person was not in danger of being eaten, he was required merely to leave the community and go alone, unattended and forgotten, out into the desert.

Since the advent of the Industrial Revolution in the Western World, many of the elderly and the ill have met not dissimilar fates. Child labor in the factories has not differed so greatly in its effects from the custom of infant exposure in primitive Rome; large numbers of persons in failing health have been dispatched by unsafe machines, dangerous explosives, coal dust or other noxious matter in the atmosphere; and physical deformities, which used to evoke reactions of superstitious dread in earlier societies, subsequently became occasions for mockery, ridicule, and sadistic farce, completely effective to exile the victim from his tribe in a psychic sense and send him off to expire in the desert.

On the other hand, in a surpassing example of moral refinement, the Bible not only forbids us to put a stumbling-block before the blind, which the blind may fall over to their hurt, but further forbids us to curse the deaf—which presumably the deaf could not even hear.[2] When one encounters a standard as sensitive as this and considers the myriad unnecessary cruelties inflicted on disabled persons almost everywhere, one's rational capacities are quite liable to be overwhelmed.

If we are to evaluate disability reasonably and soberly, I think we must begin by directing our gaze not on the disabled but on the remainder of society—on those who are usually considered "able." What do we see then? That every one of the so-called "able" is in some respect or other and in some degree disabled. We are all partially disabled, because mental and physical perfection—like all other perfections—is only for diagrams. The old among us suffer from a thousand ailments and degenerations, slow reflexes, insecure gaits, weak perceptions.

The young, even the healthiest of them, carry the ordained disabilities of youth, which include heedlessness, impetuosity, absorption in passionate musings, and the irrational compulsion to take risks merely for the sake of thrills. Large numbers of the youth in every country are blighted with mental, nervous, or organic defects and disorders which may pass unnoticed until a military conscription system provides an occasion for medical examinations on a mass scale. Physical competence is all too often cancelled by mental or nervous handicaps, and the minority of young men who happen to excel in both mind and body will provide a substantial part of the casualty lists in periods of war. Though we are usually not aware of it, every street and avenue has among its pedestrians a full share of alcoholics, drug addicts, psychotics, congenital morons—not to mention the individuals of imperfect eyesight who would have to put on glasses to write a book or read one. And whenever a person's attention chances to flag for a moment, the finest natural endowments can become entirely useless to him; at any street crossing, alert and cautious valetudinarians may survive where athletic but inattentive youths will be struck and killed. Finally, we must allow for the remorseless caprice of chance, which sooner or later surprises and disables all. In our principal case, for example, it would have been so very, very easy for chance to have spared Joseph S—— and sent him safe and unaware on his way. Who knows? That very thing may have come to pass on a thousand other occasions without his being a whit the wiser.

What is the law's attitude? It erects a standard of care to govern conduct which may have an injurious effect on other persons. Each of us is required to act like a reasonable man of ordinary prudence, that is, to observe the community's pattern of reasonable behavior. In judging whether a particular individual has met or has failed to meet the standard, the law takes his specific physical attributes into consideration and does not expect an elderly pedestrian to sprint or a fat woman to fit herself into a very narrow space. The law insists that we employ normal intelligence, normal memory, and such general information as the rank and file of the community would be assumed to have. For example, no one will be excused for being mentally dull (unless to the extent of infantile imbecility) or for not knowing that fire burns and that ice is slippery. Whatever an individual may think of the society he lives in, he is obliged to take reasonable care of the effect of his conduct on his own safety and on his neighbors' safety. If he happens to possess superior training and information, the law requires him to make use of them: a surgeon will be judged like a layman when he drives his car but not when he performs an operation. Even then, of course, no one holds him to a criterion of infallibility.

According to the law's assumptions, a "reasonable man" will not be callous to the special risks that he may inflict on people he knows are partially disabled. If he notices someone tapping his way along with a cane, he may be expected to take appropriate precautions to avoid inflicting an injury on him; he will not rely on the other's being able to see his approach. Our "reasonable man" must also realize that a partially disabled person is exposed not only to greater risks by reason of his disability but also to the penalty that any injury he does receive will probably cost him more severely. For example, since the loss of an eye is a severer injury to a worker with only one eye, the House of Lords (highest British court) recently held that an employer who hires a garage hand to repair automobiles, knowing the worker has sight in only one eye, must provide him with protective goggles—though no such duty would be imposed with regard to two-eyed workers.[3]

Does the law expect a blind man to meet the same standard as one who can see? It does; but although the standard is the same one of "reasonable prudence," when applied to a blind man it is necessarily adapted to his physical attributes, including his special disability. A reasonable man who happens to be blind will not be heard to say he has never heard of using a cane or being guided by a companion. Of course, even if he takes these precautions, he may nevertheless suffer an injury which normal vision would have avoided; but then a jury will be legally entitled to find that he exercised the care of a prudent person in his particular condition, and the verdict will stand.[4] In the law's appraisal, a blind man is not of a different species from one who has the sight of his eyes. A blind man is simply another member of the total society; he must take suitable and reasonable precautions for his and others' safety. So must a man who is too short,[5] or too heavy, or whose reflexes are slowing with the years; so also must every one of us.

There is, however, one grievance Joseph S—— might be inclined to express at this point. He might say, "A cane; well, yes. A companion; perhaps—although few in my position could afford to hire one. But when the Pennsylvania Supreme Court recommended a 'seeing-eye' dog to me, it only rubbed salt in the wound. Does the state offer to purchase one for my use and to pay for the dog's food and care? Until it does, I prefer to lose my case on the Superior Court's opinion—that is, simply for lack of a cane." If these were his thoughts, we can hardly disagree with them. The moral responsibility rests with the legislature in every state to offer every possible assistance to the blind.

What of the law we have been summarizing? I suggest it has certain implications which, while designed primarily for the physically handicapped, are pregnant with meaning for all morally sensitive persons. These are:

First, there is a moral duty to make reasonable use of the facilities of one's society, to share in its tangible and intangible progress, to mitigate one's human incapacities and augment one's human capacities by employing the socially available resources. This is an aspect of the ubiquitous moral obligation to exercise intelligence.

Second, there is a moral duty to avoid imposing unnecessary guilts on others. A cane or some similar device is a notice which the blind man owes to others, to help them regulate their conduct toward him. In sum, one must do whatever can reasonably be done to reduce the burden of one's incapacities on all persons whc may be affected by them.

Let me express these thoughts in a different way, using the Biblical phrases we have already mentioned: When the Bible says, "Thou shalt not put a stumbling-block before the blind," it addresses not only the seeing but the blind as well; when it says, "Thou shalt not curse the deaf," it addresses not only those who have hearing but the deaf as well. So interpreted, it anticipates and agrees with the posture of our modern law: Persons who are afflicted and disabled must not be categorized even by themselves as an inferior or pitiable species. They are, on the contrary, men in all essentials like their neighbors—with the needs, duties, dignities, and singular potentialities of the genus.

But when these sober and reasonable things have been said, it is necessary to add that this section is not intended to bring satisfaction of conscience to the defendant Peter Sn—— or to other persons in his position. The section they should digest is the immediately preceding one, the one entitled "The experience of magnanimity."

2. DEATH

In 1876, Mark Twain composed a tentative sketch or outline of a blood-and-thunder story, entitled "A Murder, A Mystery and A Marriage" and offered it to William Dean Howells, then the editor of the ATLANTIC MONTHLY, proposing that some other famous authors such as Bret Harte and Howells be invited each to write an independent version of a final chapter which would present his own denouement. The plan was to publish Mark Twain's plot along with the collection of different solutions. After some correspondence between Twain and Howells, the scheme was abandoned, although notations in Twain's diary indicate that he may have intended to revive it at some later time. When Mark Twain died in 1910, the manuscript was not found among his papers.

The manuscript next appeared in 1930 in the estate of Dr. James Brentano Clemens (no relative of Mark Twain's), a New York collector who died in that year. How he had acquired it could never be ascertained. Subsequently, when Dr. James Brentano Clemens' widow died, the manuscript was sold at auction in 1945 along with the rest of his collection. Lew D. Feldman, having bought it at the sale, asked the trustees under Mark Twain's will for permission to publish. Though permission was refused, Feldman went ahead with the process of publication, whereupon the trustees sued for an injunction to prevent his doing so.

The highest court of the State of New York held unanimously that Feldman had no right to publish. The right of first publication is a right different from that of ownership of the paper manuscript. Since Mark Twain had never intended that the manuscript should be published in the form he had drafted, Feldman could not have bought the right to publish.[6]

This case has been very consciously selected because under its surface appearance of confidence and simplicity there are implications of the profound confusion which overwhelms judges along with all other men when they confront the subject of death and death's consequences. Death, we are about to see, perplexes the law no less than it does the other institutions of society, and although out of sheer necessity the judges do attribute this or that specific legal meaning to the ending of human life, their truths are truncated truths and the assumptions they act upon can be nothing more than fragmentary guesses. Like the rest of us, they hear or fancy they hear meaningful voices in a reverberating corridor on the other side of a door, yet they cannot quite make out a single phrase. It would be well, then, for us to expect little of the law and to accept whatever it may offer with a sort of modest but determined skepticism. This is no subject for sanctimoniously pat answers.

Let us try at least to remove two age-old curtains from our line of vision. The first of these is the matter of interment practices —an ancient example of intelligent men's capacity to confuse what is conventional with what is essential in moral concerns. Herodotus, for example, thought the following incident demonstrated beyond doubt that a man could live only by the customs and practices he might become familiar with in his own country:

> *Darius having summoned some Greeks under his sway, who were present, and asked them "for what sum they would feed upon the dead bodies of their parents." They answered, that they would not do it for any sum. Darius afterwards having summoned some of the Indians called Callatians, who are accustomed to eat their parents, asked them in the presence of the Greeks, and who were informed of what was said by the interpreter, "for what sum*

they would consent to burn their fathers when they die?" but they, making loud exclamations, begged he would speak words of good omen. Such then is the effect of custom: and Pindar appears to me to have said rightly, "That custom is the king of all men." [7]

Some ages later, Montaigne with all his insight and sagacity likewise argued that the diversity of interment practices proves that morals are nothing more than established local conventions. Perhaps he chose his evidence from burial practices just because the classic statement of a universal and eternal moral law, so often quoted from Sophocles' *Antigone*, happened to arise in a controversy over Antigone's right to inter her brother. Be that as it may, our study has taught us that we can respect customs without equating morals with them, and that we can honor Antigone's devotion to her dead brother and her determination to give him what she considered a suitable burial without committing ourselves either to any specific form of interment ceremony or to any claim of universality and eternity in the position she so bravely maintained. There is precious consolation in hearing familiar incantations and performing solemn rituals, which only a tyrant would deny to a bereaved relative or friend. Obviously, the ritual must suit the expectations of the persons whom it would console, and these will vary greatly. What Montaigne should have seen is that, however widely the forms of ceremonious convention may vary, the elemental plight of bewildered grief does recur universally in human experience. It is a short life or a cold one that is not mutilated at some point by bereavement.

The second curtain has been no less troublesome. It consists in our superstitious tendency to emphasize the circumstances under which a person dies. What a nest of moral errors we have here! Some of us still admire the early Scandinavians who went lustfully to war, convinced that a warrior who might die in battle would be forthwith transported to the delights of Valhalla. Others credulously infer that a political or religious creed must be true and right if its supporters, however misguided they may be, are willing to die for it. Then there are those who infer that a long, virtuous, and happy life has been completely ruined just because it happens to end in a final fortnight of suffering from disease. Still others will disregard the guilts and vices of a lifetime if the villain only confesses and repents on his deathbed, that is, when the sins he renounces are manifestly no longer accessible to him. And even the more rational among us are wont to evince a peculiar curiosity about a deceased person's last hours and moribund gestures. The fortuitous "last words" of a famous man are considered with reverential awe, while the sage advice he may have given at the peak of his powers is ignored.

In such ways as these, men are likely to succumb either to the dramatic awe that the thought of death inspires or to the foolish hope that they can somehow get a peek through the door. This superstitious susceptibility has prompted our judges to exercise measures of caution when a witness offers to testify to some deceased person's "dying declaration." They fear—rightly—that the testimony will gain a credence it may not deserve, particularly since there is no possibility of testing it by cross-examination. Some legal writers criticize the strictness of the rule governing the use of a "dying declaration"; they insist the statement of a man who knows he is dying is highly trustworthy for every purpose. But, in jury cases at least, the law on this point should not be changed to any radical degree: the dying are all too frequently disposed to err if not to falsify, the jurors all too easily moved to believe accusations from such a source.

The law's chief concern with death is in filling, as effectually as possible, the social and economic gap which death occasions. By provision for succession of estates and guardianship of minor children, it endeavors to mitigate the upheaval in family relationships; by money awards for death caused by a hazardous occupation or by negligence, it establishes a partial substitute for the support the family would have received from the deceased; by levy of inheritance taxes, it restores to the political community some fraction of the capital which during his lifetime he had accumulated out of its resources and under its protection. In other words, the law's general objective is to set up a series of transitional counterparts for the social and economic functions of the deceased person, so as to provide as much continuity as possible to the ongoing family, the ongoing business, and the ongoing social economy. It is interesting to notice how basic these preoccupations have been in American history: William Penn's 1676 Charter of West Jersey, his 1701 Pennsylvania Charter of Liberties, and the Pennsylvania State Constitution of 1790 each expressly provided that the property of a suicide must not be forfeited to the sovereign but must pass to the suicide's heirs as though he had died a natural death.

Here, of course, is the reason why our principal case presents such an exceptional degree of interest. An author's right to withhold his manuscript from publication is just about as subjective and personal a right as the law knows; it relates, we may say, directly to his personality. Its exercise depends on his unique aesthetic judgment, for which he is accountable to no one; in short, it depends on his arbitrary will. Yet, the fact remains that, in our principal case, the New York court proceeded to enforce the right as staunchly as though Mark Twain had not been dead some forty years.

How intimately personal the right to withhold publication can be! It seems that back in the 1840's, during the halcyon years of their marriage, Queen Victoria and Prince Albert used to make etchings together, preparing the plates in their private apartments and occasionally having a few impressions run off at a printer's for their own amusement and the delectation of a very few in the court circle. A knave of a printer's assistant surreptitiously ran off some copies of his own, which eventually came into the hands of William Strange, a respectable publisher. Mr. Strange announced a public exhibition of the royal etchings, adding respectfully to his descriptive catalogue:

> You must not be the grave of your deserving: England must know
> The value of her own. 'Twere a concealment
> Worse than a theft, no less than a traducement,
> To hide your doings.—Shakespeare.

Prince Albert having brought suit, the court not only enjoined poor Strange, it denounced him roundly. As for the descriptive catalogue, that too must be suppressed. "It concludes," said the Vice-Chancellor, "with an intimation, not that the pamphlet or the acquisition of the means of composing it, was or is, but that the abstaining from such proceedings would be 'worse than a theft.' That is, however, in poetry." [8]

While Prince Albert, of course, was alive at the time, that was not the decisive factor. A subsequent case involved the letters of James McNeill Whistler. During his lifetime, Whistler had authorized Mr. and Mrs. Joseph Pennell to write his biography and had given them extensive conferences in order to foster the project. When he died in 1903, the Pennells applied to his friends to show them his letters, so as to complete the picture of his personality. His niece, whom he had named executrix of his will and residuary legatee, sued. She prevented the Pennells from publishing the letters, quoting them, or so much as paraphrasing them. She even sought—in vain, it is a relief to add—an injunction forbidding them to make use of any information gleaned from the letters they had already read! [9]

When we encounter a problem like this, it becomes easy to understand why Anglo-American law has attempted to reduce various conflicts of personal interest to claims for awards of money, because if there is only money at stake in the contest, the judges and legislators can develop some sort of working formula which will appease the adversaries even if it does not leave everyone completely satisfied. Avarice, if such it is, has an ascertainable and measurable price; pay it on a basis that has been fixed by custom or statute and you buy your peace. For example, the British copyright legislation contains a provision (which the United States could borrow with advantage) that when the owner of the copyright has let a book go out of print or has refused to license performance of a play, certain high judges may order a compulsory license on appropriate terms including payment of the usual royalties.[10] The very existence of this remedy may have an emollient effect on copyright-owners and induce them to employ their rights in a more accommodating manner. But there are certain other needs that cash will simply not answer. When the author has died without publishing the work and the estate refuses to grant permission, what in all fairness should be done?

This is no light dilemma. Even if we eliminate the factor of secrecy by considering situations—like the Mark Twain manuscript and the Whistler letters—where some third person holds possession of the writing, it is difficult to decide the consequences we ought to ascribe to the author's death. Granted that he possessed the highly arbitrary right to forbid publication as long as he lived, that he was entitled to withhold a writing from the public because he desired to safeguard his aesthetic reputation, to avoid political jeopardy, to spare the sensibilities of friends and acquaintances, to prevent being sued for libel, to await a more propitious literary market, or—merely to indulge a perverse whim. But once the author has died, prospective readers may well feel they have been patient quite long enough and are entitled now to satisfy their cultural demands and their natural curiosity. They will likely rebel against the presumptuous executor or heir who forbids publication, denominate him or her a "dog-in-the-manger," and prepare a plaintive list of the treasures they have been denied. Did we not insist in the last chapter that an author can only offer back to the community what he has taken from it and reshaped? If that is so, then the community seems to have a just demand on the executor or heir for access to the unpublished writings. (This argument would be considerably more cogent if Americans would evince greater interest than they do in reading a good author's *published* writings. While seconding the complaint that certain poems of Emily Dickinson, who died in 1886, were not made public until 1945,[11] one can yet wonder how many published poems of comparable value lie neglected on the shelves and indeed how many copies of that 1945 volume are in active use at any given time.)

Let us hear the other interest, the family's. Authors and other artists display their feelings, experiences, and emotional intimacies to the literate part of the community in a sense and to a degree that is hardly matched by any other pursuit—certainly not by the so-called "public men," who would rarely run the risk of similar candor. Usually, the creations and disclosures of the literary artist are drained away from what might otherwise have been a satisfactory personal existence, and it is the members of his immediate entourage who generally pay in one way or another for his emotional sustenance, the maintenance of his energies, and the combustion of his nervous reserves. If he becomes famous, the great world, which understands him so little, cares for him less, and embraces him along with a thousand others while it coquettes with his and their eventual successors and supplanters—this great, inconsiderate world stamps into his private circle, boorishly thrusts those who love him aside, and expects them to express gratitude for the invasion. When death finally claims the author, the ones who have cared for him expect that they will at least be permitted in peace to serve as trustees of his standards, his wishes, and his fame. Perhaps they have had to cover a thousand indiscretions, infidelities, and villainies of one sort or another while he lived; now, they may say, let there be privacy, security, and repose for all concerned. Perhaps they value other things more than the public's curiosity. In any case, since he is no longer able to defend his reputation or fulfill his personal duties, who will do so if they do not? Artists being what they generally are, their heirs may be said to have bought and paid for the absolute right of veto over the release of unpublished works.

If there is anything like a demonstrably valid solution for this dilemma, I have not found it. Merely allotting money will not satisfy the heirs' private and personal interest; nor, on the other hand, will the general community accept certain old judicial dicta which indicate it may be excluded from unpublished works perpetually. I would therefore suggest we take our lead from some analogous legal situations, that is, situations which involve collision between a public interest and a private interest associated with the personality of a deceased individual.

The first analogy would be found in our law of criminal libel. Under the law, it is considered a crime against the good order of the community to defame a dead person or vilify his memory because doing so may scandalize and provoke the relatives or friends who have survived him. This implies, of course, that there is a time limit on the recognition of these rights of personality.

Just what should that time limit be? I suggest we can find a practical guide in the famous old rule of law that Anglo-American lawyers call "the rule against perpetuities." Stripped of technical subtleties and refinements, "the rule against perpetuities" amounts to this: any trust or condition or other control a man may exercise by will over his estate (except the part he may leave to public or charitable purposes) will not be permitted to endure beyond the lives of persons he designates in his will from among all those who happen to be *alive when he dies.* When the designated persons of the living generation have passed on, the hand of the dead loses all the force the law allows it to exert.

Somewhere within the lines marked by these analogies, we could develop a tolerably fair solution for the dilemma we have been considering. We could, in effect, uphold the heir's or the trustee's veto power over unpublished works provided the vetoer was himself alive at the time the author died or represents some living person who was alive at that time. And when the time arrives that there is no longer such a person, we could insist with justice that any responsible individual or firm should be entitled to publish the work. Probably the publisher should be required to pay royalties to the author's estate, but for a much shorter period than the usual copyright term.

It is intriguing to apply this perspective to our principal case. If we do, we find that, although each of the three courts in the New York judicial hierarchy issued a full-length opinion, none of them saw fit to mention two very significant facts in the case: first, that Mark Twain's daughter Clara was one of the suing plaintiffs in addition to the trustees under his will; and second, that Mark Twain's will contained a statement that his daughter Clara (along with Albert Bigelow Paine, who died before this litigation arose) was familiar with his desires concerning his literary productions and should be consulted "as to all matters relating in any way" to them. With these additional facts in the situation, we can respect the court's decision as upholding the individual's interest without trenching to excess on the community's.

Thinking of himself as an individual existing in irreducible uniqueness, a man can draw some interesting inferences from what the law does to meet the emergency of death. Though compelled to resort to substitutes which are often inadequate, it emphasizes above all the performance of his obligations to the living. The law concerning death is *life-oriented,* shaped to the needs of the living and the preservation of an ongoing social continuity. If one chooses to, one may infer that such is the real nature of our immortality—to fall from the tree of life and dissolving, fertilize its roots. The law is solicitous of the interests and sensibilities of those among the living who were tied to us. We may survive death as individual, phenomenal existences by continuing in their conscious lives. There is for us a sort of post mortem life and a post mortem dying, as we live on in their activities and as we finally expire when they too cease to be.

Our subject has, however, another and different aspect, for as yet we have considered only the consequences of the *fact* of death—without a word about the meaning of the *thought* of death. Obviously the two are not the same. The thought of death is to death itself as a largo strain of muted violins is to an utter and vacuous silence—a silence which we habitually attribute to others and not to ourselves. Is it any wonder that heretofore our discussion has seemed so cool, so remote from dismal reflections about the final hour, the way life wrenches itself out of its house in the body, or the haste with which the flesh proceeds to putrefy and dissolve into dust? There was no need for the analysis to emphasize anything "morbid" as long as the death we were concerned with was someone else's. Now, however, when we turn to inspect the thought or prospect of death, everything changes its focus. Suddenly, as Horace put it, *de te fabula narratur*—the tale that is to be told concerns you, yourself; the ultimate and terminal spasm you feel in imagination is your own spasm; you are the one whose chair and books will remain here, acknowledging their former master no more; the identity which fades into complete oblivion is now none other than yourself. It will not serve any more to repeat, "All men are mortal; Socrates is a man; therefore Socrates is mortal." For henceforth not Socrates but you must be the man to fill out the syllogism.

There are some who may find this posture appalling, for the visage of death assumes exceedingly different expressions to different men, as it does to the same man at different periods of his day and lifetime, terrifying him in the small, uncanny hours of the morning, challenging his pride and beckoning to his curiosity at high noon, and strangely suggestive of comfort and release during the pause of stillness when the world holds its breath just before sundown. To those who may find themselves frightened by the prospect of death but who are not so overcome with panic that they cannot attend to the voice of reason, Epicurus offered these famous words of reassurance:

> *Accustom thyself to believe that death is nothing to us, for good and evil imply sentience, and death is the privation of all sentience; therefore a right understanding that death is nothing to us makes the mortality of life enjoyable, not by adding to life an illimitable time, but by taking away the yearning after immortality. For life has no terrors for him who has thoroughly apprehended that there are no terrors for him in ceasing to live. Foolish, therefore, is the man who says that he fears death, not because it will pain when it comes, but because it pains in the prospect. Whatsoever causes no annoyance when it is present, causes*

> *only a groundless pain in the expectation. Death, therefore, the most awful of evils, is nothing to us, seeing that, when we are, death is not come, and, when death is come, we are not.*[12]

For the purpose for which they were spoken, these still remain very wholesome words; nothing need be subtracted from them. "Death is nothing to us," said Epicurus to the frightened spirits, and surely if a state of panicky fear were the only possible reaction to follow from contemplating the meaning of death, it would be far wiser to banish the thought permanently and insist that it could never mean anything in our lives. But since modern psychology has emphasized the fact that fear can attract the human spirit as well as repel it and that the grisly thought of death possesses a certain perverse fascination of its own, there is not enough for us in Epicurus' analysis, which considers the thought of death merely in terms of the terrors it may occasion and the techniques available for calming them. Assuming that you who read these lines are among the stauncher minds and are able to reflect on the subject of death—even your own death—without succumbing completely to fear, you will desire our inquiry to proceed farther; and so it shall now.

Can we obtain any indication or assistance from the law? On first impression, it would appear that we cannot, because law which occupies itself so busily with provisions of one sort or another to meet the exigencies which arise from the fact of death, this very expedient and life-oriented system of law seems to care little about the mere imaginative prospect of death or the kind of thoughts men may entertain in contemplation of their final hour.

Yet even when our concern is with the thought instead of the incidence of death, the law is not without some interesting hints. For example, is it not instructive to observe that when an American lawyer or judge uses the technical phrase "in contemplation of death" he refers almost invariably to a transfer of property which the owner has made for the purpose of circumventing the government's inheritance taxes? The law provides that if the circumstances of the particular transaction indicate that the owner acted as he did "in contemplation of death," then his estate does not escape the inheritance tax levy on the property he gave away during his lifetime.

What purposes do the courts usually consider "life motives" which would avoid the tax; what are "death motives" which would incur it? Here we receive some revealing answers: by and large, the courts say the act of retiring from business does not indicate a death motive; nor does the act of donating a major portion of one's property to children or faithful employees (provided one reserves enough to support himself). In other words, according to the judges' cheerful picture of normal American behavior, the desire for leisure or sheer idleness is a manifestation of the will to live, and so too is the desire to provide comfort and security for one's family and business assistants.

Then what would be considered a "death motive"? What does convince the courts that the specific case involved a "contemplation of death"? If at the time of the transaction the owner should appear to have been highly aware of inheritance taxes and preoccupied with reducing the tax charges on his estate, the court will most probably consider him actuated by "death motives." According to the courts, in the thinking processes of the normal American, the prospect of death is associated with taxes and the two are regarded as jointly distasteful. As far as I know, no judge has ever assumed that an American man of property might discuss the topic of taxes with his lawyer and accountant in order to make sure he is paying his full patriotic share of the cost of government. So much for that strangely unphilosophic phrase "in contemplation of death."

There may be rather more enlightenment for us somewhere in the American law on the subject of suicide. If our approach were of a purely sociological nature, the statistics of suicide would probably provide us with considerable new information about the national mores, which have shifted from one time to another in significant ways. For example, we are now told the typical median embezzler of entrusted moneys is found to be much younger than his counterpart in past generations and much less disposed to commit suicide by way of reaction to the shame of exposure.[13] What data like these tend to show is that pecuniary honesty having sagged, there is not much left of the shame which used to be associated with pocketing other people's money or even, among more strait-laced families, failing to pay one's ordinary borrowings and debts. It is not that contemporary mores have kept embezzlers alive by making suicide more disgraceful or horrendous. On the contrary, if the attitudes of, say, the seventeenth century are contrasted with those of our times, another's suicide, which was then regarded as an unforgivable affront to law and religion, is now looked upon by most Americans as little more than an occasion for raised eyebrows.

Whipping the dead has always been a popular practice for bigots, who are by nature rather slow to understand that what they happen to be doing is futile. Until the nineteenth century, English law not only treated the act of committing suicide as a felony but also required that the suicide's corpse be interred ignominiously under a public highway. Whether this mode of burial did more to reduce the incidence of suicide than to disrupt vehicular traffic we do not know. Be that as it may, other savage legal punishments were inflicted on the living, that is, on the suicide's family, who were deprived of their right to inherit his property, which would be forfeited to the sovereign. William Penn, as we have seen, did what he could to end this barbarous practice and eventually his more civilized view prevailed both in England and in the American states; though who can doubt that in his own day Penn must have been denounced from many a pulpit as a man who advocated that people should go about killing themselves?

Western society has never quite known its mind on the subject of suicide, for even in those centuries when the law merely copied the churches' attitude of anathema and detestation, suicide under certain circumstances was not only permitted but might be hailed with honor. While urbane and cultivated individuals of the sixteenth and seventeenth centuries bowed in memory of the several heroic suicides reported by Plutarch, the calm self-execution of Seneca and other noble Stoics, and the supreme example of Socrates' death, what were the churches teaching along with their fulminations against suicide? They taught: that Saul, first king of Israel, having fallen on his sword because he was convinced that God's favor had departed from him, was thereupon praised with sweet songs of lamentation by his successor David; that the blood of martyrs who had deliberately sought out death to bear witness to their faith had become the seed of Christianity; that Jesus had chosen to be put to death for the salvation of others though at any stage of the tragedy it had lain within his power to halt the proceedings against him; and that various perfervid individuals who by extremes of asceticism and abstinence had hastened their own departure from this life, deserved to be canonized.

Suicide, a detached observer might fairly infer, was some sort of special aristocratic preserve on which the rank and file of humanity were forbidden to poach. If such it was, it has since gone the way of most other aristocratic possessions, that is, it has not been destroyed but distributed, popularized, and made accessible to all and sundry. In many American states, neither suicide nor attempted suicide remains a criminal offense even on the statute books; and in the states which still list attempted suicide as a criminal act, prosecutions therefor are virtually unknown, for if a man is despondent enough to elect death for himself, he is not likely to be deterred by a mere threat of imprisonment.

So it is that most of the modern American law cases dealing with suicide disclose two rather modest policies on the judges' part, neither of which should astonish us. (1) So far as possible, the act of suicide should not be permitted to impair the interests of the surviving family. For example, if a life insurance policy contains a provision that the proceeds will not be paid in the event of suicide, almost invariably the judge will rule that in this clause suicide means "self-killing while sane" and he or the jury will find that the insured killed himself while temporarily insane. (2) The act of suicide must not be converted into a tool to defraud others. For example, if the insurance policy provides for double indemnity in the event of accidental death, the courts will deny the double payment where the death was not accidental as claimed but really the result of a suicidal act.

In other words, the courts believe the living should not lose by reason of the suicide, neither should they make a windfall of it. In order to reach this very reasonable position, American judges have had to engage in some difficult legerdemain. On the one hand, there is a traditional presumption in the law that every man is sane and understands what he is doing, unless the contrary should be shown; and if this presumption were to dominate the subject, most self-killings would have to be classified as "suicide while sane"—with disastrous results for the families concerned. But on the other hand, modern courts have developed and applied a so-called "presumption against suicide," which according to the judges rests on the universal operation of the instinct of self-preservation. (It is interesting that this presumption against suicide, as expressed in the generality of judicial utterances, does not assume that human life is particularly desirable or happy; it holds merely that, in the absence of evidence showing a deliberate self-killing by a sane person, we should adopt some other explanation of the mode of death.) Thus if a case arises where the fact that the deceased has killed himself is too manifest to be disregarded, the only way to accomplish the court's purpose is to push aside the established presumption of sanity and determine that the instinct of self-preservation must have failed because this particular individual was out of his mind when he took his life. In many instances, the result has to be reached on very flimsy evidence of temporary insanity, which the judge fortifies as best he can with some rather unscientific tributes to the usual efficacy of the instinct of self-preservation.

This area of the law is in a rather uneasy state. Since modern standards of reasonableness and decency have put an end to the practice of punishing the surviving relatives, there does not seem to be much else that the legal system can possibly do about the problem of suicide. Judges do not claim to have jurisdiction over departed spirits, perhaps because the living keep them busy enough.

Nevertheless, I feel convinced that the law is able to provide us with moral guidance on this subject as on others, and that the maxims we need will be near at hand once we recognize that a suicide is merely a type or specimen of homicide. Whoever kills himself kills a member of the human genus. He commits a homicide; and according to the general rule of our law, a homicide must be considered criminal unless it is "justifiable" or "excusable" (as in cases of self-defense or unavoidable accident). Since we are not concerned here with merely accidental self-killings, our central question comes down to this:

Can self-killing ever constitute an act of self-defense, which might make it morally "justifiable?"

Let us assume that self-defense justifies you in killing an aggressor who attacks you without provocation and clearly intends to kill you. (St. Augustine stated that even the urgent necessity of individual self-defense cannot provide a moral although it may provide a legal justification for homicide; [14] but many moral leaders have disagreed with him, to which I would append that this statement of his is an instance of the kind of utopian and impossible standard that tends to defeat its own aims.) Accepting the proposition that, in order to save himself, a person may warrantably kill an assailant bent on murder, we can deduce when suicide should be considered morally justifiable. It will be justifiable only if demonstrably necessary for self-defense, that is to save the intrinsic self from destruction when no less extreme action will suffice. If there remains no other way to save the self's authenticity from sure and impending debasement or dehumanization or exploitation as an instrument of evil, then the act of suicide becomes justifiable, because it will preserve the generic integrity of the individual though at the cost of ending his private capacities and of destroying whatever within him is unique and ongoing. When circumstances conspire to exact such a gruesome choice of any human being, it behooves the remainder of mankind to abide the outcome in humble silence, for until a man has crawled his way through that same valley, he can understand nothing of its unique and solitary terrain, and those few who have undergone the experience and remain alive are not likely to utter judgments concerning the course taken by others.

This discourse about the law and suicide brings us at last to the entrance of our subject's principal chamber, where the thought of death waits in its profoundest moral significance. But even here as we enter together, permit me to suggest that the aspect of mortality we are about to behold, although it is the most important, should not be taken for the entire meaning, which our finite nature does not enable us to apprehend at once in any single setting or context. We never see the whole of a capital concept at one time, at least not so far as it can be communicated in words or symbols even to ourselves. One might put it that we can only walk around the elephant, for if we want to look at his back and his belly, his tusks and his tail, his right side and his left side all at the identical moment, then we shall have to cut him into sections and he will not remain an elephant. Remembering that there is a right side and what it looks like while we look at the left side and mentally construct the complete animal is the best we can do; this approaches reasonably close to a view of the whole and in any event it has the advantage of leaving him intact as an elephant. Apparently he observes us in much the same way. The critical difference between him and us is that we human beings have projected certain special kinds of wholes—the all-important abstract and essential kinds—which he does not seem able to formulate. And while religious pessimists have long argued that there must be something congenitally defective in our human composition because we can never quite enclose or comprehend any of the abstract wholes we have conceived (such as life and death and love and virtue), it seems more accurate as well as juster to conclude that man has made a godlike creature of himself by fabricating any abstractions at all. Glory to the man who first seized fire from the heavens, and greater glory to him who first laid hold of the concept of fire! Nevertheless, though we may be gratified with this genius of ours to conceive of wholes, let us remember—at least for the immediate purpose—that, in any single perspective, what we are witnessing is only a facet, an aspect, a part.

The thought of your own mortality comes now and says that

the wild and tempestuous beasts—the desires, lusts and fears, the anxieties and longings—which so continually in your life take the bit in their teeth, dash away madly first in one direction then in another, shake the reins out of your hands and toss you about helplessly, these headstrong beasts can be disciplined and brought to a temperate pull toward a purposeful destination. Confronting the thought of death, they will become subdued within you, for suddenly the self-loves and self-hates find themselves harnessed to a destiny which the entire genus must learn to acknowledge. Let the inflamed stallion paw the ground, let him rise snorting and rampant if he will: the thought of inevitable death can fall upon him, cling to his back like a great, black leech, and draw his fevered blood until he is ready once more to obey judgment, his master.

The old proverb says that death levels all ranks; and so it does, for no man can find a way to buy it off. But the thought of death possesses an even greater power. Where death can only terminate, the thought of death can moderate; where death can only destroy, the confrontation of death can purify; and where death must of necessity treat every man the same way, it is the excellence of the thought of death that a wise man can discover deep truths in it where a fool will see nothing but a Gorgon's head.

Come, look at your own life through this dark glass, the thought of death, which, though admittedly it takes most of the color out of what you behold, will nevertheless dull the glare your passionate egotism has cast over the scene to dazzle the eye of reason. Now, at least in outline, you can see the essential direction of your journey, the countenance you have gradually formed out of the one you began with, the triviality of the concerns that customarily fret you, and the worthlessness of your striving, in your insecurity, to impress other individuals who, in their several insecurities, have been trying pathetically to impress you. Here is an anodyne for almost every fear you have ever known, for were not almost all of them fears for the safety of some interest which you claimed as a private and unique personality? If then you will pause long enough to see your career as an infinitesimal participation in the life-stream of the genus, you will scarcely believe that these concerns and fears can be of lasting moment. In due perspective, they are only a petty local parade of figments and appearances. Surely, when thinking about death has convinced you most thoroughly of your equality with the myriads of your congeners, you will put aside the illusion that a desire possesses some special validity and right to be satisfied because it happens to be yours instead of another's.

But is there not something here which is reminiscent of the very beginning of our study and the inferences we drew from American law concerning the value of being alive, the case of seaman Holmes in the long-boat, and the "morals of the last days"? Indeed there is; we have finally come full circle, for in death our end, precisely as in birth our beginning, we remain under conscience's generic commands. Working on us through tranquilizing thoughts of death, the moral constitution suggests continually that at times and intervals we ought to cease repeating "What am I?" in order to look both near and far and inquire "What is man?" At times it is salutary to review every ephemeral desire in the spirit of humility which comes from acknowledging the sure approach of the ultimate hour. When he is reminded of mortality, the wise man, withdrawing to an inner retreat of his own, contemplates the unfolding of his particular destiny with sedate and imperturbable detachment. Quietly he surveys its course *sub specie humanitatis,* under the aspect of an enduring and universal human community.

3. INTERIM COMMENTS

On embarking to explore the moral values in American law, we drew much-needed inspiration and courage from one of Francis Bacon's eloquent passages, which we adopted for our enterprise as a sort of motto. Bacon had referred in heady terms to "that New Continent" where "the trial must by all means be made," and he had assured his readers that "there is hope enough and to spare." Now we seem, as it were, to have traversed the long continental coastline of the good-in-law from its beginning at the point of birth to its end and culmination in death. Rich and various we have found it, far too much so, in fact, for any attempt to summarize its profile in a short and tidy phrase. Since it was not our purpose to discover a formula or a system, we have tried persistently to keep our eyes open for inconvenient as well as convenient data. No system having been taken along with us, none has been brought back, and, at the risk of disappointing those who do not recognize gold unless it is first minted into pocketable coin, we propose to report only a few tentative observations which may indicate what we have and what we have not accomplished.

In the first place, there is no harm in repeating that the coast we have followed covers only a portion of the terrestrial globe. That is to say, there are vast and important areas of human life and interest which, because they have only the remotest connection with morals, are beyond the proper scope of an investigation like ours. Fortunately in every life there are a thousand kinds of delight and a thousand kinds of pain which remain morally neutral and indifferent, for a healthy and muscular conscience requires long intervals of relaxation and sleep, lacking which it is liable to become repressive and guilt-ridden. Moreover, moral philosophy has never ordered things so successfully at home that it should be tempted to imperialistic invasions of other areas of human activity.

One of the most interesting inquiries has to do with the so-called "principal cases" and the other legal materials we have analyzed. The principal cases, we should freely concede, possess no syllogistic force at all in morals. They were not selected for their demonstrative qualities; they were not even selected for their intriguing illustrative qualities. It is fundamental to the method of our study that they were selected for their *prismatic* qualities. The criterion of selection has been very simple: Are the data of this specific case—its legal data as well as its factual data, for all combine together to give the case its distinct attributes—are these data likely to make an effective prism which will catch the undifferentiated, white light of the good and disperse it in multiple colors and rays—precise, decisive, and responsible? In brief, would the case give us a richer moral spectrum? I find now that I have generally expressed agreement with the decisions reached in the principal cases; perhaps one is more likely to perceive the prismatic value in a judicial opinion if one agrees with its conclusion. But when the discussion of the principal cases took us to related holdings in other cases, disagreement was expressed so frequently and, at times, so vehemently that we can hardly be charged with a credulous or uncritical approval of the present state of American law.

Before our exploration was launched, we decided it would probably involve certain characteristic advantages and certain necessary hazards. We anticipated that: Where the general notion of good might seem excessively abstract or vague, the good-in-law would be able to supply dramatic projection and the urgently desired quality of precision; that where the notion of good might seem neutral or irresolute, the good-in-law could supply a model of decisiveness; and that where the good had been exalted to utopian altitudes, the good-in-law could anchor it down to responsibility. Any of these would be a fair and legitimate test to determine the practical usefulness of an enterprise like ours.

While we were agreeing on the advantages to be hoped for, we likewise took note of the losses we might find ourselves incurring. We feared our vision might be obscured by forensic contests between opposing trial lawyers, more interested in winning a victory than in advancing the cause of justice; and we also dreaded the courts' proverbial absorption with fine-spun distinctions and technicalities. These two misgivings do not seem to have been confirmed, at least not yet. But since they are likely to emerge more prominently in the law governing procedures and trials than in the law governing substantive rights, we must carry our alertness forward to Part III.

Here and there, we have encountered instances of Philistine standards both in the law and in popular attitudes and practices. The instance of tax-cheating is far and away the most alarming.

In the setting of our times—with taxes on incomes, gifts, and estates established at the high rates which our national debt and international obligations demand—the future of the existing property-tenure and business-enterprise system depends directly on our maintaining a close correspondence between the tax-dollars due according to the statute books and the tax-dollars actually collected by the government. Steeply progressive taxes constitute the system's most effectual palliative not merely for the objective ills caused by inequality of wealth and income, but even more for the corrosive envies, discontents, and cynicisms that inequality inspires. The degeneration and wretched decline of other nations which were once great powers in the world should warn the United States: A country's morale rots away when the rank and file of its people become convinced that, even if high taxes should be inscribed somehow on the statute books, most of the more prosperous citizens would find a way to avoid paying and the main burden of government would still remain on the backs of the working masses. This disillusionment even America is not rich enough to afford. And apparently there is only one primary preventive which we can employ. Unless every year some of the worst tax-evaders among the "respectable" social classes (merchants, lawyers, accountants, doctors, farmers, labor leaders, housewives, manufacturers, police officers, clergymen, etc.) are exposed, prosecuted, and required to serve moderate prison sentences, there is no genuine prospect that most of the other taxpayers will ever learn to practice honesty in their returns or that workers whose taxes are withheld and remitted directly to the government will regard the process as anything but a form of exploitation.

Our findings have continually emphasized the moral freedom of the individual human being. The dimensions of this freedom are remarkable. Again and again, we have seen that the good-in-law rests not only on freedom to act or not to act, to act with due care or act negligently, to rise above or fall below the level of an external standard (what we may call "freedom of the minor premise"); in large measure, it also rests on the extraordinary additional freedom to legislate by one's own behavior and define the elevation of one's own personal standards (what we may call "freedom of the major premise"). These freedoms and moral powers belong to each of us, if only we exercise intelligence and wisdom and judgment. Our first moral duty is to think.

From ancient times, moralists have debated whether the generality of mankind are or are not too selfish to attain the practice of virtue. But this is not the really decisive question. Instead, it might have been more profitable to investigate whether the generality of men are too flabby of will, fitful of purpose, and torpid of wit to attain even the practice of selfishness. For as Bishop Butler wrote most astutely, "The thing to be lamented is, not that men have so great regard to their own good or interest in the present world, for they have not enough; but that they have so little to the good of others." [15]

PART THREE

Moral Guides in the American Law of Procedure

IX

The Forum

1. DUE PROCESS OF MORAL DECISION

> *"I present you with a Key. . . . A little Key may open a box, where lies a bunch of keys."*
> ROGER WILLIAMS, *A Key into the Language of America (London 1643)*

According to the lawyer's way of thought, this should prove the most important part of our study. The law of rights covers a province which the bar is required to share with laymen, at least in many parts and measures; but the law of procedure is felt almost universally to be the peculiar realm of the professionals. *How* to enforce a claim of right by invoking official action, *how* to set the machinery in motion with a reasonable expectation of just results, and *how* to use accepted general propositions so as to dispose satisfactorily of a concrete problem or controversy: these are the habitual and characteristic concerns of the lawyers. Our review of the law of rights disclosed, first, the different and multiple gradations of moral standards; second, the opportunities every one of us enjoys for individual moral creativeness; and third, the incessant moral duty to exercise intelligence, the fullest and best intelligence our minds and hearts can muster for the purpose. Now, taking these great propositions for granted, what can American law teach about the *method* to be followed in making a moral decision?

Though I have a key to offer for the reader's use, I respect him too much to go about choosing the doors he would desire to unlock with it. In this, as in all other aspects of practical judgment and wisdom, there are strict limits to what any human being can expect to communicate usefully to his fellows. Wisdom is neither dry nor cold but moist and warm; it resides not only in the head but throughout the body, in the veins, the glands, and the dispositions of nerve and muscle. It can never be reduced to a formula or transferred in so many words from a speaker to a listener. And for this impossibility we should rejoice; it is an indispensable condition of learning to be free. If the key I offer were an infallible one, lawyers trained in its use would never make the mistakes, utter the fatuous opinions, or commit the brutal injustices many of them do. And, on the other hand, if the key were quite useless as an aid to wiser and juster moral decisions, then civilized society could not possibly continue in existence. The key I present is "due process of moral decision."

The best part about "due process of moral decision" is that everyone of normal mental endowment can employ it. Thus, it may be claimed, nature has furnished the moral life with a distinctly democratic foundation—not in the sense of rule by arithmetical majority but in the more fundamental sense of the equality of human individuals. Thomas Jefferson used to say that one who wanted the answer to a moral problem should not consult a professor of ethics but a farmer. As Jefferson saw the model farmer of his day, he meant a man of experience in dealing with nature, business, and neighbors, of independent understanding stiffened by skeptical shrewdness, and of a cautiously optimistic faith. Our position is that there are absolutely no moral experts or authorities, whether they call themselves priests, ministers, rabbis, farmers, or professors. There are only levels and gradations of judgment, resolution, warmth, sensibility, and kindliness. The key of "due process" is for everyone's hand.

What is due process of moral decision? Can we set down a formal definition? (There are people who would not permit a lifeguard to save them from drowning until he had first given a satisfactory definition of the word "rescue.") The United States Supreme Court has refused again and again to define "due process of law," because what "due process" requires in one set of circumstances it obviously does not require in another and different set, say, an emergency. A precise formulation would only freeze the law before various unanticipated situations could be allowed for. We may find it profitable to follow the Supreme Court's example. First let us see how the methods we call "due process of law" regulate the conduct of criminal prosecutions in American courts.

Here are the main requirements of due process: We must not accuse anyone of an act violating some standard of behavior unless he could have ascertained the existence and meaning of the standard before he committed the act. We must let him know what he is accused of doing and must give him a fair opportunity to collect his evidence and then to present it. The judge and jury who hear his case must be unbiased and attentive; and, especially where the accusation is a grave one, the accused is entitled to the assistance of a counsel and advocate. Moreover, even after an accused has been found guilty, due process of law requires that we provide some sort of remedial procedure to uncover and correct any serious error that may have been committed in the trial of his case.

These are basic requirements of due process as applied in American law. Anyone who returns now to the preceding paragraph and reads it a second time will recognize that the requirements apply, point by point, to the formation of defensible judgments in the life of morals. The moral parallels are clear in almost every instance. The only exception, I believe, is the requirement that an accused have the assistance of a counsel or lawyer in his defense. While this one is no more important than the other rules of due process, it is a bit less obvious as a moral admonition and deserves to be explained.

The point here is that, under due process of law, if an accused has no means of procuring an advocate of his own, the judge must provide him with counsel by appointing a competent lawyer to present his evidence and plead his cause. In the moral forum, of course, the whole process takes place within a single psyche; the judge and jury operate internally. Sometimes the psyche includes not merely the judge and jury but the accused as well. But whether the accused be the same or a different personality, the judge must take care that he is provided with counsel to plead on his behalf. Otherwise there is no due process of moral decision.

The counsel, it goes without saying, is a subjective one, operating within the same mind that summoned him to service. His duties—like due process itself—depend on the nature and exigencies of the particular case, the severity of the moral issue, and the extent of the penalties that may be imposed. But in every case, without exception, it is his duty to remind the judge and jury of the accused's *generic* rights, I mean the rights of the accused under the moral constitution. For everyone can perceive his own uniqueness—that is easy. The miracle takes place (it is no less than a miracle) when imaginative projection uses genus as a bridge over which we pass to see and defend the irreducible uniqueness of another. Often, it is enough when the perception of the genus takes us to the threshold of the other's uniqueness; often there is so little beyond the doorway that we need only recognize that, though very unlike our own, it is nevertheless a private doorway. But all this requires an inner advocate's voice to point insistently toward the bridge of common genus, and to plead for fairness and understanding. Providing counsel for the accused is one of the marks of a cultivated moral forum.

If these are the methods men ought to follow in arriving at moral decisions, why do they err so often and why is due process violated continually in the forum of conscience? Due process is by no means easy to achieve; nothing excellent ever is. And among the chief adversaries to its application, there are four which impede almost all moral arbiters, including even the most conscientious. These adversaries can be labeled in the same way the early Greeks labeled the constituent elements of the physical universe: the adversaries of earth, air, fire, and water.

The adversary of *earth* stands for all the familiar manifestations of crass egoism which debase human beings and turn them into moral moles. Oh, that this adversary needed a lengthy and elaborate description to be understood!

Different in appearance and yet dangerously similar in substance is the adversary of *air*. This is the one that overcomes some of the best, subtlest, and most exalted minds. It manifests itself in a feeling of high elation which is accompanied by a sense of the unimportance, if not the unreality, of all transitory human conflicts and interests. In such a mood, the mundane drama seems to become a mere passing pageant, and the joys and sufferings of human beings are reduced to episodes in a stage play. Every truth is matched and spun about by an opposite truth. No one is quite right, no one quite wrong, nothing here on earth quite worth the spirit's preoccupation. Ralph Waldo Emerson knew the condition and described its cure. He noted in his Journal, "When the mountains begin to look unreal, the soul is in a high state, yet in an action of justice or charity things look solid again."

And then there is the adversary of *fire*, by which I mean the many passionate heats that rise to deflect and befog our vision. Who can withstand the logic of sexual attraction, the syllogistic force in the contours of a bosom, a belly, or a well-shaped thigh? Against adversaries like these, due process needs all the resolution a judge can gather.

Fourth, *water* represents still another species of inimical force. Water stands here for thought that meanders because it is not properly banked, or overflows in freshets because its pace has become incontinent. It stands for imprecise analysis, carelessness of inference, and resort to guesswork. Likewise, water may be taken to symbolize the excesses of sentimentality that dazzle a man's judgment with tears just when he needs clarity of moral vision.

In this sense, it would be no hyperbole to regard due process of moral decision as a victory of aspiring mind over earth, air, fire, and water. The victory is not available to complacent or slothful personalities. "None shall see the truth," Roger Williams wrote, "but the soul that loves it, and digs for it as for treasures of gold and silver, and is impartial, patient, and pitiful to the opposers." In moral decisions, if the truth comes at all, it does not come as a gift but as wages for strenuous digging.

How much is this victory of due process worth? Surely no sophisticated thinker will expect accuracy and certainty in moral inquiries of the degree we get—or believe we get—from the physical sciences. If what is generic in human beings facilitates the making of generalization. what is unique in them offsets it, and the most generic of human qualities is this very uniqueness. Thus statistical studies can help us, but only a little; empirical verification can test our assumptions, but only the ones that least need testing; and the values that really mark the problem as a moral one are somehow lost when we take the case out of a germ-laden world into an antiseptic and sterile clinic. Sometimes we can follow scientific method and repeat the experiment in order to observe results on the periphery of our moral problem. When we approach the moral nucleus, however, testing by means of repetition becomes completely impossible in most circumstances, because we cannot push a human being at will through identical and successive sets of choice, impulsion, and consequence. In the forum of conscience, therefore, the sciences have to serve as official consultants, informing the judge on contributory matters within their specialized competence. Rarely if ever can the scientist's answer amount to a complete disposition of a moral problem.

If not scientifically correct, are the results of due process correct at all? Most of us would be content with considerably less than scientific precision provided we knew the results would serve the practical purposes of our moral transactions. If a man can find his mouth in the dark, he can eat without an accurate anatomical chart. The question is whether we can trust the findings of due process to this modest extent or whether we are no better off with due process than we are without it.

In a series of brilliant juristic studies, Judge Jerome Frank has presented a critique which he calls "fact skepticism." Drawing on an opulence of data, he has shown how easily our trial courts can err in their most basic duty, which is finding the facts of the case.[1] Suppose the judge is wholly honest and unbiased; suppose the jury is the same; and suppose the testimony in court is entirely free of deliberate perjury. These are very ambitious suppositions, particularly the last one; yet even if we make all of them, we still find ourselves far removed from a reliable path to the truth of the matter. For, as Judge Frank has demonstrated, there are many other traps and snares along the way. Of these the most common are: (1) the witnesses' weak powers of observation; (2) the witnesses' weak powers of memory; (3) the witnesses' weak powers of narrating what they do remember; and (4) the judge's and jury's weak powers of observation, memory, and narration—since they too are called upon to sit as witnesses, i.e., witnesses of the trial proceedings.

For example, take the final appearance of Molière. Molière, who was not only one of the greatest dramatists of his or any other era but also a distinguished actor, had written a fine comedy called *Le Malade Imaginaire*. It was the fourth performance and he played the principal role. He died that evening. The best wits and brains of the most cultivated capital of the world were in attendance. Everyone appreciated the dramatic irony of the situation: the artist had imitated death so perfectly that death then and there had claimed him for her own. And yet, despite all these circumstances—circumstances almost unparalleled in their combined concentrative force—we do not know nor shall we ever know precisely what happened to Molière that evening. Some contemporary accounts say he collapsed during the performance, some after it was over; some say he coughed up great clots of blood on the stage, others say nothing of blood; and so on in respect of every dramatic detail.[2] What did occur on the illuminated stage before those attentive, highly sophisticated, and articulate spectators? If we cannot answer with positive assurance in Molière's case, we may well doubt we ever can.

In Judge Frank's scheme of thought, "fact-skepticism" has never been put forward as a warrant for despair or for cynicism. On the contrary, his writings present several optimistic proposals for the reform of American court procedure, so that findings of fact shall become less vulnerable to error. For in a court trial a man's life or liberty may be at stake, and an unjust conviction puts a dreadful blot on the whole community. At times, we know, men have been unjustly convicted, innocent men have been imprisoned or even executed. And due process of law has not prevented these instances from happening. An honest mistake of identification, for example, can hang an innocent man despite the most meticulous and fair-minded trial of his case.

Now, if the outcome of court trials were completely unreliable, we might as well close our courts—at least until we could find other, more dependable procedures. But no one carries the criticism to that extreme conclusion. Though opinions may vary concerning the scope of "fact-skepticism," everyone favors keeping the courts open and applying due process in them. Some very naive or arrogant judges, thrusting "fact-skepticism" aside, choose to believe their own fact-findings are always true. More and more American judges, however, do subscribe to "fact-skepticism" in greater or lesser degree. I think most of them would say, "It would be absurd to claim that I know whether the driver of that car was or was not going eighty miles an hour at the time of the accident. The evidence has been too conflicting to permit any such precision on my part. All I can conscientiously find is that he was driving unreasonably fast. Fortunately for me, that is all I need to find in order to dispose of the case. Probably there was perjury in the testimony on both sides; some of it the lawyers exposed on cross-examination. I have done my very best—my painstaking and experienced best—to ascertain what I could from watching the witnesses and attending closely to the evidence. Call the next case."

Turning back to the sphere of morals, we shall find that "fact-skepticism" will mark and influence our views in almost every remaining portion of this book. Sometimes the influence will be explicit; at other times, implicit. It will scarcely ever disappear. For we shall be discussing subjects like compromise (where "fact-skepticism" exerts a powerful impulsion) and the formation of rational inference (where, above all, there is constant and imperative need for "fact-skepticism"). But while "fact-skepticism" accompanies us from this point, so too does due process of moral decision.

We shall see that due process affords the only justification we can ever find for daring to exercise moral judgment. There are occasions when we possess no moral right to pass judgment at all; there are no occasions when we possess the right to pass judgment without due process. To presume to judge without due process is to sink to the level of the beasts, whereas to use due process and err by misadventure merely proves again that we are unable to operate like electronic machines.

2. THE FREEDOM TO DECIDE

It began as a small case and ended as a very great one. In September, 1670, William Penn (the heroic Quaker) and William Mead were tried at Old Bailey for agreeing to hold and for holding an unlawful assembly in Gracechurch Street, London. Things being as they were during the reign of Charles II, a quick and sure verdict of "guilty" was expected. The presiding magistrates consisted of the Mayor, the Recorder of London, and sundry Aldermen—more talented as bullies than as jurists. But Penn and Mead declined to be cowed. The evidence against them was transparently inadequate and they were not timid about asserting their procedural rights. Inspired by the example, the jury refused again and again to hold the prisoners guilty. The magistrates' threats and bellowings proved futile. Finally, the jurors showed their valor by announcing a defiant verdict of "not guilty." For this, the court fined them "40 marks per man and imprisonment till paid," and so the jurors were taken away to jail.

Several weeks passed with the fines unpaid and the jury

locked up in Newgate prison. In November, on the application of Edward Bushell, a juror whose manly conduct throughout the case deserved enduring fame, the king's judges made formal inquiry into the grounds for imprisoning the jury, and decided unanimously that the fine and incarceration were contrary to law. The jurors were liberated immediately. Chief Justice Vaughan said in the course of his opinion:

> I would know whether any thing be more common, than for two men students, barristers, or judges, to deduce contrary and opposite conclusions out of the same case in law? And is there any difference that two men should infer distinct conclusions from the same testimony? Is any thing more known than that the same author, and place in that author, is forcibly urged to maintain contrary conclusions, and the decision hard, which is in the right? Is any thing more frequent in the controversies of religion, than to press the same text for opposite tenets? How then comes it to pass that two persons may not apprehend with reason and honesty, what a witness, or many, say, to prove in the understanding of one plainly one thing, but in the apprehension of the other, clearly the contrary thing? Must therefore one of these merit fine and imprisonment, because he doth that which he cannot otherwise do, preserving his oath and integrity? And this often is the cause of the judge and jury. . . .
>
> A man cannot see by another's eye, nor hear by another's ear, no more can a man conclude or infer the thing to be resolved by another's understanding or reasoning.[3]

WHILE so many of the works of men pass quickly into oblivion, this great case remains fragrant and sweet-smelling after nearly three centuries. It was good English legal doctrine in the reign of Charles II, and it is good doctrine today in all quarters of the globe where due process of law is an established standard. "Bushell's Case," as it is rightly named, forms an inherited part of the American legal system.

It is important to understand that the bullying magistrates who tried Penn and Mead were, in all probability, thoroughly sincere and devoted public officials. There is no reason to doubt their desire to do justice as they saw it. From their point of view, trouble-makers like Penn and Mead *must* be guilty of fomenting disorder; therefore, Bushell and the others on the jury *must* be acting in sheer perversity when they resisted the court's instruction to bring in a verdict stating what every "right-minded" and "loyal" subject already knew. Whatever the sworn testimony in the case might or might not show, the men on the jury ought to demonstrate their respect for constituted authority. To these magistrates, a verdict of acquittal seemed tantamount to condoning the defendants' behavior.

Bushell's Case established for our law that sincerity alone is not enough. Sincerity of conviction cannot be enough to justify dispensing with due process. It is not enough because we simply cannot become so certain of "facts" represented to us that we may execute judgment on another person without affording him the benefit of inquiry by due process. Bushell's Case has erected due process in Anglo-American procedure on a firm and enduring foundation of fact-skepticism. It incessantly admonishes, "Lose your heat, little man. Others have been dogmatically certain before you, and they have been mistaken. Impossible in this instance? Perhaps. We need not discuss the question until you have appointed counsel for the accused, have prompted him to do his very best, and have attended patiently to his plea. There is no man so righteous that he can never err on the facts."

Moreover, Bushell's Case implies that we ought to rationalize and discipline the methods we employ to ascertain what are the true facts of the situation. The measure of factual accuracy men can hope to attain is too limited to warrant paying an unrestricted price for it in other moral values. Even if we could expect to learn more about the case before us by torturing the witnesses until we were satisfied they had told all they knew, nevertheless we should not be justified in buying the knowledge at such a price. Instead, we place, as it were, a ceiling-price on truth. We desire truth; truth is glorious to possess, use, and contemplate—but certainly not at an unlimited cost. There are, for example, confidences and decencies we cannot ask men to violate—though by doing so they would materially assist us in ascertaining the truth. Anyone who really understands the teachings of fact-skepticism will find it easier to respect social decencies and to adhere to the methods of due process. For testimony obtained by means of torture has all the unreliabilities of voluntary testimony—with the incentive superadded to commit perjury in order to escape suffering.

How far shall we carry the logic of fact-skepticism? Is there no such thing as a true report of the facts of a controversy? I believe that the more intelligent and self-critical American jurists would tend to agree thoroughly with George Santayana's description of the truth about a reported fact:

> *The experience which perhaps makes even the empiricist awake to the being of truth, and brings it home to any energetic man, is the experience of other people lying. When I am falsely accused, or when I am represented as thinking what I do not think, I rebel against that contradiction to my evident self-knowledge; and as the other man asserts that the liar is myself, and a third person might very well entertain that hypothesis and decide*

> *against me, I learn that a report may fly in the face of the facts. There is, I then see clearly, a comprehensive standard description for every fact, which those who report it as it happened repeat in part, whereas on the contrary liars contradict it in some particular. And a little further reflection may convince me that even the liar must recognize the fact to some extent, else it would not be* THAT *fact that he was misrepresenting; and also that honest memory and belief, even when most unimpeachable, are not exhaustive and not themselves the standard for belief or for memory, since they are now clearer and now vaguer, and subject to error and correction. That standard comprehensive description of any fact which neither I nor any man can ever wholly repeat, is the truth about it.*[4]

Now, if there is any single practical corollary of fact-skepticism that stands out more obviously than all the others, it is that capital punishment should be abolished in American law. Of course, there are many cogent moral reasons for abolishing the sentence of death. These we need not particularize here, because we are not attempting to develop a program of law reform. For our purpose it is enough that execution is the only completely irremediable punishment the law can inflict. Death alone can never be reversed, or compensated for, or mitigated. When society commits this unique kind of wrong, there is no one to whom it can go later on its knees to beg forgiveness if it should discover it has erred. For even when the right person is convicted, the court may still err as to the degree of his culpability and mental competence. Capital punishment would be hard to defend in a society of the omniscient; in a human, fallible society which grows continually more aware of the implications of fact-skepticism, it is quite intolerable. And in our private controversies which involve the exercise of moral judgment, the same considerations apply: to the extent that a private moral condemnation may inflict irreversible punishment or at least partly irreversible punishment, the person who assumes to act as judge should first chasten himself with the admonitions of fact-skepticism. The more fateful the risk, the more doubtful and humble the wise judge will be.

In many courts of the Anglo-American system, there are at least three degrees of what is called "the burden of proof." Where a person is sued on an ordinary civil claim (for example, for breach of contract), the case against him needs to be proved only by a "preponderance of the evidence." If, however, he is charged with malice, fraud, or some other form of wrongdoing which may entail extensive penalties, then even in a civil court the proof must rise to the level where it can be considered "clear and convincing." And should he be indicted and tried for committing a criminal offense, the proof of guilt must be "beyond a reasonable doubt."

Even proof beyond a reasonable doubt should not result in a moral condemnation when the individual judge who hears the case is so corrupt that he loses the right to decide it. Of course, this condition does not imply that the accused is innocent; it means merely that due process entitles him to a fair trial in an honorable court. To be sure, some individuals will remark with a sigh that an honorable court does not exist among sinful men. With soulful glances toward heaven and away from earth, such persons are prone to quote from Jesus' Sermon on the Mount, "Judge not, that ye be not judged." They are ensnared, I fear, by loose thinking and sentimentality, that is, by the "adversary of water."

If "Judge not" had been intended to mean we are in all cases too corrupt to pass moral judgment, it would have been an almost nonsensical admonition. It would have appeared strangely self-contradictory, because in that outrageous interpretation it would itself amount to a judgment of condemnation on the character of the whole human species. Jesus was too discerning to intend anything like this; he had pronounced too many judgments of his own and had endorsed too many which had been pronounced previously by other men. He did, I submit, intend precisely what he said: "Judge not, that ye be not judged. For with what judgment ye judge, ye shall be judged; and with what measure ye mete, it shall be measured to you again. . . . Thou hypocrite, first cast out the beam out of thine own eye; and then shalt thou see clearly to cast out the mote out of thy brother's eye." Or, as we have been saying in less inspired terms: Each instance of moral judgment is an act of moral legislation binding on the one who judges and legislates. Thus every judgment is a self-judgment of the judger. The only way not to be bound by the resulting legislation is to abstain from making the judgment. A forum should cleanse itself thoroughly before it presumes to pass judgment on anyone else. Yet, once all these teachings have been complied with, there remains not the slightest injunction against finding a mote in another person's eye if the mote is really and demonstrably there to be found.

For most people, I think, the real difficulty is not of the watery variety we have just been considering. Moral evaluation is much more often made difficult by our starting from rigid assumptions about the quality of man's nature. There is something so tempting about a generalized optimism that calls men "fundamentally good" or an equally generalized cynicism that finds them "fundamentally evil." It is an interesting fact that in almost every literary era a writer of limited talent could develop a reputation for sagacity simply by saying unfavorable things about common human traits. Anyone who expresses himself hopefully on the subject may be regarded as well-intentioned but rather naive. To be esteemed for insight, you must dwell with a certain crisp, amused coolness on the follies and vices of mankind. "Futility of futilities" will be your motto, to be pronounced urbanely and with detachment. You will teach men to enjoy the passing hour and forget the cares of the morrow. A few perverse souls, it is true, may suspect that if you believed quite thoroughly that all was futility, you would not take the trouble of saying so.

Why is it that we think so well of the pessimists and cynics? One can only speculate, but I believe it is because we are grateful to them for relieving our own guilts. The daily and hourly practices of civilized intercourse require us to behave at least superficially as though our neighbors were honest, benevolent, and peaceably disposed. Meanwhile we infer the inhibited vices and aggressions in their bosoms from our consciousness of similar impulsions in our own. Yet social convention forbids us to burn incense at the altar of the infernal deities; if we were to do so publicly, we should lose the confidence of our friends, our share in the benefits of solidarity, and eventually our credit at the bank and the grocery store. And so, smiling, we suspect as we suspect, yet continue to do as we do. Hence it is that when some writer stands boldly before that prohibited shrine and proclaims that therein reside the gods men really worship, we feel an extraordinary respect for his discernment. This may easily exceed the value of what he has discovered or related. There is a real danger that the show of candor on his part may dazzle us into a cynical belief that the infernal deities are the only ones who intervene actively in human affairs.

All these uncritical and undifferentiated stereotypes about the nature of mankind ought to be put on the shelf. They become mere impediments and nuisances when an intelligent person, finding himself involved in a position of conflict, looks for the moral decision which will best resolve his unique and concrete problem of choice. If a generalization about the moral quality of men can have any conceivable utility, then let us leave it that men are disposed to be good and evil and mediocre in widely varying degrees under diverse, unpredictable circumstances. Let us fix our attention on the evidence in the case. For stereotypes, whether philanthropic or misanthropic, act like bullies in the same sense as the magistrates on the bench at the trial of Penn and Mead. An alert and independent jury will recognize them for what they are, disregard their claims, and proceed to exercise genuine freedom of judgment.

There is an ancient legend that illustrates this important point. It seems that when God was about to create the first man, the angels in heaven formed themselves into parties or factions. One group approved of creating man, the other strongly opposed. Mercy said, "Let him be created, for he will be merciful." Truth said, "Let him not be created, for he will be all lies." Righteousness urged, "Let him be created, for he will perform righteous deeds." Peace replied, "Let him not be created, for he will be full of contentiousness."

What then did the Holy One do, according to this legend? He is said to have done two things. First, to the amazement of the ministering angels, He took Truth, His own seal, and flung him to the earth. Then, He said to the ministering angels, "Why do you continue to dispute? Man is already made."

There are many meanings to be uncovered in this story; and surely one of them is that even the angels speak in vain when they utter universal stereotypes about man. Even the angel of Truth proved unworthy when he said man would be all lies, for there could not be truth in saying "all."

Let us suppose now that we have liberated ourselves from the control of these bullies—the judicial bullies who fulminate from the bench, and the stereotype bullies who seek to subdue our critical faculties. Can the law indicate further procedures which may be followed to advantage in the making of moral decisions? I suggest it can. Most of us are familiar with the fact that the law of evidence in American courts is exceedingly technical, with a wealth of special rules and fine distinctions. Many Americans visualize a court trial as a scene where the lawyers are continually rising to object to some item of evidence and to declaim the magical incantation, "Irrelevant, incompetent, and immaterial." What is this "Irrelevant, incompetent, and immaterial"? Has it any useful reference for purposes of wise moral decision?

Most men are able to grasp what is meant by "irrelevant," however much their understanding of the term may be contradicted by their practice. At least when some other person poses a point that has no logical connection with the issue, we show we are capable of identifying and resisting irrelevancy. Hence the mystification in the law of evidence derives principally from the other two terms, "incompetent and immaterial."

Every item of evidence which is logically relevant to the case possesses some degree of materiality; but if the degree should happen to be so slight that time and effort would be wasted in considering it, the item may be excluded from consideration on the ground that it is too unimportant, it can prove too little that is not already known; in a word, it is "immaterial." Materiality measures the extent to which we might feel willing to rely on the evidence. It deals with the question, "Is this evidence strong and firm enough in relation to the remainder of the proof to assist in supporting the weight of such and such a decision which would entail such and such damages or penalties?" Once it is decided that an item has relevance, the chief *moral* concern will be with its materiality.

In a law court, once we hold that a piece of evidence is "incompetent," we treat it with the same disdain as though it were irrelevant and exclude it completely. "Hearsay evidence" is the best-known example of what American lawyers mean by "incompetent." Under the rule against hearsay evidence, Jones will not be permitted to testify that Brown killed Smith when the only basis he has for his statement is that White told Black, who told him (Jones) that Brown had done so in White's presence. This sort of testimony, which amounts to little more than gossip, is not allowed to reach the jury at all.

But in the moral forum within the individual psyche, it is almost impossible to exclude incompetent evidence from consideration. Though we can perhaps close our eyes to it, nature has not equipped us to close our ears. If we must first examine the item in order to decide whether it is competent or incompetent, then we have learned of its existence and can hardly succeed in banishing it altogether. As a practical matter, we have let it into our consciousness. Thus we cannot imitate the protected position of the jury in regard to "hearsay" or other kinds of incompetent evidence.

The working solution in the moral forum is to convert questions of the competence of evidence into questions of its materiality. Suppose a statement is a mere bit of hearsay, or suppose a paper bears a man's name but there is no proof he composed or signed it. In law, the items would lack competence; in morals, what they lack is materiality. We cannot avoid knowing about them, but we can avoid extending credence to them. We can insist that the hearsay statement be corroborated or that the handwriting on the document be verified. This would only show a proper respect for the integrity of our own moral judgment.

Even in the law courts some classes of hearsay evidence will be admitted. These exceptional classes of hearsay are the ones that pass the dual test of *necessity* and *trustworthiness.* In other words, hearsay evidence may be considered competent if long experience shows that there is no better way of discovering the circumstances and that the total situation tends to vouch for the truthfulness of this class of hearsay statement. For example, no one knows the date of his own birth except from hearsay, and the same is true of many other facts about pedigree and relations that we learn from family conversations. These statements are deemed competent evidence mainly because experience leads us to expect them to be trustworthy. The same criteria can be applied to evaluate hearsay evidence in the forum of moral judgment. We may test its materiality by inquiring: (1) Does this particular hearsay statement acquire some degree of materiality out of sheer necessity, because no more direct evidence can be found? (2) Does it acquire materiality because there are especially cogent reasons to vouch for the sincerity and reliability of the source? These are good, probing questions, calculated to foster the search for factual truth and safeguard us against reckless or passionate credulity.

When we come to examine the psychology of deciding, we can hardly fail to notice that there is something about it that is distinctly feminine, or at least more obvious and explicit among women than men. There is something every woman appears to know about the process of making up one's mind and forming a decision. Perhaps I may put the secret this way: We discover what we want mainly by confronting and rejecting the available alternatives. The primary conviction consists in recognizing what one does *not* desire or accept or approve. Having identified this, one proceeds, by corollary, to make an affirmative commitment.

But there is more to what every woman knows about the decisional process. We discover our decision by means of confronting the alternatives, well enough; but this process, if confined to a single psyche, may become so entangled in the conflicts of competing subjective impulses that often nothing results but confused indecision. Endless debate with one's self can lead to a state of inanition—the inner forces come so nearly in balance that none seems capable of forming a decisive structure.

What occurs to catalyze the process is very simple and familiar. Some other person is asked to express a choice. He or she does. Forthwith, the inner structure falls into shape, in direct or inverse response to the other's presentation. The advocate outside has accomplished what the contending voices within had failed to do—he has won the case or has unwittingly exposed all its weakness. The choice I hear from outside I know is mine, or I know is not mine. In any case, once I have heard it, I feel certain I know. The inner judge gains precisely the detachment it needs to distinguish the harmony from the discord.

But these are the culminative steps, which should be held steadfastly in suspense until the completion of due process in the inquiry. To seek the final structure before one has analyzed every material part of the evidence is to go begging for alms of error. In effect, freedom to decide amounts to little more than freedom to apply due process and stand responsible for the outcome. This is man's dignity.

3. THE SKILLS OF COMPROMISE

In 1952 a profound dilemma confronted the Justices of the United States Supreme Court. Racial segregation in public schools (i.e., schools maintained by states, cities, or counties) dated back to the beginnings of public education in the United States. Segregation was gradually abolished in most states of the Union, but it remained a uniform and established practice in the schools of the South. By 1952 the wickedness of the practice had become evident to large numbers of white and non-white Americans in every part of the country.

In an 1896 decision the Supreme Court had found nothing unconstitutional in "separate but equal" facilities for whites and non-whites; but from 1938 on, through a variety of oblique references in other cases, the Justices had intimated that their view of the matter had changed and that the days of segregated public schools were numbered. It became increasingly clear that the Court was prepared to prohibit segregation as violating the Constitutions's guarantee of "equal protection of the laws" to all persons. When, therefore, a contention to that effect was brought before the Court in 1952 by certain Southern Negroes on behalf of their children and of others similarly situated, the big problem was not WHETHER *to declare segregation unconstitutional, but* HOW *to proceed to do so. For there was no secret about the impassioned—not to say menacing—opposition of state and local authorities and of substantial segments of the populace in the Southern states. The educational structure and deep-seated habits of a whole region were involved. Yet did not logic and law dictate that the enforcement of segregation must be either constitutional or unconstitutional? And if segregation was held unconstitutional, must it not be outlawed as fast as a pen could inscribe the signature on a decree? Such was the logical dilemma facing the Court. There did not seem to be any possibility of a middle ground.*

Two years passed, during which additional signs and portents were provided to indicate that the old rule of "separate but equal" was about to be discarded. By the time the decision was finally announced on May 17, 1954, the public mind had been so well prepared that there was little room for surprise or for the superfluous resentment which surprise can cause in circumstances of this sort. True, a few less sophisticated observers did express astonishment—at the Justices' extraordinary unanimity, for there was only one voice heard from the bench, the voice of the Chief Justice on behalf of the entire Court. What the Chief Justice said showed implicitly that the Court had discovered a middle ground between the constitutionally valid and the unconstitutionally void.

As one would expect, the bulk of the Court's opinion was devoted to demonstrating that segregation was unconstitutional and that various earlier statements to the contrary were, for one reason or another, either irrelevant or no longer binding on the Court. Thus, on principle segregation was condemned to death and executed. On the other hand, in actuality, how was the difficult and complex transition from segregated to unsegregated schools to be effected? At the end of the Court's opinion the threefold solution was disclosed: (1) all the interested parties—not merely the prevailing parties—were invited to participate in recommending and framing a suitable line of procedure and were allowed several more months for their heads to cool; (2) the Court indicated that the procedure to be adopted must be flexible enough to conform to varying local needs and conditions; and, most important by far, (3) the Justices revealed a clear preference for "an effective GRADUAL *adjustment." In other words, between the constitutional and the unconstitutional, the Court created a middle space by inserting the wedge of* DURATION.[5]

LIKE other political democracies, the United States provides an excellent setting to study the skills of compromise. In a free society, we demonstrate how autonomous we are mainly by shaping our own compromise choices to reflect our personal standards and values. From day to day, our experiences remind us that we cannot make a moral decision without sacrificing at least part of one desire for another. It becomes second nature to surrender today's good in order to insure tomorrow's, or to accept a portion of what we want in order not to lose the whole of it. Though by means of wise decisions we may succeed in maximizing the good that is preserved, some measure of loss is virtually certain to result. Thus it becomes a mark of civic maturity to practice the arts of accommodation.

Lawyers employ these arts in every detail of their professional work. Sometimes, it is true, they seem to overdo the virtue and put an excessive premium on getting matters settled and extinguishing controversy. Perhaps their preoccupation with the peace and order of society tends to make most of them more accommodating than we can approve. However that may be, the bar does deserve special credit for devising model techniques for the attainment of compromises. The more sophisticated lawyers are accustomed to look on rules of law not as eternal truths but only as adjustments established rather tentatively in order to compose conflicting social interests. In this way, they learn to anticipate the changes that are sure to emerge from time to time. And—as Max Weber pointed out—when the trend of social evolution in a specific field is not yet precise enough to warrant pronouncing a rule of law which might draw a sharp line, the Anglo-American system strives to keep the adjustment adaptable and elastic by submitting cases of this kind to the jury instead of the judge. Our legal machinery continually develops ingenious new methods to foster the spirit of compromise. In the Children's Courts, Fair Employment Practices Commissions, and Labor Relations Boards, we have institutionalized our hopes of conciliation and cooperation.

The most imposing accomplishments would be found in the area of adjustment which has always belonged to the lawyers, that is, the settling of cases out of court. Exact statistics do not exist, but it is safe to say that over half of the controversies that could be taken to court never are litigated. Moreover, even where suit is begun, probably not more than five per cent of the cases are tried and determined finally by the courts. Our judicial systems could not operate at all if the skills of compromise did not relieve them of most of their potential business.

Our principal case, which holds that racial segregation is unconstitutional in public schools, will not be classified in the law digests under the rubric of "compromise." Yet, properly understood, the disposition of the case constitutes a compromise of the most enlightening kind. It is a compromise in terms of the *temporal* dimension.

There is an important distinction between "time when" and "time during which." The former is the familiar time reference in moral discussions, particularly discussions that have a relativistic turn. The "time when" a moral transaction occurs forms part of the aggregate background or milieu in which it is set. We are likely to evaluate the transaction against the total background, which of course is spatial and cultural as well as temporal.

But the duration or "time during which" a transaction occurs is one of the critical dimensions of the transaction itself. Frequently its inmost nature is determined by how long it lasts. A good that evaporates too soon is hardly worth while to us; an evil that passes quickly enough seems more like a shadow or a salutary warning. A metaphor that lingers can become a creed. Stretch out a pleasant appetite and you may have a ravenous lust. If an event possesses any human reference, one of the factors interpreting its value is its duration. Duration is a moral dimension.

For this reason, duration can be manipulated, as the Supreme Court manipulated it in the School Segregation decision, to insert what amounts to a wedge between *either* and *or*. Without the temporal dimension, the opposing categories ("valid" or "void") seemed inexorable. By working with the implement of duration, a gradual tapering-off may be devised, conforming on the one hand to the change in regional mores and on the other hand to the Negroes' generic rights. Radical adjustment requires the use of time, which may be made into an ally or an enemy, depending on the experience and judgment one brings to the occasion. For this reason individuals who can think only in terms of "immediately" and "forever" will not acquire the skill.

When we seek to reach a compromise, it is not so much our interest in the pending conflict but rather the other interests of our existence—the ongoing and as yet intact ones—that we are most at pains to protect. Experience points out incessantly that, no matter how absorbing today's climax may appear when it is confronting us, tomorrow will follow in due course, bringing its own set of personal rounds and household duties. Mature people learn to expect anticlimax and provide for it. Though it be sadly true that the father of the family has come home drunk and beaten the children, the beds must nevertheless be made. And, we know, the very mourners who swear at noon that they can never touch food again are the first ones to sniff the evening fragrances that drift in from the kitchen. If we acquire any single bit of wisdom from the day-to-day relationships of the family home, it is that through compromise and accommodation one may prepare as best one can for the arrival of assorted anticlimaxes.

Now for the techniques. In Francis Bacon's wily little essay *Of Negotiating,* we are told, "It is generally better to deal by speech than by letter; and by the mediation of a third than by a man's self." This is concrete advice and also very sound. There is considerably more to Bacon's recommending "mediation of a third" than he set down in this cursory essay of his.

For one thing, in every process of negotiation, no matter

how rabid the claimant may feel, it is indispensable that he remove himself a few inches from the claim and look at it for a moment from the vantage point of a third person. Thus, if only for the moment, he may achieve some semblance of detachment and some approach to impartial evaluation. It is his opportunity to view and understand the other side of the case. Biased though his view may be by resentment or selfish calculation, it is an opportunity none the less that only negotiation could evoke. Negotiation invites fact-skepticism to set to work, and fact-skepticism in turn prompts a re-examination, if not of the nature of the injury, then at least of the damages actually incurred.

In order even to begin the process of negotiation, the claimant must pass some sort of tentative judgment on the persuasiveness of his own evidence, the force of his adversary's defenses or counterclaims, and the total impact the case would probably have on the mind of an impartial third person. These necessities may serve to chasten the claimant when no other influence can.

In the course of this experience, a claimant may suddenly discover that the greater part of his excitation comes from believing that a thing has value equal to one's desire for it. Most of the things we consider desirable are held to be so only because we do in fact desire them, because we happen to have attached our will to securing them, and possibly because the attachment has been reinforced by someone else's opposition. It is the greatest insight of Oriental philosophy to have seen that an individual can school his concupiscent will to turn and detach itself from its objects. Doing so, the will may be liberated to pursue ends which are enduringly useful and valuable. What is it that causes the majority of human conflicts? Is it the essential value of the thing contested? Clearly not, for we know there are amicable means of sharing either our lacks or the goods we possess. In most instances, it is rather a clash of one attached will against another attached will, a collision between two egoisms on the rampage. But should either of them pause long enough to criticize and evaluate the object at stake in the conflict, he may eventually turn aside from the whole sorry scene, bemused perhaps that he had ever thought it worthy of his heat. And if fact-skepticism does not take his analysis quite so far, it may at least bring him to strike hands on a reasonable price of compromise and to resume friendly business or personal relations with his erstwhile adversary.

The adversary too deserves close examination. Somehow we find the process of negotiation requires us to think of him in a new perspective. Our wrath has reduced him from a human being to an abhorred, perverse, and spitefully motivated object. Now it is necessary for us, in some degree at least, to re-personalize the adversary. Otherwise there will be no hope of locating a common ground, a corner where our mind and his may consent to meet. And so, as Bacon observes in most Machiavellian terms, we must study the man with great care. "Men discover themselves," he says, "in trust, in passion, at unawares, and of necessity, when they would have somewhat done and cannot find an apt pretext. If you would work any man, you must either know his nature and fashions, and so lead him; or his ends, and so persuade him; or his weakness and disadvantages, and so awe him; or those that have interest in him, and so govern him." One must understand him not merely as the occupant of an adverse position but as a total personality. And to negotiate successfully one must treat him as such.

This implies that the skilled negotiator will indulge in a certain measure of prolixity and even of digressiveness. He is prepared to devote time, patience, and much meandering talk. There are faces to be saved, doubts to be artfully insinuated, and little witticisms to be dropped at the expense of human nature and particularly of irreconcilable quarrelers. If the conflict is over dollars, the offsetting human values must be made vivid; if the conflict is over offended pride and injured sensibilities, the insignificance of the dollar consequences must be suggested. To express these things curtly or brusquely would be worse than not saying them at all. To develop them slowly and discursively shows a proper respect for the firmness of the opponent's principle, for only firm principle would require so much discussion to become relaxed. Meanwhile, for obvious reasons, the skilled negotiator endeavors to steer the negotiations away from the weak spots in his own position and the lacerated spots in his opponent's.

All this requires a tactful and patient perception of "time during which" the negotiations should be conducted. And to it must be coupled an equally active sense of the "time when" they may best be initiated. Rabelais tells us about a father who had won a reputation for settling controversies among the people of his vicinity. His son then tried his hand at the same pursuit and failed completely. Deflated by the series of failures, the puzzled son finally came to ask his father for guidance. Then the secret was disclosed: The father had always abstained from intervening or suggesting a composition until the conflicting parties had fought each other so long at law, had spent so much money on the litigation, and had suffered so many intermediate checks and disappointments in court that, in contrast to their initial bravado, they had become ready, nay anxious, to escape with even a shred of pride and a modest residue of cash. All the son's failures had been due to having intervened in the early stages, while the blood was still running too hot. As Bacon concluded, "In all negotiations of difficulty, a man may not look to sow and reap at once; but must prepare business, and so ripen it by degrees." Nevertheless, remarks like these are to be taken as pointers, not hard and fast rules. There is no substitute for an alert sense of timing which responds to the individual affair, for in many instances if accommodation is to be effected at all, it should be broached forthwith.

Though timing is important, it is by no means the only skill that is needed. For when the propitious moment arrives, one must be prepared to propose some method or medium of settlement which will accord with the nature of the controversy. The history of every mature legal system illustrates our point. The goal of the search is to discover some basis of sharing or compensation which, in the specific time and culture, can be regarded as commensurable with the nature of grievance. "An eye for an eye," which appears to us like a barbaric maxim, was in its day merely a primitive rule of commensurability. It marked a substantial advance over the earlier practices, which were "a life for an eye" and "the lives of a whole tribe for an eye." Eventually, the law reached the level of evolution where money-damages were employed to compensate the injured person and his family. In this way they would be induced to abstain from taking vengeance in violent forms. The evolutionary background helps to explain why our present legal system seems at times to be offering money in exchange for goods with which, we feel deeply, money should not be made commensurable—goods like affection and reputation. But, aside from these exceptional situations, there is no questioning the social need for some kind of crude commensurable—if possible an arithmetical one, like money or working hours or acres of land—to supply the medium for negotiation of compromises.

There are compromises that may be called "linear" and others that may be called "quadratic." A linear compromise occurs when Merchant Jones claims Manufacturer Smith has broken a contract, causing Jones so much loss in expected profits. This is a matter of the same medium (dollars) from beginning to end and therefore the easiest type of compromise to develop.

The quadratic compromise may involve a division of spheres of influence between two imperial powers, or a division of territories between two corporate monopolies, or an agreement, express or implicit, between husband and wife that he will manage the office and she the home. The medium of compromise appears to be geographic in these instances, but spatial division is intended only as a method for the allotment of interests, resources, and authorities. Perhaps there is also, under our system, a cubic kind of compromise, which may be applied to the complex distribution of powers between Church and State. Be that as it may, once one of the parties to a controversy begins to search for an appropriate commensurable, his attitude has at least registered an advance on the road to accommodation. He begins to look away from the grievance with its roots in the past. Consequently, at that point the discussion may lose some of its invective and turn toward the practical advantages of an adjustment. The commensurables indicate just what the opponents ought to be weighing and debating if they are to arrange an eventual compromise.

Here we should take notice of a most important step in the negotiation of compromise. I shall call it "the forming of brackets." When a means of commensuration has been discovered, such as dollars or hours, the next stage consists in establishing an arithmetical bracket to localize the deliberations. It is astonishing to observe how much has been gained when a specific, arithmetical minimum of demand and maximum of offer have been accepted by the parties for the framework of their discussion. Generally, the obligor who makes an initial offer must exercise considerable tact and subtlety in order to lead the claimant into accepting it implicitly as the floor of the bracket for their further discussions. And although the claimant, on his part, may be disposed to place his minimum demand sky-high, he too will pause to consider whether a lower figure would not have a better prospect of acceptance for the ceiling of the bracket. In the early stages of negotiation, these lower and upper limits must be introduced with great delicacy and an air of irresolute tentativeness. Once introduced—no matter how arbitrary they may have seemed previously—they form a firm and defined frame. If a compromise eventuates, it will not pass above the ceiling or below the floor; more than that, it is rather likely to gravitate to a point not far from midway between them. By "the forming of brackets" the grievance and resistance, originally poles apart, acquire fixed arithmetical limits.

This process is so beneficial to the welfare of society that the courts do their utmost to foster it. It is the law's policy to encourage settlements. For example, in order to provide a relaxed and private atmosphere for the conduct of negotiations, the courts will generally refuse to admit evidence of the making of an offer of compromise. Thus a party is enabled to make an offer without fearing that it will later be used in court as an admission or concession of liability on his part. In moral as well as legal controversies, this policy of tolerance is well worth emulating.

When we come to consider the kind of rhetoric that expedites a process of negotiation, there are two maxims that seem to me most useful to apply. First, whenever possible, the person speaking should advance his contentions in a representative capacity, that is, on behalf of some person or group other than himself.[6] Second, whenever possible, the speaker should endeavor to represent interests and principles which include the adversary's interests and principles. The first of these maxims introduces a rational, more detached and impersonal element into the debate; it cools the discussion by substituting an unoffending abstract right in the place of a personal enemy. The second maxim goes farther: it appeals from one of the interlocutor's aspects to another of his aspects, for example, from his selfishness to his generosity, or from his outraged sensibilities to his impulses of grace. Francis Bacon said it is better to employ "the mediation of a third," and certainly it is better if the "third" can be enlisted, as though for a civil war, from among the aspects and interests of the interlocutor himself.

We may illustrate these various devices by taking a very ancient and celebrated instance of negotiation—the one related in chapter 18 of the Book of Genesis. There, as we are told, the Lord has heard that the sinfulness of the Sodomites is very grievous. Nevertheless, furnishing a divine example of the use of due process, He does not adjudge before He has investigated the facts. He says rather, "I will go down now, and see whether they have done according to the cry of it, which is come unto me; and if not, I will know." Then the following colloquy is reported to have taken place between the Lord and Abraham:

> *And Abraham drew near, and said, Wilt thou also destroy the righteous with the wicked? Peradventure there be fifty righteous within the city: wilt thou also destroy and not spare the place for the fifty righteous that are therein? That be far from thee to do after this manner, to slay the righteous with the wicked: and that the righteous should be as the wicked, that be far from thee: Shall not the Judge of all the earth do right? And the Lord said, If I find in Sodom fifty righteous within the city, then I will spare all the place for their sakes.*
>
> *And Abraham answered and said, Behold now, I have taken upon me to speak unto the Lord, which am but dust and ashes: Peradventure there shall lack five of the fifty righteous: wilt thou destroy all the city for lack of five? And he said, If I find there forty and five, I will not destroy it.*
>
> *And he spake unto him yet again, and said, Peradventure*

there shall be forty found there. And he said, I will not do it for forty's sake.

And he said unto him, Oh let not the Lord be angry, and I will speak: Peradventure there shall thirty be found there. And he said, I will not do it if I find thirty there.

And he said, Behold now, I have taken upon me to speak unto the Lord: Peradventure there shall be twenty found there. And he said, I will not destroy it for twenty's sake.

And he said, Oh let not the Lord be angry, and I will speak yet but this once: Peradventure ten shall be found there. And he said, I will not destroy it for ten's sake. And the Lord went his way, as soon as he had left communing with Abraham: and Abraham returned unto his place.

Several of the skills we have listed can be seen at work in this narrative, which presents a particularly effective illustration of the forming of brackets.[7] It is a pleasure to observe the tentativeness with which Abraham fixes his end of the bracket at fifty; the deft method he adopts to subtract only five at a time until he has ascertained his Interlocutor's reaction, whereupon he shifts to ten; the persistent emphasis he puts on the cogency of the principles he represents as contrasted with his personal insignificance; and, above all, the deliberately prolix way he appeals to one of his Interlocutor's attributes, saying, "Shall not the Judge of all the earth do right?" In all, it is a masterwork of negotiation.

What reflections the Lord may have entertained on leaving Abraham we are not told. It is possible that, if the story were to go a bit farther, it might end with some such commentary as this: "It shall be permitted them to regard Me as omnipotent, and likewise to regard Me as their heavenly Father: but it shall not be permitted them to regard Me as both omnipotent and Father in the same thought or the same deed."

X

In the Mind of the Judge

1. INFERENCE AND EVIDENCE

BEFORE the enactment of reform measures under the administration of Franklin D. Roosevelt, bank failures played a recurrent and tragic role on the American scene. During good times as well as bad, every year reported its sum of closed banking houses, ruined depositors, and—in too many instances—callously unconcerned directors. In an effort to cope with these problems, the State of Georgia had provided in its Banking Act that "Every insolvency of a bank shall be deemed fraudulent, and the president and directors shall be severally punished by imprisonment and labor in the penitentiary for not less than one year nor longer than ten years; provided that the defendant in a case arising under this section may repel the presumption of fraud by showing that the affairs of the bank have been fairly and legally administered . . ."

Another section of the Georgia Banking Act, added in 1919, declared that a bank shall be deemed insolvent (1) when it cannot meet its liabilities as they become due, (2) when the cash value of its assets is insufficient to pay its liabilities, or (3) when it fails for thirty days to maintain the reserve required by law and directed by the State Superintendent of Banks.

Construing the Banking Act, the Supreme Court of Georgia ruled that bank presidents or directors were entitled to over-

come the presumption of fraud either by showing that they had administered the affairs of their bank carefully and honestly or by showing other circumstances which would rebut the presumption. For example, if they could prove the insolvency was caused by an unexpected panic or by some officer's speculations for which they were in no way responsible, they must be acquitted.

W. D. M—— was president and director of a Georgia bank that failed in 1926. He was prosecuted for fraud and convicted under the presumption established by the statute. The Georgia Supreme Court having affirmed the conviction, he appealed to the United States Supreme Court. M—— claimed the presumption created by the Georgia statute was so arbitrary that it deprived him of due process of law. The United States Supreme Court sustained his contention unanimously and set his conviction aside.[1]

At the outset, it seems only humane to warn any and all simplistic readers, particularly those of a Marxist persuasion, that this case should be approached with care. On its face, it appears so inviting to the simplist that he is very likely to rush into a trap, exclaiming, "Aha, a typical decision of class domination. The Supreme Court of the United States thrusts the poor depositors aside and vindicates the defaulting banker. What else would be expected under a capitalistic regime?" And if it is pointed out to him that the judgment included the outstanding liberal Justices Holmes, Brandeis, and Stone in its unanimity, he may go on to insist all the more vehemently that liberals are at bottom no different from the remainder of the capitalists. Nevertheless, compassion prompts us to caution him.

For where would his attempt at dialectic lead him? Economic determinism can be a very sharp instrument—that much one must grant. But the edges are equally sharp on both of its sides, and our simplistic neighbor may inflict serious harm on himself if he plays with this case in a reckless way. Is he prepared, for example, to defend the position that the Supreme Court of Georgia, which had upheld the statutory presumption and M——'s conviction under it, must have been motivated by opposition to capitalists? Even if he is, it will not serve. For in addition he must concoct some sort of deterministic explanation for the main precedent which the United States Supreme Court followed as controlling in M——'s case. The precedent,[2] decided in 1911, arose out of an Alabama statute which had likewise created a presumption of intention to defraud—to be imputed not to a banker but to any laborer who might borrow from his employer and later fail to repay the loan. As if purposely devised to make matters more embarrassing for our simplist, the 1911 case was decided in favor of an humble, unskilled worker, an Alabama Negro by the name of Alonzo Bailey. In recent years the Court has not only reaffirmed but substantially extended the holding in Bailey's case. The legal narrative has nothing in it to comfort or encourage a disciple of simplism.

On the contrary, whenever a legislature adopts by law some rigid rule of presumption, it only underlines the importance of analyzing our habits and practices of inference more thoroughly and more skeptically. Legitimate evidence is often difficult to assemble; in complicated matters like the administration of a bank it may be more difficult; in highly subjective matters like the intention to perpetrate a fraud it may be most difficult. The easy—the lazy—solution consists in putting the burden of explanation and exculpation on the accused person. Accuse him in general and let him try to defend in particular; accuse him in the newspapers or on television and let him try to defend when he finally appears in court; accuse him often enough and evidence may be dispensed with entirely, for his name will have become linked with guilt beyond hope of extrication. And if he should happen to belong to an unpopular group—as bankers did in the 1920's when so many of them behaved like lords of the universe—the presumption will spare the community a great deal of tedious investigation and painful analysis. With the crutch of the presumption to assist their progress, prosecutors, judges, and juries would have so much less bother.

But as we have seen, the judges may resolve to spurn the use of a crutch. If they can find no rational connection between fact A, which is duly proved by proper evidence, and fact B, which they are asked to infer from it, the legislature's attempt to compel the making of the inference will fall as unconstitutional. In Bailey's case, for example, fact A was that Bailey had borrowed the money and subsequently had not repaid it; fact B, which the Court was expected to infer, was that, at the very moment Bailey received the loan, he was planning to defraud his employer by not returning it; and on that inference Bailey would be fined and sent to imprisonment at hard labor, half of his earnings to go to the county and the other half to the employer who had advanced the loan! Yet everyone knows that failure to repay a loan implies nothing dishonest in a borrower's intent at the time he received the money. In fact, it is just because most borrowers do intend honestly to perform their obligations that business and banking are practicable at all.

If there are models of rational analysis to be found anywhere in the American community, surely the judicial bench is the place we are accustomed to look for them. In our society, it is of the essence that a judge be adept at probing the evidence, digging beneath the surface of the case, discovering the vein of truth which others may have overlooked. Like many other peoples ancient and modern, Americans feel a particular confidence in their judges' capacity to see through illusions to the true circumstances that lie beneath and beyond. It is not so much a matter of scholarship in expounding the law as of wisdom in finding the facts. What, after all, was King Solomon's famous judgment, when he devised a way to distinguish the true mother from the pretender? He made no new rule of substantive law; quite the contrary, he took it for granted that the natural mother, once identified, would be entitled to the child's custody. His virtuosity consisted in bringing forth the decisive fact.

There are similar stories about wise judges and their astonishing little tricks in the mythology of many other peoples. In the process of separating good from evil, no endowment is so desirable as this almost divine gift of ripping through the appearances and revealing the hidden truth. In point of fact, according to some highly respectable authorities, when the serpent tempted Eve in the Garden of Eden and urged her to eat the fruit of the Tree of Knowledge, it did not say—as we have been taught—that "Ye shall be as gods, knowing good and evil." Not at all. It said rather, "Ye shall be as magistrates or judges, knowing good and evil." [3] If this is really what the serpent intended to say on that momentous occasion, it was paying a greater tribute to the discernment of our judges than most of them would be willing to accept, even from such a celebrated source. But beneath the compliment's hyperbole there remains a considerable core of truth. For whoever desires to "know good and evil" in a morally useful sense must strive earnestly to "be as magistrates or judges" are obliged to be. In other words, he or she will test and probe the evidence; and to that purpose will put away the crutch of irrational inference and the complementary crutch of vulgar prejudice that indolent minds love to lean upon. Which is not to deny that there are rational inferences as well as irrational ones.

Under our system, the prosecution has the burden of proving every legal element of guilt beyond a reasonable doubt. This burden, which we summarize popularly by referring to a "presumption of innocence," never shifts to the shoulders of the accused. From the beginning to the end it is the prosecution's burden to prove guilt, never the accused's burden to prove innocence. But in the process of presenting its case, the prosecution is not limited to what it can demonstrate by direct, immediate, eye-witness testimony. Inferences that accord with reason, common sense, and normal experience may, and almost always do, supply some portion of the proof of guilt. For example, where in a prosecution for murder the state must establish beyond a reasonable doubt that the accused killed *deliberately*, it may fulfill this part of its burden of proof by showing that the accused had recently threatened to kill the person he did kill. From the threats the jury may rationally infer that he acted deliberately, and if he offers no excuse or explanatory evidence, the inference will become not only rational but highly probable.

It seems fitting now to ask whether the presumptive inference of fraud in banker M——'s case was so very irrational. The High Court's decision may astonish some readers. They would point to the common knowledge that when a bank closes it doors, some sort of chicanery on the directors' part is very likely to come to light as an efficient cause of the failure. Moreover, the State law did permit M—— to rebut the presumption by showing that the affairs of his bank had been fairly and legally administered. One may argue that he of all people ought to know best whether they had been.

Come, let us reason together, the Supreme Court seems to say; and in our reasoning let us not overlook the threefold definition of insolvency which the State of Georgia added to its law in 1919. According to the 1919 amendment, a bank would be considered insolvent not only when its liabilities might exceed its assets, but also whenever it might not be able to meet its liabilities as they become due (a very different situation as we shall presently see) and even when it might, for thirty days, fail to maintain the reserves required by law and directed by the State banking authorities. Suppose unforeseen demands are made on a bank, and the depositors suddenly rush to withdraw their money at a time when the bank cannot immediately call in and collect the funds it has loaned. Pursuant to the 1919 definition, the bank would be closed for insolvency under the circumstances. But would this state of affairs even suggest that a fraud had been perpetrated? Alternatively, assume there is money to meet the flood of withdrawals but not enough left to maintain the legal level of reserves. Here again the inference of fraud seems baseless. In lawyer's jargon, there is not even a *corpus delicti*, not even proof that a crime of any nature has been committed.

That is not all. Even if there had been a sufficient basis for inferring the commission of a crime, the presumption would still remain an irrational one, because it was far too sweeping in its imputation of guilt. It comprised all the directors of a closed bank. In M——'s case there were only three, but Georgia law permitted as many as twenty-five. Without distinction or discrimination, all of them, regardless of their diverse relations to the management of the bank, would be caught in the net of the presumption.

But there was another streak of irrationality to the presumption, one that appeared most inexcusable in the Supreme Court's estimate. The accusation it made is hopelessly vague. It leaves the accused in the kind of predicament that one finds depicted in Franz Kafka's works. When M—— was indicted under this presumption, what could he do? He need only prove, responds the Georgia law, that he has managed the bank "fairly and legally," "honestly," and "in accordance with law." Oh admirable precision! Here we are concerned with the administration of nothing less complex than a bank, involving of necessity countless business transactions, thousands of loans and investments, myriads of acts, omissions, and minute decisions. Where is the point at which M—— will prepare t justify himself, what is the issue he must defend? Everything that ever took place in the bank will be considered false and fraudulent unless he proves the contrary. "He is to be convicted," said the Supreme Court by way of summation, "unless he negatives every fact, whether act or omission in the management of the bank, from which fraudulent insolvency might result or shows that he is in no way responsible for the condition of the bank." Such a burden we could not in conscience expect anyone to sustain. It does not matter how arrogantly M—— may have conducted himself in the days of his power; now that he has fallen into the hands of those who detest him, he is nevertheless entitled to claim due process of them, and they are bound to accord it to him.

In dissecting the Georgia presumption and exposing its irrationality, the Supreme Court observed a most useful maxim. It succeeded in making a correct analysis, largely because it suspended considering the testimony about M——'s actual management of the bank. As far as we can judge from the details developed in the Georgia court's opinion,[4] M—— had probably violated several State banking regulations and had executed several transactions of very doubtful propriety. He may well have been vulnerable to prosecution for these specific acts, which were brought out at his trial. The Georgia judges should have reminded themselves, however, that a banker may be guilty of this or that crime without being the cause of his bank's becoming insolvent. They allowed their view of the case to become so distorted by M——'s misconduct in these specific transactions, concerning which the indictment was silent, that they failed to grant him due process on the vague and general charge which the indictment did express.

Ought it to be said in circumstances like these: As long as he was guilty, it does not matter why he was sent to jail or on what charge? No, it ought not, if we sincerely respect our administration of justice. For we have no means of telling how M—— would have defended his dealings if the indictment had given him proper notice that these specific transactions were to be the decisive ones. Nor can we tell how the jury would have weighed the conflicting testimony if the judge had not charged that the burden of vindication fell on M——'s side. Let us insist stubbornly that we do not know these things. When the scissors have cut, it is hard to exonerate either of the blades.

In moral evaluations, the best method is to test all presumptions of this order with a maximum of temporary detachment from the detailed circumstances of the case. Otherwise, what generally results is that the evidence will seem to confirm the sweeping presumption, and the presumption will seem to anticipate the incriminating evidence. Thus all the indications in favor of the other side, all the exceptions and qualifications our analysis might point to if it applied due process, are liable to be submerged and lost. We fail to assay the presumption because our eyes are on what we consider to be the facts, which in turn we consider to be the facts because we have taken the presumption as our premise. But if we desire to reason soundly and justly, we must resolve we are not ready to identify the facts until we have first purged our minds of the irrational presumption.

There are certain occasions on which the United States Supreme Court has failed to strike down oppressive presumptions established by federal or state statute.[5] In each of these cases the Court, one may surmise, might have reached a wiser decision if it had only tested the presumption independently of whatever distaste it felt for the personality and conduct of the accused. It is the mark of a superior mind to segregate and condemn an unfair mode of accusation even when it is levelled at a notoriously obnoxious individual. But this calls for a constant will to cleanse one's intellectual apparatus by means of self-criticism. A man must entertain a hearty respect for the worth of his own judgment if he is willing to pass through a process of purgation before he undertakes to examine the evidence against one of his neighbors. Yet in conscience there is no other way to enforce the rule that a finding of guilt requires proof beyond a reasonable doubt.

What do we mean when we say "proof beyond a reasonable doubt"? Why do we insist that, without such proof, even the vilest and most detestable creature shall go acquitted and free? Some of the law's foremost authorities maintain that "reasonable doubt" is as clear a locution as can be devised and that when a judge attempts to explain it to the jurymen, he succeeds only in confusing them.[6] This may be true. At any rate, a reasonable doubt should never be defined as a doubt for which the individual juryman would be prepared to give an intelligible reason if he were questioned.[7] Often a flimsy "paper-doubt"—I am borrowing phrases from Charles S. Peirce, co-founder of American pragmatism—can be elaborated discursively and made to appear solid, while "the genuine metal" of uncertainty may resemble a vague pain that we feel deep in our bones and do not know how to describe.

Peirce was not the only pragmatist to concentrate on the meaning and utility of doubt. Another member of the famous Metaphysical Club of the 1870's was Nicholas St. John Green, a lawyer and law-teacher of great insight. Green said, "If he [the juryman] feels uneasy as to the truth of the fact in saying guilty, he has a reasonable doubt." [8] This ultimate feeling of discomfort and unease, after the evidence on both sides has been heard and considered carefully, seems to be the surest sign of the reasonable doubt.

But unless I am mistaken, there is another factor in the complex, one that the legal authorities would be reluctant to recognize. When a juryman endeavors to decide whether guilt has been proved beyond a reasonable doubt, he will usually consider not only the evidence in the case, which is all he is supposed to consider, but also the probable sentence or fine, which the law almost invariably leaves to the judge's discretion. A reasonable doubt for purposes of what sanction? he asks himself. Regardless of the judge's instructions, the juryman feels deeply concerned with the relation of the verdict to the punishment that may be inflicted. It will not avail to tell him that a reasonable doubt must in logic reach the same minimum level, whether the trial involves a fine, an imprisonment, or a sentence of capital punishment. He will not yield to this instruction, and he is right. For in a world filled with misgivings and uncertainties, the conscientious person will seek to avoid relying on a blemished certitude when by doing so he may precipitate some serious injury. The more severe the prospective punishment, the more receptive he will be to intimations that the doubt in the case is a reasonable doubt.

Why is it that we insist on being persuaded so very intensely in criminal cases? The question is of prime ethical importance. There are many lawyers who would reply by saying that our present rule has been enforced ever since Anglo-Saxon legal institutions emerged from a state of primitive barbarism. Replies of this caliber are very common. They pass well enough for history in speeches at bar association gatherings; and they are probably useful in the sense that a flourish of trumpets is useful. But, in point of factual accuracy, the requirement of proof beyond a reasonable doubt became explicit in Anglo-American law only in the latter part of the eighteenth century.[9] It was a current among the reform impulses initiated by men like Cesare Beccaria, Jeremy Bentham, and Sir Samuel Romilly. We may conjecture that the rule was originally designed to comfort and salve the consciences of civilized Englishmen on the bench and in the jury box. Under the Draconian penal laws of the period, judges and jurymen knew that a verdict of guilty could send the accused to the gallows for some offense which many sensible men even in those days considered quite expiable, if not trivial. No wonder that, as an early step in the direction of humanitarian reforms, the proof of guilt was required to attain the very highest intensity of persuasiveness—beyond a reasonable doubt.

As we see, Anglo-Saxon legal history does not furnish a sufficient answer to our question. At most, it may tend to confirm the suggestion that there is a latent bond between the severity of punishment and the degree of proof which conscientious men will look for before imputing guilt. Yet even if the facts of legal history had supported the claims of the lawyers' myths, we should not have gained very much from that circumstance. For when one turns to the strictly moral aspect of a problem, it is difficult to expect the intelligent public to embrace a principle simply because Clio—the most easily suborned of all witnesses—seems to vouch for it. There should be a better reason than the accidents of history for our insisting on proof of guilt beyond a reasonable doubt.

How one formulates the reason depends on how one chooses to pronounce the terms of the moral constitution. It can be read in the language of individual morals, as Jesus and many other religious leaders read it in their times. Using this language, one says he abstains from condemning without proof beyond a reasonable doubt because he feels himself equivalent to the accused person. He does not condemn without the acme of proof lest in his turn he be condemned without it. He realizes that like all his congeners he may unexpectedly need the benefit of every reasonable doubt; therefore he accords it. He hopes to be judged by the same standard and to be acquitted on the day of trial when, though he may appear doubtfully innocent as men so often do, he will at least appear doubtfully guilty. This would be a sufficient reason.

A socially oriented morals would probably phrase the reason differently. It would point to the mutual confidences that bind a human community together. It would emphasize the fears and divisiveness that result from men's distrusting their neighbors and anticipating evil instead of good. Moreover, it would admonish that philanthropic hopes or misanthropic suspicions are equally potent to fulfill themselves in personal relations and contacts, so that what one encounters in the behavior of his neighbors depends to a considerable degree on what one goes forth expecting. Finally, a socially oriented morals would emphasize the tie between general environment and injurious individual behavior. It would lay at least a part of the blame for any person's offense at the door of the society that had contributed to the shaping of his character. In this perspective, to impute guilt to an individual would require the highest degree of proof that he had been predominantly responsible for his own wrongful act. Without conclusive proof, a judgment of condemnation would shirk the group's obligation and reduce the group's solidarity. This too would justify our demanding proof beyond a reasonable doubt.

There is a third mode of expressing the moral constitution in this relation. Perhaps to some readers the first and second reasons may have appeared too interested, that is, too concerned with the expectation of benefits for the individual or for society. Other readers will have found nothing disadvantageous in looking for incidental utilities and benefits; to their way of thinking, a moral good can delight innumerable human noses without losing a trace of its fragrance. Fortunately, there is no need to debate the point, for the third reason, far from competing with the ones we have mentioned, seeks only to combine and merge them into a unified ideal.

When discussing the administration of justice, we are accustomed to express our special regard for "the equitable judge." The equitable judge is one of the ideal types in our society, as he has been in many others, ancient and modern. Using this ideal as an analogy and broadening its scope, Aristotle described the attributes of character one could expect to observe in "the equitable man." [10] Such a man, says Aristotle, is kind and generous, more sensible of benefits than of injuries, preferring the spirit of the law to its letter, giving consideration to the good deeds a person has normally done rather than the bad deed committed on this or that occasion, indulgent to the weaknesses of human nature, and alert to distinguish misfortune from bad judgment and both of them from moral offense. And the equitable man "is no stickler for his rights in a bad sense but tends to take less than his share though he has the law on his side." I think we may surely deduce that such a man will resolve to insist on proof beyond a reasonable doubt before he utters a judgment of condemnation. Confronted by the universal and eternal ocean of anguish that flows wherever there are men, he will not add a single drop to its tide unless justice, having removed the last vestige of a reasonable doubt, compels him.

Even then, if clemency and mercy can be extended to the convict without incurring the risk of additional harm to other persons, he will grant his utmost of mercy. But our equitable man, we trust, is no maudlin fool, and when he has pardoned a particularly outrageous injury, he will take such precautions as he can to avoid crossing the same culprit's path again. He notices that in being forgiven there resides a hurt which some who receive it are never able to forgive.

2. WHOSE DECISION?

One of the statutory requirements an alien must meet before he can become a citizen of the United States is that, for the five years immediately preceding his filing a petition for naturalization, he has been "a person of good moral character." The statute, however, does not define what constitutes "good moral character." When the question arises in a controversial case, how is the judge to formulate a standard for his decision?

On October 12, 1939, Louis R—— had deliberately put his 13-year-old son to death by means of chloroform. His reasons for this act were that the child had "suffered from birth from a brain injury which destined him to be an idiot and a physical monstrosity malformed in all four limbs. The child was blind, mute and deformed. He had to be fed; the movements of his bladder and bowels were involuntary, and his entire life was spent in a small crib." R—— had four other children at the time. The family was altogether dependent on his work for its support. He was always a dutiful father, and the nurture of the four normal children was compromised by the effort and expense involved in caring for the unfortunate one. R—— was convicted of manslaughter in the second degree, the jury recommending utmost clemency; he received a suspended prison sentence and was placed on probation, from which he was discharged in December 1945. It was conceded that, except for this act, R—— had in all respects conducted himself as a person of "good moral character."

On September 22, 1944 (almost but not quite five years after the "mercy killing") R—— filed his petition for naturalization. The District Court granted it, but the Government took the case on appeal to the United States Court of Appeals. In the Court of Appeals the order was reversed and R——'s petition was dismissed (2–1). By that time, considerably more than five years having elapsed since the date of the homicide, Judge Learned Hand added at the end of his opinion for the Court: "However, we wish to make it plain that a new petition would not be open to this objection; that the pitiable event, now long passed, will not prevent R—— from taking his place among us as a citizen."

Judge Hand's motives for denying R——'s petition were: (1) the test of "good moral character" is whether the conduct conforms to "the generally accepted moral conventions current at the time," without regard to the judges' own views and consciences; and (2) there is no way of finding with certainty what "the current moral feeling" would be concerning an act like R——'s. "Left at large as we are, without means of verifying our conclusion, and without authority to substitute our individual beliefs, the outcome must needs be tentative; and not much is gained by discussion. We can say no more than that, quite independently of what may be the current moral feeling as to legally administered euthanasia, we feel reasonably secure in holding that only a minority of virtuous persons would deem the practice morally justifiable, while it remains in private hands, even when the provocation is as overwhelming as it was in this instance." [11]

QUITE deservedly, Judge Learned Hand has long been regarded by many Americans as an outstanding jurist. He was appointed to the federal bench in 1909. In that same year there appeared

Professor John Chipman Gray's *The Nature and Sources of the Law*, one of the finest products of American legal theory. In it, Professor Gray said:

> *We all agree that many cases should be decided by the courts on notions of right and wrong, and of course everyone will agree that a judge is likely to share the notions of right and wrong prevalent in the community in which he lives; but suppose in a case where there is nothing to guide him but notions of right and wrong, that his notions of right and wrong differ from those of the community,—which ought he to follow—his own notions, or the notions of the community? . . . I believe he should follow his own notions.*[12]

He did not, however, stop at this point, but went on to discuss the questions a reflective and responsible judge might put to himself in order to refine his notions of right and wrong. The circumstance that the community's opinion differed from his should give the judge pause. He must take care to read extensively and ponder deeply. But though he should respect "custom" in formulating his views, custom as an authoritative source of law meant only what the community did. What the community or its members merely opined did not have the dignity of custom. In short, granting that the judge in cases of this sort was under duty to consult external sources, the eventual decision ought to rest squarely on his own shoulders.

Unfortunately, many influences have combined to obscure the soundness of Professor Gray's analysis. For one thing, there were, and still are, too many unthinking judges. The unthinking judge can escape responsibility for moral obtuseness by convincing himself that his own familiar biases represent the eternal verities. Whatever he dislikes is, by his test, immoral. The pleasures he no longer lusts for are automatically sinful.

On the other hand, the genuinely thoughtful judge may come to trust his own moral judgment too little. He is too sophisticated to ignore the existence of problems concerning moral standards, too well read in anthropology and history to overlook the element of relativism, and sometimes too modest to insist that other persons conform to what he considers virtuous. If he is one of us who witnessed the arrogance of American judicial dogmatists during the long period which ended in 1937 with reform of the Supreme Court, he is likely to have reacted violently to the spectacle. It was a deeply disturbing experience.

On such considerations as these, a judge's democratic loyalties may seem to compel him to accept uncritically the moral standards and beliefs of the community. And so he sets about to call "moral" what the community would approve and "immoral" what it would condemn if it could somehow be placed in the seat of judgment. And then . . .

And then his oracle stands uncommunicative and mute. Or if the voice of the people can be heard at all, it utters commands in a riotous confusion of tongues, each denouncing the others, and all contradictory and irreconcilable, babbling at him without message, guidance, or sense. What, in such a plight, is the good and thoughtful judge to do?

Beginning in 1929, Judge Learned Hand's opinions have maintained persistently that moral right and wrong must be determined only by "the common conscience," "moral feelings now prevalent generally in this country," or "the common conscience prevalent at the time." For a quarter of a century he has been reaffirming this position whenever appeals in naturalization or deportation cases came before him.[13]

But again and again and in appeal after appeal, Judge Hand has reported with dismay that, if the case presents the slightest tinge of difficulty, he can never find a way to identify the community's moral feelings on the subject. For example, he wrote in a recent opinion, "Our duty in such cases, as we understand it, is to divine what the 'common conscience' prevalent at the time demands; and it is impossible in practice to ascertain what in a given instance it does demand." [14] Rarely does one observe a judge clinging with such tenacity to a rule of decision while he himself repeatedly demonstrates its worthlessness.

In R——'s case, Judge Jerome Frank dissented from Judge Hand's decision. He contended that if the community opinion was to be decisive, then the case should be remanded to the trial judge under directions to receive additional evidence as to what the community thought. Judge Frank also suggested that "the attitude of our ethical leaders" might be the test implicit in determining issues of "good moral character."

Judge Hand warily avoided these challenges. In the next appeal [15] on "good moral character," he preferred to concede again that there was no practicable way "to conduct an inquiry as to what is the common conscience on the point. Even though we could take a poll, it would not be enough merely to count heads, without any appraisal of the voters. A majority of the votes of those in prisons and brothels for instance ought scarcely to outweigh all accredited churchgoers. Nor can we see any reason to suppose that the opinion of clergymen would be a more reliable estimate than our own." This appeal involved a member of the faculty of City College, thirty-nine years of age and unmarried, who had openly stated to the Government examiner that he had occasionally engaged in sexual intercourse with various unmarried women. With a sigh evoked by the burst of candor, Judge Hand decided that the teacher did possess "good moral character" suitable for naturalization, "so far as we can divine anything so tenebrous and impalpable as the common conscience." Yet what is this criterion of "the common conscience," to which Judge Hand has turned with repeated futility and mounting annoyance, but the creature of his own theorizing? The naturalization statute requires nothing more than five years' good moral character; it does not mention a common conscience.

We could have foreseen Judge Hand's finding himself in a state of frustration. There probably never was a civilized society so homogeneous in its standards and monolithic in its reactions as he has premised. Certainly the American community has not lacked variety and multiplicity in these regards. Our diversity is, in fact, one of our patriotic boasts.[16] We do from time to time reach a high degree of consensus when some sensational drama forces itself on the public attention, but most cases of this kind would be so obvious for moral evaluation that not even Judge Hand would feel constrained to linger with them. If an alien stabs his parents in order to accelerate the inheritance of their property and appears in court with a bloody dagger in his hand, he is not very likely to obtain a certificate of naturalization. So too if he fails to support his infant children, or makes a livelihood as procurer, or trades in illicit narcotics, or engages in acts of arson in order to collect from insurance companies—assuming he perpetrates these misdeeds within a short time before the question of naturalization arises. But should a moral issue fall anywhere near the borderline, there will be no pre-fabricated consensus to accommodate the judge. And even a very ugly deed will gradually become ambiguous to the "common conscience" as years elapse and the offense recedes into the past.

The principle Judge Hand appears to have overlooked is one we have become familiar with, i.e.: When various groups in the community present a number of diverse or opposing attitudes, there is as affirmative an act of personal enterprise and moral commitment in *selecting* one perspective from the available many as in *establishing* a perspective which one believes to be entirely original. The human conscience is not constituted to function like an inert and neutral mirror, for even when it wills to deny its own authentic impulses, it must, at very least, choose the objects it will turn to and reflect in their stead. If we appear to be enforcing what we call community opinions, it is generally because we have previously sorted out the ones we find most expedient. Doing so, we legislate standards for ourselves not a whit the less. The essential difference is that by attributing a standard to the welter of the community's conscience, we may delude ourselves that we are somehow cleansed of personal responsibility.

In the literature of morals there have been many different varieties of irresponsibility, and it would be indefensibly dogmatic to propose consigning all of them to the flames of disapproval. On occasion, even the most utopian and therefore irresponsible kind of moral exhortation may have its uses. When people of a responsible cast tend to become earthbound and insensitive in their judgments, a blast of messianic hopes or apocalyptic threats may awaken their minds and startle them out of the rut. It is a legitimate function of the irresponsible moralist to prevent his responsible brothers from lapsing into habits of complacency. But this is the utmost we can concede to him. On the other side of the score, there is the depressing fact that moral teaching has forfeited most of its audience during the modern period just because people gradually become aware of the *calculated* irresponsibility of so many pulpits. Kierkegaard described the process most vividly:

> *The parson (collectively understood) does indeed preach about those glorious ones who sacrificed their lives for the truth. As a rule the parson is justified in assuming that there is no one present in the church who could entertain the notion of venturing upon such a thing. When he is sufficiently assured of this by reason of the private knowl-*

> edge he has of the congregation as its pastor, he preaches glibly, declaims vigorously, and wipes away the sweat. If on the following day one of those strong and silent men, a quiet, modest, perhaps even insignificant-looking man, were to visit the parson at his house announcing himself as one whom the parson had carried away by his eloquence, so that he had now resolved to sacrifice his life for the truth—what would the parson say? He would address him thus: "Why, merciful Father in heaven! How did such an idea ever occur to you? Travel, divert yourself, take a laxative." And if this plain-looking man were to fix his eye upon him with unaltered calm, and holding him with this glance were to continue to talk about his resolution, but with the modest expressions which a resolute man always uses—then the parson would surely think, "Would that this man were far away!" [17]

In one respect, we can see, Judge Hand's experience served him well. While he continued to attribute authority to the "common conscience," which in turn persisted in refusing to give him a decisive answer, the Judge would not agree that a poll be taken to ascertain what the "common conscience" had to say. Here he proved worthy of his reputation for sagacity. For no one would expect Judge Hand to believe that Jones, Smith, Robinson, and Brown possess ready and considered opinions on moral problems of the twilight zone, such as arise in naturalization proceedings. No one would expect him to entertain much respect for the offhand, unreflective answers his neighbors would probably offer. Feeling no personal responsibility in the matter, many of them would blurt their opinions without waiting long enough to make sure they had comprehended the question. Even an exceptionally serious and intelligent person is liable to give a thoughtless reply if the setting in which he is questioned conveys no sense of personal responsibility. At the end, the statistics resulting from a poll may depend on whether the poll-taker has to be dismissed summarily because he happens to arrive when the family's dinner is ready for the table.

How heavy would the responsibility have been if Judge Hand had elected to shoulder it? Not so overwhelming, I suggest, as his modesty led him to fear. Professor Gray was warranted in saying that "a judge is likely to share the notions of right and wrong prevalent in the community in which he lives." We may carry the proposition considerably farther. For in these borderline situations such as R——'s case, even when a judge's notions of right and wrong may seem to disagree with those "prevalent in the community," he will always—unless he loses his sanity—find himself agreeing with and supported by a significant strand of public opinion. Taking a responsible view does not drive a judge to act in an idiosyncratic or irrational manner. Irrationality is not what we have to fear from the men we have vested with judicial office. We do have cause to fear that they will consider themselves mere mouthpieces for an amorphous popular mass, without identity or location. How does one go about finding the chimera of "common conscience" in order to call it to account?

Judge Hand would reply again that he must do what the "common conscience" demands. Plaintively he has concluded that "it is impossible in practice to ascertain what in a given instance it does demand." Perhaps this impossibility would have been evident from the outset if the judge had fixed his attention more closely on the test Congress asked him to impose in naturalization cases. The legislation applicable to R—— did not mention acts of euthanasia. Congress has not required the judges to decide whether euthanasia is or is not moral.[18] It has required them to decide, in each individual application for citizenship, whether the applicant has been of "good moral character" for five years. Thus R——'s case did not properly present an occasion for evaluating euthanasia in general. What it did present was a duty to evaluate R——'s moral character in particular.

Obviously, on this approach it would be quite impossible, as Judge Hand admitted, to ascertain what the common conscience demands "in a given instance." It would be impossible not only because there is no way of nailing down the community's general standards of moral evaluation, but even more significantly, because the community cannot conceivably know the myriad circumstances of R——'s or any other applicant's unique personal biography. The community may possibly pass an informed judgment on a single act; in the case of a famous or notorious individual, it may have become familiar with his public reputation; but the community can never have the knowledge which the judge must glean and assemble in order to pass judgment on the totality known as "character." Character, especially when the term is addressed to a period of five years, is the composite product of innumerable influences, impulses, overt manifestations, and private intentions.

Perhaps it will be argued that the community can at least say that a man who has done such and such an act of violence cannot have a good moral character. Even if this be granted, it would never indicate when the man does have a good moral character. But to grant it would be to discard considerations that moral teaching has stressed since civilization began—considerations having to do with upbringing, background, environment, and temptation; considerations antecedent to the intention that accompanied the act; considerations of reformation and personal rehabilitation; and those most sacred considerations associated with repentence, mercy, and forgiveness.

Speaking through the naturalization statute, the community

says to the judge, "Ascertain whether this man has had good moral character for the past five years." Judge Hand's approach attempts to return the task to the community, and the attempt proves vain. Nor can it be made to appear plausible by saying that the community expects its naturalized citizens to be only as good in character as the average native citizen, for to be as good as the average native citizen does not mean to be as good according to the *judgment* of the average native citizen. The act of individual judgment must belong to him who bears the name of judge.

A judge evaluates "moral character" in one way or another every time he listens to a witness testifying before him. That is the way he decides whom to believe and what testimony to disregard. What is new and special in connection with naturalization is the heightened duty to judge after most painstaking investigation of all the circumstances, after sympathetic understanding of unique individual motives, and after careful criticism of the judge's own customary biases. This is indeed much to ask, but acquiring American citizenship may be considered equivalent to entering into a social communion, and someone, it seems, must be charged with the duty of testing the fitness of the proposed communicant.

Generally speaking, it is the best and finest of judges who afflict themselves with the whips of doubt while their inferior colleagues remain in a state of complacency. What the community needs most is the moral leadership of such a man as Learned Hand and the full benefit of his mature and chastened wisdom. The community is perhaps not at fault when it calls upon him and those like him to test and determine the good moral character of aliens who wish to join its ranks. The path of personal responsibility, thorny though it may be, remains the only path anyone has ever found to wise and righteous judgment.

There is a delightful incident of men's responsibility and self-reliance recounted in the Babylonian Talmud.[19] The story culminates with peals of hearty laughter ringing and reverberating through empyrean and firmament. As the scene of the episode opens, we find ourselves attending a court conference of rabbinical sages; and we observe that one of the most distinguished among them, Rabbi Eliezer by name, is engaged in heated argument with his colleagues over a delicate, technical point in the interpretation of the law.

After exhausting all his resources of precedent, distinction, analogy, and citation of textual authority without convincing any of them, Rabbi Eliezer becomes desperate and cries out, "If the law agrees with me, let this tree prove it!" Thereupon the tree leaps a hundred cubits from its place, some say four hundred cubits. But the other judges calmly retort, "No proof can be adduced from a tree." Then he says, "If the law agrees with me, let this stream of water prove it!" At this the stream of water flows backwards. The others rejoin however, "No proof can be adduced from a stream of water." Again he calls out, "If the law agrees with me, let the walls of the house prove it!" Whereupon the walls begin to fall, but Rabbi Joshua, one of the sages present, rebukes them, saying, "When scholars are engaged in a legal dispute, what right have you to interfere?" And so they do not fall, out of respect for Rabbi Joshua, nor do they resume the upright, out of respect for Rabbi Eliezer, but remain standing and inclined. Finally Rabbi Eliezer says, "If the law agrees with me, let it be proved from heaven!" At that moment a Heavenly Voice cries out, "Why do you dispute with Rabbi Eliezer, seeing that in all matters the law agrees with him?" For a space the assembly sits transfixed, but almost immediately Rabbi Joshua rises from his seat and exclaims, "The law is not in heaven! It was given on Mount Sinai. We pay no attention to a Heavenly Voice."

Soon thereafter one of the rabbis happens to meet the prophet Elijah, who, having been alive when he was transported into the celestial regions, remains able to converse with mortals. The prophet is asked, "What did the Holy One, blessed be He, do at that point?" Elijah replies, "He laughed with joy, saying 'My sons have defeated Me, My sons have defeated Me.' "

3. THE COSMIC MEANING OF DECISION

In the resolution of our own moral problems, we too can scarcely rely on receiving testimony from a tree or from running water. There does not seem to be the faintest reason for inferring that the distant stars and galaxies are interested in our continued existence, or that the moral constitution we value so highly is able to penetrate into the reaches of space or control the destination of macrocosmic and microcosmic forces. And if in our international hatred and folly we should commit the crime of annihilating our species completely, which I do not expect we will do, then by means of some vital evolutionary power a new form of life will emerge sooner or later and make its bid for leadership in the cosmos. We are utterly dispensable to the galactic scheme.

This, however, was always so. It does not demonstrate that we have fallen in any respect or have lost a more important status by lapsing into sin. So far as we can form an objective estimate of the species we belong to, human beings do not seem to be characteristically or predominantly evil. If there is any common trait to be found among us, I suppose it would consist in fickleness and instability. We seem able to astonish ourselves at times by exertions of extreme righteousness and again by sudden outbursts of vice. Rather frequently we veer about like cocky weathervanes in a fitful wind. But this does not mean that we are pointing toward corruption with more constancy than toward virtue.

It has long been preached that men feel acutely conscious of guilts and imperfections in themselves because they sense an earlier state of innocence and grace from which they have degenerated. As noble and ardent a thinker as Blaise Pascal adopted this reasoning. To elucidate the point, Pascal asked, apparently confident that there could be no reply, "Who is unhappy at not being a king, except a deposed king?" A fine metaphor this is; yet if his hypersensibility had not prevented him from experiencing more of the world's ways, Pascal might have found a response for himself and for us. He might have said, "Everyone is unhappy at not being a king, except those who are intelligent and mature enough to subdue the appetite for absolute power. And the same immature mentalities that would desire to play the part of kings would likewise desire to return to a mythical Eden and an innocence which has left no persuasive proof it ever existed."

The evidence afforded by human behavior being full of conflict and disorder, different minds or different moods will attend to one portion of it and ignore the remainder. Surely, it is not coherent enough to require a verdict condemning the whole species. In the successive chapters of our study, man has hardly seemed to maintain the posture we should expect of "a deposed king." In point of fact, he has never seemed to maintain any characteristic posture very long or consistently. In his present cultural situation, he would seem most nearly to resemble a type of *parvenu*—proud but insecure, rich beyond his most voracious hopes, distrustful of the scenes to which he has raised himself, and aware that the struggle for existence in his new environment will require more of imagination, discipline, and refinement than he has previously been called on to exhibit. It is an equivocal position.

Yet, as our survey shows recurrently, the living generation of men always hold a supreme cosmoplastic *opportunity*. Though they may blunder and falter on the way, as long as they live the capacity remains with them to create moral standards superior to those their fathers evolved. In the annals of our species, it has never been enough simply to stand still and cling to the past. The prophets of past ages deserve honor precisely because they surpassed their predecessors in applying the moral constitution to the problems and conflicts of the cultures in which they lived. The moral evolution they carried forward acknowledges no line at which to halt. Everything we have learned from the ancients needs to be refined through modern experience and employed toward producing still better moral decisions. In certain respects the sciences of man and society have advanced beyond anything the classic prophets could have known; the ends and purposes which a modern community conceives for itself have expanded in a magnificent arc; the duty thus becomes manifest to evolve wiser moral legislation and make use of the past advisedly as a means of pressing beyond it. Meanwhile, the moral constitution abides with each of us to assist in determining whether any new departure we contemplate will probably cause an advance or a loss of ground.

As we have seen, arithmetic and statistics will furnish little guidance. In the realm of morals, it is rare that an authentically decisive factor can be reduced to measurement or quantity. Yet many of our contemporaries, intoxicated with statistics, believe that progress is impossible in any endeavor without the use of numbers, quantities, and graphs. In this they are badly confused.

For the truth is precisely opposite. The moral commonwealth

deserves our reverence for remaining as free as it is from quantification. It has refused to surrender its concern with quality for a mess of arithmetical pottage and, by refusing, it has saved the individual human spirit from dissolving into the conglomerate mass. In morals, there is no basis for saying that ten good decisions are worth ten times as much as one. What is one good decision worth? It may be transient and ineffectual; or it may be so charged with inspiration that it reaches the loftiest moral plane. The test of moral value will always be qualitative. When, for example, any human being, however obscure, decides to follow the more benevolent of the courses presented before him, the dynamic good in his choice explodes and penetrates through all the communities of men. By merely seeking to ascertain what is righteous we can bring the quality into existence, where it persists until we learn, as we may, to form still more humane decisions.

It is of the nature of righteous judgment that the judge should aspire to see his own wisdom transcended by those who come after him. With the advantage of further observation and experience, our successors can be counted on to surpass and supersede the moral decisions established in our time, including the ones set down in this book. Let them accept the yoke of due process and personal responsibility. Bearing it resolutely, they can scarcely fail to bring the standards of their society closer to the living spirit of the constitution. And when they have won their way to a more eminent plane, they may feel disposed to look back on the judgments in this book with tolerant forbearance. The task will never be complete. Yet daily it summons every human being to join in creating the happier world of justice, kindness, and compassion.

Acknowledgments

It was Hon. Herbert F. Goodrich, distinguished United States Circuit Judge, who first suggested my exploring American law to discover moral values and guides. I am sincerely grateful to Judge Goodrich for his interest and kind encouragement.

Anne Aldrich Mooney, of the District of Columbia Bar, has verified the statements of law in the manuscript in order to safeguard against material inaccuracies. I am obliged to her for this characteristically fine assistance. For invaluable help and painstaking care in connection with the manuscript, proofs, and indexes, Paula Gross deserves my praise and hearty thanks.

There is a special pleasure in recording my indebtedness to Bernard Perry, Edith Greenburg, and others on the staff of the Indiana University Press for their extraordinary skill, cooperativeness, and cordiality.

For the opinions expressed in this book no one but the author is responsible. They are not to be attributed to any other person or to any institution.

EDMOND CAHN

A Short Bibliography on Law and Morals

James Barr Ames, "Law and Morals," 22 Harv. L. Rev. 97 (1908).

Edmond Cahn, *The Sense of Injustice* 93–123 (1949).

Felix S. Cohen, *Ethical Systems and Legal Ideals* (1933).

A. L. Goodhart, *English Law and the Moral Law* (1953).

John Chipman Gray, *The Nature and Sources of the Law* cc. XII and XIII (2d ed. 1921).

Leon Petrazycki, *Law and Morality* (H. W. Babb trans. 1955), v. VII of 20th C. Legal Phil. Series.

Roscoe Pound, *Law and Morals* (2d ed. 1926).

Roscoe Pound, "Law and Morals—Jurisprudence and Ethics," 23 N.C.L.Rev. 185 (1945).

Gustav Radbruch, "Law and Morals," in *The Legal Philosophies of Lask, Radbruch, and Dabin* (K. Wilk trans. 1950), v. IV of 20th C. Legal Phil. Series 78.

T. V. Smith, "The Right as the Legal," in *Constructive Ethics* bk. I, c. 3 (1948).

S. E. Stumpf, "The Moral Element in Supreme Court Decisions," 6 Vanderbilt L. Rev. 41 (1952).

"Symposium—Ethical Values and the Law in Action," 12 Ohio State L.J. 1 (1951).

"What Should Be the Relation of Morals to Law? A Round Table," I J. of Pub. L. 259 (1952).

FOR ADDITIONAL REFERENCES, CONSULT:

Roscoe Pound, *Outlines of Lectures on Jurisprudence* 80 (5th ed. 1943).

Notes

FOR PAGES 62 TO 70

CHAPTER III

1 United States v. Holmes, 26 Fed. Cas. 360 (C.C.E.D. Pa. 1842).
2 'Erubin 13b in the Babylonian Talmud, Seder Mo'ed III, 86 (London, Soncino Press 1938).
3 This distinction was familiar to the Talmudic sages. For example, see Baba Bathra 130b in the Babylonian Talmud, Seder Nezikin IV, 545 (London, Soncino Press 1935).
4 Biddle v. Perovich, 274 U.S. 480 (1927).
5 Hubert Winston Smith, "Psychic Interest in Continuation of One's Own life: Legal Recognition and Protection," 98 U. of Pa. L. Rev. 781 (1950).
6 Benham v. Gambling, [1941] A.C. 157.
7 Discussed in Jerome Hall, *General Principles of Criminal Law* 396 (1947). See also Queen v. Dudley, L.R. 14 Q.B.D. 273 (1884). It should be mentioned that Lord Coleridge, who in Queen v. Dudley spurned the rule stated in the Holmes case, obviously misunderstood it. He had not read the report but relied on Stephen who in turn had paraphrased a digest by Wharton. Thus Coleridge received the impression that the Holmes case stood for choice by "ballot," i.e. by voting, which, as Stephen said, would indeed have been a "grotesque" idea.
8 J. F. Stephen, A *History of the Criminal Law of England*, II, 108 (1883). Cf. the supposititious case of two men swimming for a plank that can support only one of them, a very old topic in the literature of ethics.

9 Benjamin N. Cardozo, "What Medicine Can Do for Law" in *Selected Writings of Benjamin Nathan Cardozo* 388 (M. E. Hall ed. 1947).

10 Railway Company v. Stout, 17 Wallace 657 (1873).

11 *Politics* 1260a (Barker trans. 36) (1946). The bracketed words are supplied by the translator.

12 United Zinc and Chemical v. Britt, 258 U.S. 268 (1922).

13 McKee v. Gratz, 260 U.S. 127 (1922).

14 W—— v. T——, 85 N.E. 2d 246 (1949).

15 *Reason in Society* 45 (1905).

16 Jeremy Bentham went so far as to consider parental commands as instances of law-making.

17 "Preface to the Metaphysical Elements of Ethics" XII(C) in Kant's *Critique of Practical Reason and Other Works on the Theory of Ethics* 312 (T. K. Abbott trans. 1927).

CHAPTER IV

1 R—— v. State, 107 P.2d 813 (1940).

2 For a summary analysis of laws governing sex relations, see Ploscowe, *Sex and the Law* (1952).

3 S—— v. S——, 260 N.Y. 477, 184 N.E. 60 (1933).

4 V—— v. M——, as abstracted in Bouscaren, *Canon Law Digest* 1917–1933, 523 (1934) Simpson and Stone, *Cases and Readings on Law and Society*, bk. 2, p. 946 (1949).

5 B—— v. B——, [1948] A.C. 274, [1947] 2 All Eng. R. 886.

6 London *Times*, Feb. 6, 1948.

7 K—— v. K——, 20 N.J. Misc. 52, 23 A.2d 800 (1942).

8 In Fletcher v. Peck, 6 Cranch 87, 3 L. Ed. 162 (1810). The Chief Justice was discussing an entirely different subject.

9 Wilton v. Webster, 7 C. & P. 198 (1835).

10 The rules are assembled in Butterworth v. Butterworth, [1920] P. 126.

11 Heck v. Schupp, 394 Ill. 296, 68 N. E.2d 464 (1946).

12 P—— v. P——, 50 N.M. 224, 174 P.2d 826 (1946).

CHAPTER V

1 E—— v. Saks & Co., 226 P.2d 340 (1951).
2 W. E. H. Lecky, *History of European Morals from Augustus to Charlemagne* (New York: 1875) I, 144.
3 Ultramares Corp. v. Touche, 255 N.Y. 170, 174 N.E. 441 (1931); Candler v. Crane, Christmas & Co., [1951] 2 K. B. 164 (C. A.).
4 For this episode I am indebted to a footnote in Coleridge's *Biographia Literaria,* c.V.
5 Tuttle v. B——, 107 Minn. 145, 119 N.W. 946 (1909).
6 *Rhetoric* 1391a.
7 In a footnote to his *Methodology of Pure Practical Reason,* Kant wrote: "One need only reflect a little and he will always find a debt that he has by some means incurred towards the human race (even if it were only this, that by the inequality of men in the civil constitution he enjoys advantages on account of which others must be the more in want), which will prevent the thought of *duty* from being repressed by the self-complacent imagination of *merit.*"
8 Block v. Hirsh, 256 U.S. 135 (1921); Marcus Brown Co. v. Feldman, 256 U.S. 170 (1921).
9 Home Bldg. & Loan Ass'n v. Blaisdell, 290 U.S. 398 (1934).
10 Blaisdell v. Home Bldg. & Loan Ass'n, 249 N.W. 334, 343 (1933).
11 M—— v. S——, 249 N.Y. 458, 164 N.E. 545 (1928).
12 For an encouraging move in this direction, see Abrams v. Allen, 297 N.Y. 52 (1947).

CHAPTER VI

1 Steele v. Louisville & Nashville Railroad Co., 323 U.S. 192 (1944).
2 Bentham, *The Limits of Jurisprudence Defined* 91 (C. W. Everett, ed. 1945).
3 Brotherhood of Railroad Trainmen v. Howard, 343 U.S. 768 (1952).
4 Several States have enacted express legislation to forbid racial discrimination by labor unions as well as by employers. And Congress enacted in 1951 that an employer and a union who make a "union shop" agreement cannot apply it "with respect to employees to whom membership is not available upon the same terms and conditions as are generally applicable to any other member or with respect to employees to whom membership was denied or terminated" except for

non-payment of union dues. 45 U.S.C. § 152(11); 29 U.S.C. § 158(a)(3).

5 Shelley v. Kraemer, 334 U.S. 1 (1948).

6 United States ex rel. Iorio v. Day, 34 F. 2d 920 (1929).

7 United States ex rel. B—— v. Reimer, 113 F. 2d 429 (1940). Later, in Jordan v. De George, 341 U.S. 223 (1951) the United States Supreme Court (6–3) confirmed the view of the majority in our principal case.

8 Satire XIII, lines 100 *et seq.*

9 Marsh v. Alabama, 326 U.S. 501 (1946); Tucker v. Texas, 326 U.S. 517 (1946).

10 This passage is, of course, from the Funeral Oration, Thucydides, *The Peloponnesian War* bk. II, c. VI (Crawley trans.).

11 *Journals of the Continental Congress* 1774–89, I, 105–113 (Wash. 1904).

12 Reynolds v. United States, 98 U.S. 145 (1878).

13 Girouard v. United States, 328 U.S. 61 (1946) rehearsing the three previous cases. In the first of them, Holmes had commented on the contention that a pacifist could not be "attached to the principles of the Constitution of the United States," which the naturalization statute required, by saying: ". . . if there is any principle of the Constitution that more imperatively calls for attachment than any other it is the principle of free thought—not free thought for those who agree with us but freedom for the thought that we hate." 279 U.S. 654–5.

14 West Virginia State Board of Education v. Barnette, 319 U.S. 624 (1943), overruling Minersville School District v. Gobitis, 310 U.S. 586 (1940).

15 From his essay on "Civil Disobedience."

CHAPTER VII

1 Wagner v. International Railway Co., 232 N. Y. 176 (1921).

2 Luke 10:25–37.

3 *Don Quixote,* Part I, cc. XXII and XXX.

4 E. g., New York Vehicle and Traffic Law § 88(10).

5 Part I, c. IV.

6 Book I, c. XII.

7 Book III, c. I.

8 "The Failure to Rescue: A Comparative Study," 52 Col. L. Rev. 631 (1952) where the literature of the subject is collected.

9 *Leviathan,* Part I, c. XIII.

10 Shostakovich v. Twentieth Century-Fox Film Corp., 196 Misc. 67, 80 N.Y.S.2d 575, aff'd, 275 App. Div. 695, 87 N.Y.S.2d 430 (1948). A good but rather partisan treatment of the law on this subject is to be found in Katz, "The Doctrine of Moral Right and American Copyright Law—A Proposal," 24 So. Cal. L. Rev. 375 (1951). See Judge Jerome Frank's concurring opinion in Granz v. Harris, 198 F. 2d 585, 589 (1952).

11 UNESCO Copyright Bulletin, II, no. 2–3 (1949). For analysis of this report see the Katz article, cited in note 10.

12 Crimi v. ———, 194 Misc. 570, 89 N. Y. S.2d 813 (1949).

13 *Ethics,* part v, note to prop. x (Everyman's Library) 208.

14 I have paraphrased a remark in Burton's *Anatomy of Melancholy.*

15 E—— v. F—— Life Ins. Co., 41 N.W.2d 422 (1950).

16 Post v. Jones, 19 How. 150 (1856).

CHAPTER VIII

1 S—— v. Sn——, 26 A.2d 452 (1942), affirming 24 A.2d 61 (1942).

2 Leviticus 19:14.

3 Paris v. Stepney Borough Council, [1951] A.C. 367. Moreover, once the defendant has been found negligent, he is legally chargeable for all the harm his negligence brought on, even though the plaintiff's injuries were aggravated by his own predisposition or weakness. Owen v. Rochester-Penfield Bus Co., 304 N.Y. 457 (1952).

4 Davis v. Feinstein, 88 A.2d 695 (1952), where the injury took place despite use of a cane; Harris v. Uebelhoer, 75 N.Y. 169 (1878), where the injury took place despite reliance on a companion. Leaving the question of contributory negligence entirely to the jury would not necessarily result in a verdict for the blind plaintiff. In Weinstein v. Wheeler, 15 P.2d 383 (1932), the blind plaintiff's case was submitted to three different juries, and each of them found against him.

5 Mahan v. State to use of Carr, 191 A. 575 (1937).

6 Chamberlain v. Feldman, 300 N.Y. 135 (1949), affirming 84 N.Y.S. 2d 713 (App.Div.), which reversed 79 N.Y.S.2d 42 (S.Ct.).

7 Herodotus 187 (Bohn Class. Lib. 1904). For Pyrrho on the same theme, see Diogenes Laertius (Loeb Class. Lib.) II, 497 (1931).

8 Prince Albert v. Strange, 2 De G. & Sm. 652 (1848), aff'd, 1 Macn. & G. 25 (1849).

9 Philip v. Pennell, [1907] 2 Ch. 577.

10 Chafee, "Reflections on the Law of Copyright: II" 45 Col. L. Rev. 719 (1945), an exceptionally valuable commentary.

11 Ibid. 731–2. In 1954 certain of Miss Dickinson's intimate letters were made public for the first time. M. T. Bingham, *Emily Dickinson: A Revelation.*

12 Diogenes Laertius (Loeb Class. Lib.) II, 651 (1931). The passage is beautifully elaborated by Lucretius in the final 200 lines of his third book.

13 See booklet *1001 Embezzlers—Post War* (U.S. Fidelity & Guaranty Co. 1950).

14 St. Augustine, *De Libero Arbitrio,* bk. 1, c. V, (Tourscher trans. 25–9) (1937).

15 This illustrious sentence appears in § 40 of the Preface to Joseph Butler's *Sermons* (1726). *The Works of Bishop Butler* (J. H. Bernard ed. I, 19) (1900).

CHAPTER IX

1 *Courts On Trial* (1949) is the most complete statement of Judge Frank's analysis.

2 Some of the conflicting versions are given by Bayle, who also provides a very affecting account of Molière's relations with his wife. *Selections from Bayle's Dictionary* 183–202 (Beller and Lee eds. 1952).

3 Trial of William Penn and William Mead, 6 How St. Tr. 951; Bushell's Case, id. 999, Vaughan 135 (1670).

4 Santayana, *Scepticism and Animal Faith* 266 (1923).

5 Brown v. Board of Education, 347 U.S. 483 (1954). The Court's opinion and order of May 31, 1955 made this solution explicit.

6 In negotiation, as every experienced lawyer knows, it is almost indispensable to have someone "to go back to," someone to blame for being "vindictive and harsh," someone whom one must "induce" to recognize the opponent's point of view, someone to "consult" about a sudden and possibly deceptive proposal. Clients would shudder if they knew how their lawyers depict them in these parleys. They are generally kept away from the negotiations—in their own interest.

But the utility of a representative capacity extends much further.

In his *Autobiography*, Benjamin Franklin explains how the funds were raised for America's first public library:

> *The objections & reluctances I met with in soliciting the subscriptions made me soon feel the impropriety of presenting one's self as the proposer of any useful project that might be supposed to raise one's reputation in the smallest degree above that of one's neighbours, when one has need of their assistance to accomplish that project. I therefore put my self as much as I could out of sight, and stated it as a scheme of a number of friends, who had requested me to go about and propose it to such as they thought lovers of reading. In this way my affair went on more smoothly, and I ever after practised it on such occasions; and from my frequent successes, can heartily recommend it. The present little sacrifice of your vanity will afterwards be amply repaid. If it remains a while uncertain to whom the merit belongs, some one more vain than yourself will be encouraged to claim it, and then even envy will be disposed to do you justice, by plucking those assumed feathers, & restoring them to their right owner.*

7 Some learned commentators have suggested that the eventual compromise figure of ten may have been implied from the outset, because ten is the smallest number of men who will be rcognized as a community under Hebraic law. Perhaps this point is more than a bit anachronistic.

CHAPTER X

1 M—— v. Georgia, 279 U.S. 1 (1929).

2 Bailey v. Alabama, 219 U.S. 219 (1911).

3 Genesis 3:5 uses the Hebrew word ELOHIM, which the standard translations render either "gods" or "God." On reflection, the reader will see that there is nothing peculiar in the word's being so ambiguous. In English the great difference of meaning between "the Lord" and "the lord" depends on a mere matter of capitalization. Even this aid is unavailable in certain other tongues whose usage requires that both, or neither, be capitalized. So in Hebrew the word's significance may vary with its context. There are a number of exceptional places in the Bible where ELOHIM was recognized by the classical Jewish commentators as meaning "the magistrates, the mighty, the judges, the rulers," etc. From this reading the Jewish Publication

Society translation, published in 1917, derived a radiant line for the beginning of Psalm 82: "In the midst of the judges (ELOHIM), He judges." In the King James version, the phrase is rendered "among the gods," which does not seem very enlightening.

Interpretation of the serpent's prediction (Genesis 3:5) as referring to "judges" instead of "gods" apparently began with the ancient Aramaic translation called the Targum Onkelos. This rendition is approved by Maimonides in Bk. I, c. II. of *The Guide of the Perplexed.* Some analogous references of curious interest will be found in *Encyclopedia of Biblical Interpretation* (M. M. Kasher, ed.; translated under editorship of Rabbi H. Freedman I, 121, 182) (1953).

The interpretation has its parallels. In John 10:34–5, Jesus had explained his mission by referring to the Law which "called them gods unto whom the word of God came." John Calvin, in his "Institutes of the Christian Religion," quoting this passage, says that magistrates are called "gods" because they act as God's viceregents in making laws and judging wisely and equitably.

John Selden, a truly erudite jurist, discusses the widespread use of similar pretentious terms (e.g., *dominus*) by emperors, kings, and nobles. See his *Titles of Honor* (1614) part I, c. IV.

If it is objected that nothing in Eve's previous experience had prepared her to understand the meaning of "judges," one can only respond that she must have been equally vague about the threatened punishment of "death."

4 M—— v. State, 166 Ga. 563 (1928).

5 E.g. Casey v. United States, 276 U.S. 413 (1928); Leland v. Oregon, 343 U.S. 790 (1952).

6 Wigmore *On Evidence* §§ 2497, 2511 (3rd ed. 1940).

7 Judge Jerome Frank, dissenting rightly in United States v. Farina, 184 F.2d 18, 21–24 (2d Cir. 1950).

8 For a fine account of Green's contribution, see Philip P. Wiener, *Evolution and the Founders of Pragmatism* c. 7 (1949). The quoted sentence is from p. 205 of Green's *Essays and Notes.*

According to a recent statement of the United States Supreme Court, a reasonable doubt should be defined "in terms of the kind of doubt that would make a person hesitate to act." This statement appears in the course of a very careful and enlightening analysis of the kinds of inference that are permissible in income tax prosecutions. Holland v. United States, 348 U.S. 121 (1954).

9 See note 6.

10 *Nicomachean Ethics* 1137; *Rhetoric* 1374.

11 R—— v. United States, 165 F. 2d 152 (2d Cir. 1947). In this section, I have revised and restated portions of my previous discussions. 1952 *Annual Survey of American Law* 765 [on skepticism in American jurisprudence]; *Freedom and Authority In Our Time* (L. Bryson, L. Finkelstein, R. M. MacIver, and R. McKeon, eds.) (1953) 201, also in 51 Col. L. Rev. 838 [a more detailed analysis of Judge Hand's series of "good moral character" opinions].

Although in technical taxonomy R—— v. United States is not a case of procedure but of substantive law, considerations of concinnity have persuaded me to present it at this point. If a further excuse is needed, I submit that Judge Hand has supplied it. That is to say, against the background of his doctrine, the case is made to resemble one in which a jury (the community) has handed the judge a confused and ambiguous verdict. In general, when there is to be decided which is the proper organ to dispose of a case, our law treats the identifying of the legitimate organ as a question of procedure.

Readers should not be misled by the circumstance that R—— was able forthwith to file a new and unexceptionable petition for naturalization. Judge Hand's holding announced a rule for general application. Like all his utterances, it possesses weighty influence as a precedent.

12 The discussion I refer to begins at p. 287 (2d ed. 1921).

13 For details, see 51 Col. L. Rev. 838 (1951).

14 Johnson v. United States, 186 F.2d 588, 590 (2d Cir. 1951).

15 S—— v. United States, 177 F.2d 450 (2d Cir. 1949).

By the 1952 Immigration and Nationality Act, Congress directed that certain defined classes of persons shall not be found to have good moral character. 8 U. S. C. § 1101.

16 Never better said than by John Locke: "Men may choose different things, and yet all choose right." Locke's *Essay* bk. II, c. XXI (in the author's final revision, 4th edition, 1700, or any subsequent edition).

17 Kierkegaard, *The Present Age* 100 (A. Dru and W. Lowrie trans.) (1940).

18 For an illuminating analysis of statutory provisions relating to euthanasia, the reader is referred to Silving, "Euthanasia: A Study in Comparative Criminal Law," 103 U. of Penn. L. Rev. 350 (1954).

19 Baba Mezia 59b.

Index of Names

NAMES OR INITIALS MENTIONED IN CONNECTION WITH CASES APPEAR IN SLANTING TYPE. ALL OTHER ENTRIES ARE IN ORDINARY TYPE.

Topical Analysis